ALEXANDER ZINOVIEV: AN INTRODUCTION TO HIS WORK

Also by Michael Kirkwood and published by Macmillan

ALEXANDER ZINOVIEV AS WRITER AND THINKER (*editor with Philip Hanson*)
LANGUAGE PLANNING IN THE SOVIET UNION (*editor*)

Alexander Zinoviev

Alexander Zinoviev: An Introduction to His Work

Michael Kirkwood

Senior Lecturer in Russian
School of Slavonic and East European Studies
University of London

M

First published 1993 by
THE MACMILLAN PRESS LTD
Houndmills, Basingstoke, Hampshire RG21 2XS
and London
Companies and representatives
throughout the world

ISBN 0–333–55621–6

A catalogue record for this book is available
from the British Library.

Typeset by Ponting-Green Publishing Services
Sunninghill, Berkshire

6003704729

Printed in Great Britain by
Antony Rowe Ltd, Chippenham, Wiltshire

For Alexander Zinoviev, my friend and
(unwitting) mentor

Contents

List of Abbreviations

G	*Gorbachevizm*
ING	*Idi na Golgofu*
IS	*Il superpotere in URSS*
K	*Katastroika. Povest' o perestroike v Partgrade*
KKR	*Kommunizm kak real'nost'*
MDMCh	*Moi dom – moia chuzhbina*
SB	*Svetloe budushchee*
TGF	*The Grand Failure*
TM	*The Madhouse*
TRC	*The Reality of Communism*
TRF	*The Radiant Future*
VPR	*V preddverii raia*
YH	*The Yawning Heights*
ZhD	*Zheltyi dom*
ZV	*Ziiaiushchie vysoty*

Introduction

This is not a book in the 'life and works of' mould. Zinoviev's output to date, not counting his professional work, occupies over a metre of the shelf space in my study. This volume will take up probably less than three centimetres. A full discussion of his work in one volume is quite obviously impossible. I have essayed a partial discussion of some of his work.

I have been prompted to write this book by an awareness of the fact that Zinoviev is undervalued, both as a writer and as a commentator on Soviet affairs. He is a 'difficult' writer who makes great cognitive demands on his readers and also a writer who constantly broadcasts his opinion of Western Soviet studies scholarship by dismissing it *in toto*. Not surprisingly, he has been virtually ignored by the vast majority of Western Sovietologists. This is a major source of concern to me, for Zinoviev has contributed more to my understanding of the Soviet Union than the rest of Russian literature and Soviet studies scholarship put together. I do not exaggerate.

Given the constraints of space, I have been obliged to be highly selective in my treatment of this writer. Of the various approaches which I could have adopted (thematic, chronological, genre-based, biographical) I have chosen a combination of the chronological and the genre-based. The reasons for my choice were dictated by the readership I had in mind.

The book has been written for people who have a good command of Russian and who are interested, professionally or otherwise, in the Soviet Union and how it works. With the exception of the first two chapters, each chapter examines an individual book. An English translation for all of these books bar *Konets kommunizma?* (*The End of Communism?*) is, or shortly will be, available. I earnestly recommend, however, that the works should be read in their original Russian version if at all possible. Given the fantastic rate at which developments in the Soviet Union are taking place, it seemed to me important that I should present Zinoviev's views on these events. That consideration partly explains the selection of works examined in the last three chapters. However, there are two major reasons for choosing to examine individual works in chronological order. One was the desire to chart the evolution of Zinoviev's 'model' of Communism from its inception. Another reason resides in the complexity of the structure of the works themselves. The sad fact is that many readers do not 'stay the course', particularly as regards the larger works such as *Ziiaiushchie vysoty* (*The Yawning Heights*) and *Zheltyi dom* (*The Madhouse*). I have therefore tried to help the reader by producing a kind of *vade mecum* for each of the books examined.

It may be thought presumptuous of me to assume in advance that the reader of Zinoviev will require any particular assistance. However, there are good grounds for my assumption. First, by writing in an amazingly discontinuous fashion, he makes incredible demands on the reader's short-term memory. As I discuss in detail in future chapters, his works are compendia of short texts, accompanied by a title. A work like *Zheltyi dom* contains over 800 of them. Keeping track of what is going on in a Zinoviev 'novel' is a major undertaking. Secondly, his works are entirely innocent of lists of contents and/or indexes. This constitutes a major handicap for the reader, since Zinoviev, more than any other writer I can think of, requires the reader to refer back constantly to what has gone before, without, however, providing him or her with any obvious means of so doing. At that mundane level, therefore, this book should be of assistance, since I try to provide a 'reader's guide' to help in the negotiation of Zinoviev's vast intellectual terrain. To that extent, description takes precedence over analysis.

I make no apology for that, since it seems to me that at the present stage of Zinoviev scholarship what is required is an effective mode of access to his work as a preliminary to productive analysis. I am the more persuaded of this view by my perception that various literary critics have made questionable judgements about Zinoviev's work which seem to have their origin in a less than thorough acquaintance with it. Part of my purpose, therefore, has been to discuss and evaluate the reception of his works by the literary-critical establishment, offering my own response where appropriate.

In an important sense, however, Zinoviev is a writer *sui generis*. Indeed, he seems to me to be a remarkable, if unwitting, example of a writer who fits, more closely than anyone else I can think of, the model adumbrated in that school of literary criticism associated with Roland Barthes and Michel Foucault. To borrow a phrase from the social sciences, he does not write within any of the conventional 'paradigms', yet he writes on matters literary, historical, political, sociological, philosophical, aesthetic, moral and religious, in a mode which defies genre classification. In that sense he is indeed a 'scriptor' producing 'écriture', to borrow terms defined by Barthes in his essay 'The Death of the Author'. Perhaps an unconventional writer requires unconventional treatment.

This book is unconventional in the sense that it tries to discuss the issues which Zinoviev raises from a perspective which is not 'paradigm-specific'. Zinoviev is writing for the intelligent non-specialist. This book examines his work from a non-specialist point of view. My selection of individual works from Zinoviev's vast output has been determined by my sense of their relative importance. They constitute in my opinion the 'essential' Zinoviev. Excluded are well-known works such as *Gomo sovetikus* (*Homo Sovieticus*) and *Idi na Golgofu* (*Go to Golgotha*), as well as works of arguably little or no interest such as *Para bellum* or *Gosudarstvennyi zhenikh* (*The State Suitor*). One major omission is *V preddverii raia* (*On the Threshold of Paradise*), a huge book which was published while Zinoviev was still in Moscow. This 'book' in fact was Zinoviev's literary archive, smuggled out to the West and published in unrevised form, and for that reason I decided reluctantly to leave it out. I have with much less reluctance decided to ignore the huge number of articles which Zinoviev has written for an astonishing range of Western (and, increasingly, Soviet) publications. Much of what he writes in these articles replicates ideas treated in the books I have selected for examination. I have also made no reference to his numerous public appearances on radio and television, nor to the notorious interviews with George Urban and Georges Nivat, published respectively in *Encounter* and *L'Express*. These constitute, to my mind, the 'inessential' Zinoviev.

The format of this book is simple. Chapters 1 and 2 introduce the man and his method of writing. The remaining chapters discuss individual works in chronological order, for the reasons given above, covering almost equally the Brezhnev and Gorbachev eras. All quotations are given in English, but the Russian has also been supplied in the case of excerpts taken from *Ziiaiushchie vysoty, Svetloe budushchee* (*The Radiant Future*), *Zheltyi dom* and *Katastroika*. All unacknowledged translations are my own. I have used the Library of Congress system of transliteration.

POSTSCRIPT, 2 SEPTEMBER 1991

I am grateful to the Macmillan Press for granting me the opportunity before the typescript goes to press to comment on the momentous events which have taken place in the Soviet Union since I wrote this book, particularly the events of the failed coup of 19 August 1991 and its aftermath.

Actually, these events do not materially affect the arguments set out in this book. Zinoviev himself predicted a coup and provides at least part of the explanation for its failure. The coup was the logical outcome of the process of 'counter-*perestroika*' which is discussed in Chapter 9, and at least part of the explanation for its failure is the unreliability/untrustworthiness of comrades, a theme which runs through Zinoviev's whole *oeuvre* and which is discussed in Chapter 8. The antics of Gennady Yanaev, a man in whom Gorbachev put his trust, recall the figure of Suslikov, Gorbachev's right-hand man in *Katastroika*.

The aftermath of the failed coup has also been in tune with Zinoviev's view of Communist society. Boris Yeltsin's instincts were authoritarian and anti-democratic, reflected in his move to shut down newspapers and ban the activities of the Communist Party.

More serious for Zinoviev's theory of Communism are Gorbachev's suspension of the Communist Party and the historic session of the Congress of People's Deputies on 2 September 1991, at which Gorbachev and the leaders of ten of the fifteen Soviet republics signed a joint declaration outlining proposals for what is in effect the controlled dissolution of the Soviet Union. Zinoviev has always maintained that one of the constitutive features of a communist society is a unified, centralised system of power. Currently, the Soviet centralised system is in the process of being destroyed.

However, one of Zinoviev's key distinctions is between what he calls the 'froth' of history and history's more important, unseen currents. The failed coup, the banning of the Communist Party and the 'joint declaration' referred to above may well be examples of that 'froth'. The Soviet Union's chronic problems remain. There are still many opponents of capitalism and believers in the egalitarian principles of the Communist ideal. Such private enterprise as exists is increasingly in the grip of various mafias. The administration of a territory as large as the Russian Federation with its population of some 147 000 000 (1989 census) is likely to require a centralised system, albeit under another name.

In short, it is too soon to say with certainty that the system has been destroyed for good. Zinoviev has always maintained that the Communist system is unreformable. So far he has been proved right. An attempt is currently being made to destroy it. It is too early to be sure that that attempt has succeeded. But even if it does succeed, it does not mean that Communism cannot be resurrected. For Zinoviev, Communism is based on the communalist instincts of people who are required to live in large numbers in complex societies. These instincts are natural and must be restrained by various forms of social control (see Chapter 3). Finally, ingrained habits die hard. The Soviet population cannot be expected overnight, or even in the next ten years, to forget patterns of thought and behaviour ingrained in them since birth. Having been told for generations about the evils of capitalism and the 'falseness' of Western democracy, they are unlikely to embrace wholeheartedly the new philosophy which denigrates virtually the whole Soviet experience and exaggerates the virtues of Western capitalism. As Zinoviev has frequently pointed out, the Soviet population cannot have the benefits of capitalism without its considerable disadvantages.

We are entering the post-Soviet era. It would be comforting to think that it was also genuinely the era of post-Communism. No one can predict the future, but if I were asked to say which was the more likely, a successful transition to a post-Communist, market-oriented, enterprise culture on the territory of the former Soviet Union, or a return to a centralised, authoritarian, anti-democratic system, albeit with a different ideology (let us say 'humanist'), I would reluctantly opt for the latter. I hope I am wrong.

Part One
Prolegomena

1 Homo Sovieticus[1]

Alexander Zinoviev is a man of contradictions. He is small in stature, yet powerfully built. Of artistic temperament, he has a razor-sharp analytical mind. An ardent individualist, he was always a conscientious member of his collective. His energy is phenomenal. In the course of his professional life he has written over two hundred books and articles on the logical structure of scientific language in an environment in which the non-scientific language of ideology was paramount. A controversial figure in philosophical circles in Moscow, he has become a controversial figure in literary circles in Munich, where he now lives. His writing likewise contains a mass of contradictions. Since the publication of *Ziiaiushchie vysoty,* his monumental anatomy of Communist society, he has written a further twenty-four books and countless articles on the nature of Communism, the earlier works describing its defects, the latest works defending it. Some of his works are gigantic, highly complex in their structure, polyphonic in their tone, unique in their exhaustive description of a particular way of life. Others are short, stylistically monotonous, devoid of any distinguishable literary merit, exaggerated, *annoying* – this is particularly true, it seems to me, of works like *Para bellum* and *Gosudarstvennyi zhenikh* (*The State Suitor*).

What accounts for the inconsistency? Why does a man whose scientific field *par excellence* should have trained him to avoid such temptation indulge in the wild generalisations which pepper his books and articles, especially since he came to the West? Is it frustration, engendered by his low opinion of Western Soviet studies scholarship? Is it his feeling that the practice of science has now been taken over by the masses to the point where 'real' science is swallowed up in an ocean of pseudo-science, of mediocrity? Is it good old Russian *razmakh*, the 'Dammit-let-it-rip' urge to make a scene, to ruffle the susceptibilities of those whose pedantic scientism confines them to the study of trivia? Or is it simply the desire to shock, *tout court?*

Zinoviev himself provides one possible answer:

3

I can express an opinion and defend it in one context, and, in another, assert quite the opposite. This is not because of a lack of principle. It is a desire to look at something from a different point of view, to look at a different facet of a particular problem. Sometimes I am motivated simply by a spirit of contrariness. The fact is that I am not doctrinaire. I am not a prophet, nor a politician, nor a decorous professor. I live in the medium of language. This medium is complex, contradictory, fluctuating. In this medium there are no established formulae, nor will there ever be. There is one unshakable principle: seek the truth and resist coercion, for if you do not, you are not a human being.

                                                      (Zinoviev, 1979c:17)

This is certainly an accurate self-assessment. There is ample evidence in Zinoviev's writing to corroborate it. The question is: what motivates him? His character? His training in the dialectic method?

Perhaps part of the explanation lies in the ongoing battle between his sharply analytical mind and his energetic, creative, *artistic* talent, reflected in his style of writing, drawing and painting. His cartoons are magnificent. Some of the paintings which adorn the front of his books are so striking that they are almost literally breathtaking. His most famous one is the picture of two rats tied together by their tails, shaking each other simultaneously by the hand and throat. That arresting picture adorns the front cover of his book *Kommunizm kak real'nost'* (*The Reality of Communism*). In a few strokes he can conjure up very funny, yet very thought-provoking, pictures of life under Stalin or life under Brezhnev or life under Gorbachev. Yet the same inspiration and skills that allow him to produce memorable cartoons occasionally let him down in the realm of the written and spoken word. Some of his verbal descriptions are as unforgettable as his cartoons. Others retain the hyperbole in contexts where hyperbole is conventionally anathema, and are consequently a disaster. His tendency to make sweeping, unscientific, irrefutable statements about complex questions is particularly noticeable in the interviews which he has given in recent years, and has not done anything to enhance his reputation – rather the reverse. Yet he is continually invited to appear on television or to give interviews to a host of representatives of the world's press. And it is easy to understand why. Whatever he says, no matter how much one might disagree with him, he always provides food for thought. This food may be unpalatable to some, but it is always appealing to others. Moreover, since he does not fit easily into any part of the political spectrum, he cannot be hijacked by the right or left. He continues to be his own man, aware that his views are controversial, yet undoubtedly glad of that.

No doubt another part of the explanation could be found if one were to take a 'dialectical' perspective. His vices, for instance, are arguably an extension of his virtues. We have already hinted at this by suggesting that his talent for drawing cartoons occasionally lets him down in contexts in which such talent is inappropriate. His great sense of his individuality, which drives him to make extreme statements, and which therefore limits the extent to which he is taken seriously by Western experts on the Soviet Union, helped him to survive in a collectivist environment, and helped him also to detach himself from it, allowing him to describe it the more objectively. His innate honesty and refusal to duck historical issues have allowed him to write magnificently about what Soviet life is like, yet also to cause offence, when he refuses to condemn Stalin and historic events like the collectivisation of Soviet agriculture. His fearless determination to confront issues when they need to be confronted, not merely when it is safe to do so, is balanced by an equally fearless determination to drop them when they become uncontroversial or 'safe'. Thus he stopped being an anti-Stalinist on the death of Stalin, attacked Brezhnev mercilessly while the latter was still in power and has been equally merciless in his criticism of Gorbachev. In the case of Gorbachev he was critical of him long before it became fashionable, and if he continues to be bitterly opposed to Gorbachev and his policies, that is because he is afraid that *perestroika* ('*katastroika*', as he calls it), may bring the Soviet Union to its knees. Thus we are confronted with the current paradox that one of the most effective critics of Soviet Communism that has ever lived is currently engaged in a struggle to prevent its collapse. A man whom Suslov appar-

ently wished to see executed for having dared to publish a
book like *Ziiaiushchie vysoty* in the West has recently been
quoted in public, and with approval, by no less a figure than
Egor Ligachev.

Who, then, is Alexander Zinoviev? What were the forces
which shaped him? What influences were particularly powerful? How much did 'character' play a part in his development, how much pure chance? What was the balance
between 'nature' and 'nurture'?

Nature was kind to him in several ways. He was endowed
with formidable intelligence, creative talent, and a great
deal of courage. From his father he learned how to paint
and draw, from his mother how to read and write. These
artistic and intellectual skills were nurtured and developed
in a strict moral environment in which the individual was
expected to work toward the common good. Young Alexander from an early age experienced the tension between
the needs of the individual and the demands of the collective.

He was born in 1922, the sixth of eleven children, in the
village of Pakhtino in the Chukhloma district of Kostroma
region. Two of his siblings died in early childhood, two in
adulthood. Zinoviev has four younger brothers and two
elder sisters. His father was a house-painter and decorator
and worked mostly away from home, returning only occasionally to the village, as Zinoviev puts it, 'to help my
mother with the harvest and with the business of pro-
creation' (Zinoviev, 1989a:323). Family life, therefore, was
very much organised by Zinoviev's mother. She came from a
village nearby, the daughter of a quite well-to-do business-
man who owned several houses in St Petersburg.

Zinoviev was clearly deeply influenced by his mother,
Appolinaria Vasilievna. He writes of her in his memoirs with
real affection and respect, drawing attention to her intelligence and religious beliefs which formed and shaped the
patterns of behaviour in that large household. The children
were expected to help in the business of running it. From an
early age they worked in the fields, conscious that their
individual efforts were directed towards the common good.
In the evenings their mother would read to them, tell them
stories, attend to their spiritual and moral development.

From an early age, therefore, Zinoviev was brought up not only to believe in the ideals of Communism, but actually to enact them in practice. The fact that these ideals were presented as Christian only emphasised the extent to which they were morally desirable.

The Zinovievs were well-known and respected in the district and people often came to call. Zinoviev recounts that often all the important personalities of the district spent time with them, from the local Party officials to the local priest. Often both the officials and the priest could be seen deep in discussion in the *krasnyi ugolok*, the corner of the room reserved for the display of holy pictures.

Since Zinoviev had learned to read and write at home, when he went to school he went straight into the second year. If he had no inkling before then, this was early evidence that he was a cut above the average. This evidence was almost immediately reinforced by the ease with which he learned and the impact he made on his teacher, who encouraged his mother to send him to Moscow to be educated, since the village school did not have enough to offer him.

Zinoviev's father and grandfather had been living in Moscow for increasingly lengthy periods, and had in fact finally been allocated a room measuring ten square metres in a damp basement. Other members of the family had gradually joined them. First it was the oldest brother Mikhail, who then married and acquired a family. Alexander was sent to join them in 1933. Then a sister and another brother arrived. Within the space of a few years there were eight people living in that one room.

It is very difficult to imagine what it must have been like to live in such cramped accommodation day after day. The term which seems closest to a definition of that particular household containing four generations is 'commune', and one suspects that it provided Zinoviev with early experience of the workings of the 'communal laws' which would later become the cornerstone of his theory of Communism.

Whether that is the case or not, it is certainly true that Zinoviev was largely left to his own devices. His father was often away on some job, his brother had his own family to worry about, and no doubt the desire to spend as much time as possible out of that basement was irresistible. It was not just a question of dreadful accommodation. There was also hunger, dirt and cold. His clothing was threadbare, he was plagued by lice and often he had to go barefoot. He maintains that the first time he had a bed to himself and ate out of his own bowl three times a day was when he was arrested in 1939 (Zinoviev, 1989a:323).

He seems to have spent his time reading, walking the streets of Moscow and visiting his friends. By his own account, he was from the very beginning attracted by tales of adventure, and would seek to model himself on his romantic heroes, trying to fashion himself in their image. It is easy to imagine the young lad escaping from the squalor of his surroundings into an exotic world of mountains and forests, medieval towns and villages, castles and keeps, riding into battle with his heroes, rescuing princesses, robbing the rich to help the poor, vicariously experiencing the sense of virtue which comes from battling against injustice and helping those less fortunate than himself. This boyhood predilection for the romantic, the adventurous, the heroic has never left him.

But he was also very much in touch with the real world. Given his cramped surroundings, it is not surprising that he spent much of his time wandering the streets of Moscow, mainly on his own, but often as one of a gang, acquiring a measure of street-wisdom sufficient to permit him to handle various kinds of incident and coming into contact with a wide range of different people who were by no means uncritical of the new post-Revolutionary regime.

Most of his classmates lived in circumstances similar to his own, but some, the 'aristocrats'–the children of powerful officials–did not. One of his friends lived in an apartment which had many more rooms than occupants, a staggering discovery for young Sasha on his first visit. He seems to have had more than one 'aristocratic' friend, and the growing evidence of inequality (an inequality, moreover, which had arisen since the Revolution and which was patently not a 'survival from the past') only strengthened his desire to see the ideals of Communism realised in practice.

The main substitute for family life, however, was his life at school. In his estimation, the Soviet school before the

Second World War was the 'best in Russian society', an intriguing remark upon which he does not elaborate (Zinoviev, 1987b:38). There is no doubt that his talents flourished there. He soon distinguished himself academically, showing a particular interest and talent for mathematics and appreciation of literature. To these twin interests could be added his talent for drawing, a talent sufficiently obvious for him to be recruited to the service of the school wall-newspaper.

Zinoviev's interest in literature, of course, was nothing out of the ordinary. The literacy campaigns of the 1920s, the cultural revolution, the official emphasis on the role of Soviet literature in the formation of the 'new man', combined with the misery of most people's circumstances, opened the world of books to millions of Soviet citizens who entered it with alacrity and enthusiasm. During the 1930s the Soviet Union had begun to publish and republish the classics of world literature, and Zinoviev read Goethe and Schiller, Lessing, Thomas Mann, Holbach, Diderot, Voltaire and many others as part of his syllabus. He also read widely outside the syllabus: Hugo, Balzac, Stendhal, Milton, Swift, Hamsun, Anatole France, Dante, Cervantes ...

Interesting from the point of view of his own development as a writer are his preferences in the field of classical Russian literature. His favourite writers are Griboedov, Lermontov, Saltykov-Shchedrin, Leskov and Chekhov. He was not particularly fond of Turgenev, Dostoevsky or Tolstoi, although he had favourite passages which he read repeatedly, for instance the 'Legend of the Grand Inquisitor' in *The Brothers Karamazov*, or the historico-philosophical passages in *War and Peace*. Perhaps if he had to choose two writers, they would be Lermontov and Chekhov, the former appealing to his romantic side, the latter to his penchant for satire. Of course he also studied Soviet literature: Serafimovich, A. Tolstoi, Maiakovskii, Sholokhov, Fadeev, Blok, N. Ostrovskii, Furmanov, Bagritskii and others. He claims to have known almost all of Blok, Esenin and Maiakovskii by heart (Zinoviev, 1989a:325).

Zinoviev's account of his school days makes for fascinating reading. A lad of obvious talent, he early on revealed an inability to conform. For instance, schoolchildren like the young Alexander were taught to venerate old revolutionary heroes like Spartacus, Robespierre, the Decembrists and others. Their teachers were still fired with post-Revolutionary enthusiasm and encouraged the children to identify with the downtrodden and the oppressed. It was typical of young Sasha that he would agree to identify with Spartacus and the other slaves, but only from the point of view of a 'free' Roman soldier with 'progressive' views. He refused to be a slave himself. His idealism, however, was not in doubt. His devout sense of collectivism, inspired by his mother's teaching about one's duty to help others, and consolidated by the Revolutionary ardour of his teachers, resulted in Zinoviev's becoming a dedicated Communist, ready to put his talent and energy at the service of the community. At the same time, in a context of alleged equality, his awareness of obvious material inequality was complemented by a growing awareness of an inequality deriving from injustice.

Zinoviev has always been a defender of the thesis that genuine merit should be recognised and acknowledged, and an opponent of the practice whereby mediocrity is wherever possible allowed to masquerade as talent. Gradually he became aware of instances of unfair treatment in his school's assessment procedures. He was good at mathematics – indeed his teachers told him he was the best – yet weaker pupils received preferential treatment in official examinations. He realised that he lacked 'protection', that his parents had no 'clout'. Those who had, the children of Party functionaries and bureaucrats, were at a distinct advantage compared to those who had not. Grades were inflated, failure condoned, unruly behaviour excused, prizes unfairly awarded, and so on. At the same time, genuine merit was not publicly acknowledged if those who displayed it did not have the backing of influential parents. Such injustice deeply upset young Zinoviev, yet at the same time stimulated him to seek to explain why it flourished in a society in which injustice was theoretically not supposed to exist.

There are other examples of his non-conformity, a non-conformity which, if anything, was enhanced and strengthened by his discovery of the gap between ideology and reality. He had, for instance, the temerity to draw a cartoon

of Stalin for the wall-newspaper. It was sufficiently un-
flattering for the school authorities to ask him whether such
a caricature was deliberate. Zinoviev innocently maintained
that he had drawn Stalin to the best of his ability. This
incident brought his work for the wall-newspaper to a
sudden and permanent close. On another occasion he wrote
a short story influenced by Chekhov's 'Vania' which received
praise from his teacher, but it was felt that it contained the
seeds of sedition, and he was advised not to write any more
(Zinoviev, 1989a:324). Perhaps the most amusing incident,
however, relates to the appearance of Stalin's Constitution
in 1936. Zinoviev's sense of injustice, combined with his
sense of fun, led him to draw up his own 'Constitution', in
which he inserted clauses such as 'The idle and the stupid
shall have a right to the same marks as the most industrious
and brightest', or 'The workers have the right to carry out
their obligations'. His 'Constitution', a few copies of which
he circulated, created panic in the school, and he was given
two weeks suspension, since he was too young to be arrested
(Zinoviev, 1987a:85).

This combination of humour and intelligence, already
clearly evident when Zinoviev was still a young lad, to which
could be added a strong sense of his own worth plus a desire
for the recognition which he felt was his due, would increasingly force him out of the collectivist mould within which
the forces of Soviet society were trying to confine him. His
romantic sense of adventure and honour, his inability to
suppress his ego, his awareness of his artistic and intellectual
talent would make it impossible for him to conform. Already
his 'Constitution' demonstrated his ability to ridicule the
official ideology and confront people with evidence about
their society which they would have preferred to ignore.

Zinoviev maintains that he had already developed his
own, albeit intuitive, view of Communism while still at
school (Zinoviev, 1990a:90–1). What is not clear, however,
is how Stalin fitted into his conception at that stage. Zinoviev was to be an anti-Stalinist up to the death of Stalin, after
which his anti-Stalinism would lose its point and the target
of his opposition would become the nature and structure of
Communist society itself. While still at school, however,
young Alexander hated Stalin enough to want to kill him. In

his memoirs he recalls how he and some friends planned Stalin's assassination. One can easily imagine the combination of hardship, deprivation, a sense of injustice, the desire to perform a selfless act of courage, which might motivate idealistically inclined young people who thought that the removal of Stalin would somehow result in fundamental systemic change. Of course, nothing came of the project, although Zinoviev solemnly records on a note of bathos that the plan failed since they could not find a weapon (Zinoviev 1990a:122).

Whatever the unfairness and injustices experienced by Zinoviev at school, he was nonetheless awarded a gold medal for academic excellence, and in 1939 he enrolled in the Department of Philosophy at the Moscow Institute of Philosophy, Literature and History (MIFLI). Having by then already developed his own view of Communism, he was drawn to philosophy rather than mathematics by a desire to explore the mysteries of social theory.

A combination of factors, however, cut short his studies almost before they began. Zinoviev seems during this period to have been under considerable stress. His harsh material conditions, combined with his now pronounced anti-Stalinist outlook, brought him to a state of despair, which manifested itself in recklessness. He was unable to dissemble his views at the Institute sufficiently to avoid attracting attention. His ideas became known to the staff and students, and it was only a matter of time before he was reported to the security organs. At a party to which he had been invited by his friends, he was indiscreet enough to denounce the cult of Stalin and declare himself to be a neo-anarchist. Two days later he was invited to present himself for examination at a local psychiatric hospital.

He was found to be mentally stable but in poor physical condition. Under ordinary circumstances he could have expected to be allowed to interrupt his studies and convalesce, but during the evening of the very day that he presented his 'attestation of unfitness' at the Institute he was arrested and taken to the Lubianka. An order from the Rector banned him from the Institute and at the same time he was told that he would not be allowed to study at any other institution.

Apparently he was treated well by his interrogators. Zinoviev maintains, however, that they were convinced that no one as young as he was could have developed the ideas which he was expressing and that he must have got them from someone else (Zinoviev, 1987b:58). It was decided that he should be kept under surveillance in one of the apartments that the NKVD (People's Commissariat of Internal Affairs) kept in Moscow for such purposes, in the hope that he would lead the NKVD to his source. He was promised food and clothing and a chance to convalesce.

We now arrive at one of those episodes which can be characterised as 'stranger than fiction'. Two young NKVD officers were detailed to accompany Zinoviev to his new abode. On the way, there was some confusion and Zinoviev at one point was left unaccompanied. Without thinking he just walked away.

He made his way to a railway station and smuggled himself on to a train heading East. After a year of adventures, including a return to his village, subsequent flight after his presence there had been reported, and a few months of semi-legal activity in Moscow, he was persuaded by a criminal friend to join the army as a way out of his difficulties. He enlisted (without papers) in October 1940 (Zinoviev, 1990a: 132–7).

If Zinoviev regarded himself as differing in many ways from those around him, there is one thing which he had in common with people of his generation: pride in the Soviet armed forces. He himself had a 'good' war, and was decorated several times for bravery. It is true to say that, after the theme of Communism itself, the theme of war ranks next in importance for Zinoviev. His writing about his wartime experiences is quite extensive, although this impression is only gained after a study of his entire *oeuvre*. He has not devoted any one book to the war itself, but he regularly incorporates scenes from that period into his fiction, notably in *Ziiaiushchie vysoty* and *V preddverii raia* (*On the Threshold of Paradise*). He also devotes two chapters of his memoirs to his wartime experiences. He pulls no punches, describing with his usual mixture of scorn and precision the inevitable 'hurry-up-and-wait' aspects of army life, the equally inevitable foul-ups resulting in unnecessary deaths, the incidents

of simple, unassuming bravery, counterbalanced by incidents of cowardice and callous indifference. Many of his
tales are told in verse, reminiscent of Tvardovsky's *Vasilii
Terkin.*

Zinoviev spent six years in the army, discovering very soon
that it functioned like a Communist society, as he had by
now conceived it, in miniature. At first he served in a cavalry
regiment in the East, but it was disbanded and its members
sent to the West to guard the border with Germany. Again
he found it difficult to keep his ideas to himself, and the
regimental NKVD officer began to enquire into his past. He
managed, however, to transfer to a tank regiment, apparently thanks to his assertion that he knew how to ride a motor
bike! (Zinoviev, 1987b:164)

In the general chaos which ensued after the German
invasion, all of Zinoviev's papers disappeared, including the
material gathered by the NKVD. He had thus given them
the slip completely. He suffered a serious shoulder wound
but signed himself out of hospital in order to rejoin his
comrades at the front. This act saved his life, since the
hospital was taken by the Germans, who then killed all the
Soviet soldiers in it at the time. At the end of 1941 he was
sent to a pilot-training school. Thereafter he was a pilot in
several reserve regiments. He ended up in a fighting regiment and flew fighter-bombers and the low-flying bomber
Iliushin-2, ultimately taking part in the liberation of Prague
and Berlin. He married in 1943 and his son Valerii was born
a year later. Zinoviev is highly reticent about his first
marriage, vouchsafing, however, the information that he
did not see his son until the latter was sixteen years of age
(Zinoviev, 1990a:178). Recently, however, an article in a
Soviet newspaper about his son states that Valerii regularly
began to visit his father in Moscow from about the age of
eight.[2]

Zinoviev remained in the army for a year after the end of
hostilities and considered a career as a civilian pilot. He
went so far as to pay over a hefty bribe to ensure employment. However, his outfit was scheduled to be transferred to
the north of the country and, since he did not want to leave
Moscow, he resigned his post and enrolled in the Faculty of
Philosophy at the University of Moscow.

He graduated 'summa cum laude' in 1951 and embarked on postgraduate study. His student years were very difficult. He had a series of jobs including that of stevedore, navvy, laboratory assistant, watchman and schoolteacher (he taught logic and psychology between 1948 and 1952). His marriage was dissolved in 1948. He remarried in 1951. His second wife was a fellow student who became a career journalist. Since they had nowhere to live, they had to rent privately at considerable expense and inconvenience. His daughter Tamara was born in 1954, and since his wife was constantly on assignments for her newspaper, or on late duty, Zinoviev had more than what he regarded as his fair share of looking after her (Zinoviev, 1989a:328).

In 1954 he completed and defended his dissertation for the degree of Candidate of Science on a topic connected with the logical structure of *Das Kapital.* Since he demonstrated convincingly that ninety per cent of that work was couched in terms that were ideological rather than scientific, his dissertation created a scandal and the qualification was withheld for several years. His dissertation circulated in manuscript, however, and was much admired, albeit unofficially.

About this time he obtained a post as a Junior Research Fellow at the Institute of Philosophy attached to the Academy of Sciences, at a salary that scarcely paid for his food. Hard as these years were, they were rich in incident, much of which found its way into his monumental work *Zheltyi dom* (*The Madhouse*). His job in his early years at the Institute (he would be continuously employed there until 1976) was to work with a range of mentally disturbed people whose manuscripts had been sent by the KGB to the Institute for vetting. They were of two basic types: convinced Marxists or declared opponents of Marxism. They were genuine psychiatric cases and Zinoviev got to know several types of personality which he came to believe were typical of a Communist society.

During those years he did a lot of writing of a quasi-literary sort, although it was always firmly linked to some other activity. For instance, he gave many public lectures as part of his contribution to the unpaid 'social work' which Soviet citizens are required to perform on a 'voluntary' basis over and above the work for which they are remunerated. These lectures on topical themes would often be cast in literary form, containing for instance humorous dialogue. He contributed many satirical articles and cartoons to the Institute wall-newspaper. He took part in the practice of 'oral literature', a kind of social event where participants engaged in oral literary improvisations such as telling jokes, making up impromptu verse, inventing stories, recounting anecdotes, and so on. He also made much use of literary improvisation in his school lessons. One can vividly imagine how invigorating his 'social work' and teaching must have been. Audiences must have been on tenterhooks as Zinoviev explored the limits of the permitted, no doubt often exceeding them, debating with his listeners the problems of Communism which would form the content of his future books.

He began to publish academic work in 1958. The range of his scientific work can be seen from the titles of some of his books: *Filosofskie problemy mnogoznachnoi logiki* (*Philosophical Problems of Many-valued Logic*), Moscow 1960 (translated into Polish, English, German, Hungarian, Spanish); *Logika vyskazyvaniia i teoriia vyvoda* (*Propositional and Deductive Logic*), Moscow, 1962; *Osnovy logicheskoi teorii nauchnykh znanii* (*Foundations of a Logical Theory of Science*), Moscow 1967; *Kompleksnaia logika* (*Complex Logic*), Moscow 1970; *Logika nauki* (*The Logic of Science*), Moscow 1971; *Logicheskaia fizika* (*Logical Physics*), Moscow 1972; (with H. Wessel) *Logische Sprachregeln. Eine Einführung in die Logik* (*Logical Speech rules: An Introduction to Logic*), Berlin, 1975. In addition he published some two hundred articles.

Zinoviev says that he began his systematic, scientific investigation of Soviet society in the post-Stalin years (Zinoviev, 1989a:329). He had already established in his youth that the evils in Soviet life could not be attributed to Stalin's personality, but to the Communist social order itself. However, it was only after graduation that he felt equipped to put his studies on a scientific basis and to begin to invent a methodology, and moreover a methodology for study in isolation. His field of enquiry was illegitimate and he could not envisage scientific collaboration or assistance. He was not, however, in any particular hurry. He had a full programme of legitimate research, not to mention teaching and supervision, he could not hope to publish his findings and so was content to carry out his investigations for himself.

It was about this time that he formulated his system of rules for living his life in the environment of a Communist society. This system was based on the formula 'I am a sovereign state'. It was essentially a code of behaviour which allows the individual to live with dignity and self-respect in a collectivist milieu. The intellectual foundation of his system was provided by his logico-philosophical training and his theory of Communism, tempered by his experience in the war and his own character.

The basic principles underlying his system include the following:

1. Be prepared to die.
2. Let no one humiliate you.
3. Do not inform on anyone.
4. Sin is sin, differences in degree do not exist/are unimportant.
5. Act as though God were watching you.

These rules are characteristically clear and simple, if slightly quirky from a Western point of view. Zinoviev's war experiences, quite apart from any particular psychological predisposition, prepared him to expect death. He did not believe that he would survive the war flying a Soviet bomber. (The life-expectancy of a Soviet pilot in Zinoviev's sector of the front was ten sorties.) The second rule is a difficult one to obey in a society in which the individual as such has no intrinsic worth. The practice of informing is widespread and is regarded as normal behaviour by many people. Refusing ever to inform on anyone is difficult in an environment in which it counts as normal, expected behaviour. Rule number four is at first sight surprising. We are used, after all, to the notions of 'serious' and 'petty' crime. Our legal system differentiates between various degrees of criminal behaviour, reflected in graduated systems of punishment. We are used to thinking in moral terms of degrees of 'good' and 'bad', 'right' and 'wrong'. For Zinoviev, however, deception is deception. Betraying one person is as bad as betraying

your country. Not that he puts it like that. He says simply
that there is no difference. His attitude to God is equally
simple. God for Zinoviev does not exist, but that need not
stop one behaving as though there were a God and as
though that God were watching one's every thought and
deed (Zinoviev, 1987b:68–9).

Living according to the principles of a sovereign state in
Soviet society is not easy and it is not possible to remain
unnoticed. On the other hand, Zinoviev did not go out of
his way to broadcast the scale of his project. As he puts it
himself (Zinoviev, 1989a:330); 'Imagine an ant in a huge
colony of similar ants that declares its intention of building
its own ant's nest within the common ants' nest and sets to
work accordingly. What would the others do? They would
destroy the ant, of course. The same thing would have
happened to me.' He goes on to make a point that is one of
the central pillars of his thought: 'Anyone who escapes from
the control of the collective and society is perceived as a
threat to the existence of the whole.' This, he emphasises, is
the primary reaction not of the authorities and the KGB,
but of the deviant individual's immediate entourage.

The 1960s and early 1970s were years of turbulence and
rebellion. They saw the rise of the dissident movement.
'Samizdat' and 'tamizdat' appeared. As the rebellion developed, however, so did the methods of oppression. The
Siniavsky trial is an obvious example. These years were also
turbulent for Zinoviev. Much took place in his personal life.
In 1960 his second marriage broke up, his father died in
1964, his mother in 1969. He met his third wife, Olga
Mironovna, in 1965 and they married in 1967. In 1962 he
defended his Doctor's thesis and became a full professor in
1966. In 1967 he became Head of the Department of Logic
at Moscow University. In 1968 he became a member of the
editorial board of the prestigious Soviet journal *Voprosy
filosofii* (*Questions of Philosophy*). Throughout the 1960s he
was writing and publishing and his school of logic was
achieving recognition abroad. At home, too, his achievements were recognised but more unofficially than officially.

The fact is that Zinoviev's adherence to his code made for
difficulties in his career. If his published work gained him
recognition and therefore a measure of support from the

authorities on high, his refusal to have anything to do with Marxism caused great irritation among his more immediate colleagues and superiors. After all, he was working in the Institute of Philosophy and it was unthinkable that he should not write from a Marxist viewpoint. But he did not, and that caused great resentment.

Zinoviev apparently faced opposition on two fronts. On the one hand his 'liberal' colleagues, who were making a career in philosophy and who were connected with the apparatus of power, were just waiting for a signal from above to start a smear campaign against him. The authorities, however, provided Zinoviev with a measure of support, partly in the spirit of the 'liberal' era, partly out of a sense of responsibility towards Soviet culture. Zinoviev, after all, was a respected scholar with an international reputation. On the other hand, the authorities constantly tried to harness him to Marxism. He was asked to write an article for *Kommunist*, the journal of the Communist Party of the Soviet Union (CPSU), but he refused, saying he did not know how to write such an article. Eventually he was offered the opportunity simply to put his name to someone else's screed. Again, he refused. He then either resigned from his position on the editorial board of *Voprosy filosofii* (Zinoviev, 1989a:332) or was removed from it (Zinoviev, 1987b:105). Of the two accounts, the first is perhaps the more accurate. Both, of course, are possible. Zinoviev was quite capable of resigning as a matter of principle and the Editorial Board, to avoid embarrassment, would present such a resignation as a dismissal.

Another incident set the authorities against him. He refused to sack two dissident lecturers in his department. After that, he no longer had the protection of the authorities, and his colleagues could close in. Publication of his work was forbidden. His students began to experience difficulties. Lecture courses were taken away from him.

By 1974 he was almost completely isolated. That year was particularly marked by 'contradictions'. It was the year during which he was elected a member of the Finnish Academy of Sciences, an honour of which he was particularly proud since Finnish work in logic was held in high esteem. During the same year, articles were published in the

journal *Filosofskie nauki* (*Philosophical Sciences*) 'demonstrating' that Zinoviev's academic work was devoid of scientific
value. It was also the year during which he was refused
permission to take part in an international symposium held
in his own institution! Finally, it was the year in which he
wrote *Ziiaiushchie vysoty* (*Yawning Heights*).

As the Russian proverb has it: '*net khuda bez dobra*'
(literally, 'there is no evil without good'). By 1974 Zinoviev
for probably the first time in his life found himself with time
on his hands. He decided that it was time to settle accounts
with his society. By his own lights he had spent all his adult
life in service to that society. He had been a brilliant student,
had fought throughout the war, had established himself as a
scholar with an international reputation, bringing honour
not only to himself but also to Soviet scholarship. He had
lived according to an honourable code, had been an exemplary teacher and had been extremely popular with his
students. Yet he had not been accepted as fully 'sound' by
his colleagues or by the authorities. Although he was invited
many times to attend seminars and conferences abroad, he
was always refused permission to go. (His election to the
Finnish Academy of Sciences was particularly galling for the
authorities.) Finally he had had enough. He would set down
his thoughts about his society on paper.

Ziiaushchie vysoty in its original form comprises some 560
pages of smaller than average print. Yet Zinoviev apparently wrote the whole work in about six months. This seems
incredible, yet, as Zinoviev says (Zinoviev, 1989a:333), he
had been thinking about the subject matter for decades and
in a sense the book wrote itself.

He finished the book by the end of 1974. During the next
eighteen months or so Zinoviev continued to experience
difficulties in his professional life. In 1975 he was refused
permission to attend an All-Union conference in Kiev. In
1976 he decided to resign from the CPSU. Since that was
not accepted practice, his resignation in fact took the form
of expulsion. He was invited to take part in an international
conference which was to be held in Helsinki in June 1976
but was refused permission to travel by the Soviet authorities. He decided to launch a public protest, an event to
which he invited foreign correspondents. This act of de-

fiance cost him his post at Moscow University and led to his 'expulsion' from the Soviet Philosophical Society for good measure, although he was not in fact a member of that body.

On 26 September 1976 a Western radio station announced the publication in Switzerland of *Ziiaushchie vysoty*. The reaction in Moscow was immediate. Most of Zinoviev's friends and colleagues dropped him like a hot potato, although Zinoviev maintains that they had absolutely nothing to fear and claims that their actions were motivated not by fear but by envy (Zinoviev, 1987b:112); it was not the publication in the West of a book critical of Soviet society which upset them but the fact that the book became such an overnight success. Moreover he had demonstrated that it was precisely the 'liberal intelligentsia' who were the mainstay of the regime. It was not a society in which a ruling minority sat on the necks of a submissive population, but one in which ordinary people willingly participated in the administration of the regime, condoned the arrest and imprisonment of thousands of innocent people, helped to suppress talent and foster mediocrity, and so on.

Zinoviev's judgement is perhaps too harsh. Not everyone is capable of sacrificing a career or destroying their family's prospects for the sake of friendship with someone who, from one point of view, seems bent on a suicide course and who is something of a square peg in a round hole. It seems quite possible on the face of it that many people broke off contact with Zinoviev not because (or not just because) they envied his sudden success as a major writer, but because they were afraid of reprisals on the part of the authorities.

One can also feel sympathy for Zinoviev's family. The publication of *Ziiaushchie vysoty* had grave and lasting consequences for many of them. His son Valerii, for instance, who lived with his wife and daughter in Ulianovsk, was warned that if he did not break off contact publicly with his father he would lose his job and be expelled from the Party. He refused to do so, thereby cutting short a promising career in the militia. Zinoviev's daughter Tamara likewise refused to break off contact and was accordingly expelled from the Komsomol and sacked. She apparently has found no permanent employment to this day. His brother Vasilii, who was a military lawyer with the rank of colonel and who did not even know of the existence of the book, nevertheless refused to denounce him, as a consequence of which he was cashiered from the army and sent away from Moscow.

Zinoviev, of course, suffered as well. He had already lost his professorship at Moscow University, but he had retained his post at the Institute of Philosophy of the Academy of Sciences. However, on 2 December 1976 a Party meeting unanimously denounced *Ziiaiushchie vysoty* as an 'anti-Soviet lampoon' (accurately enough, it seems to me), although no one had actually seen it, and recommended to the authorities not only that Zinoviev should be sacked forthwith but that he should be stripped of all his degrees and titles, government awards and military decorations (Zinoviev, 1989 a:333–4).

He was sacked virtually the next day but had to be reinstated after vigorous protest in the West about his treatment. However, his expulsion from the Institute was finally effected in January 1977. In February, at the behest of the Institute of Philosophy, the Supreme Attestation Committee (VAK) of the USSR Soviet of Ministers deprived him of all his university degrees and titles. There was a certain measure of illegality about all this. For instance, VAK had no right to deprive him of his title of Senior Research Fellow (starshii sotrudnik) since that right belonged to the Academy of Sciences. And the Institute of Philosophy had no right to recommend annulment of his Candidate of Science degree since that had been conferred on him by the Faculty of Philosophy at Moscow University. Such details, however, cut no ice. In the same month his telephone was disconnected, as was that of a friend of his wife's, after his wife had used it to telephone her sister in Hungary, on the grounds that she had allowed someone to use it 'who had no right to it'! Contracts for books already prepared for publication in Poland, Germany and Bulgaria were cancelled. Honoraria were withheld.

The next two years were very difficult. On the one hand Zinoviev's material circumstances could hardly have been worse. Neither he nor his wife could find permanent work. They eked out an existence by selling their possessions, books, clothes, odd items of furniture. Occasionally Zinoviev would 'ghost write' an article for money or even 'edit' someone's doctoral thesis. They received occasional financial help from readers, usually anonymously (Zinoviev, 1989 a:334).[3] On the other hand they were the permanent object of scrutiny by the KGB, subject to harassment, threats and false rumours. Everyone who came into contact with them suffered likewise.

Adalbert and Renée Reif asked Zinoviev why, in fact, he had escaped arrest, given what he had done (Zinoviev, 1987b:114–16). Zinoviev points to various factors. The Siniavsky/Daniel trial had aroused a tremendous reaction in the West and the Soviet authorities were anxious to avoid a repetition of such embarrassing events. Also, the dissident movement was at its height. Many critical writers were managing to have their works published, and the authorities thought it preferable to expel them to the West, rather than to arrest them. Moreover, the authorities wanted to be seen to be acting in a 'liberal' fashion. In Zinoviev's case the outcome was finely balanced. According to a KGB contact of Zinoviev's, the Party's ideological chief Suslov had wanted the death penalty. Andropov, on the other hand, had apparently argued for emigration. At first it was thought that he should go to Hungary, where his wife's sister lived. Brezhnev, however, apparently decided it should be the West. At the time of these deliberations Zinoviev was still expecting to be arrested, so he was surprised when the KGB suddenly told him to present himself at OVIR (the Department of Visas and Registrations).

Zinoviev had always maintained that he never wanted to emigrate. Had there been any chance of earning his living in Moscow he would not have emigrated. However, not only was there no way in which he could afford to live in that city, he was threatened with the likelihood of arrest and incarceration for seven years in a labour camp, followed by five years internal exile. Forced to choose between Siberia and the West, Zinoviev chose the West.

When Zinoviev presented himself at OVIR, he was given two passports and told he had five days to remove himself and his family from Moscow. They hastily distributed their few remaining possessions among friends and relatives and arrived in Munich with one small suitcase containing their daughter Polina's books. Since Zinoviev had not stopped writing after finishing *Ziiaiushchie vysoty*, by the time he and his family arrived in Munich several other books were in the pipeline: *Zapiski nochnogo storozha* (*Notes of a Night Watchman*), *Svetloe budushchee* (*The Radiant Future*), *V preddverii raia* (*On the Threshold of Paradise*). Initially, therefore, he had a measure of financial security.

Their immediate impressions of life in the West were vivid and largely positive. As a famous writer and scholar, Zinoviev received many invitations to speak at gatherings all over the world, and in the first two years life was a hectic round of visits to different countries (France, England, Spain, Switzerland), meetings with people from all walks of life, interesting converations and the chance to take up invitations to address various learned bodies which had been denied to him in the Soviet Union.

The problems began as the Zinoviev family began to put down roots. Psychological and material factors combined to make things difficult, and Zinoviev admits that life in the West presented him with problems that he had not foreseen. On the one hand life in the West turned out to be much as he had expected in terms of material abundance and personal freedom. On the other hand, what he had failed to predict were the implications these things carried for the individual. Less serious was the problem of choice. Zinoviev recounts an incident involving the purchase of a pair of trousers. In the Soviet Union he might have had a choice of two or three pairs of trousers in his size. In the Western shop where he found himself the choice was so vast that he could not make up his mind and left without making a purchase (Zinoviev, 1987a:118). A more serious problem was the extent to which personal freedom in the West was accompanied by personal responsibility for affairs which in the Soviet Union were either largely taken care of by the State or simply did not exist. He was totally unprepared for the complexity of civilian life in the West. In the Soviet Union he had a passport and a workbook, which formed the totality of his personal paperwork. In Munich he had to spend what seemed to him an inordinate amount of time on such matters as making income tax returns, arranging mortgage agreements, dealing with various agencies, banks and other institutions.

Psychological adjustment was one thing. Much more immediate was the problem of actually earning a living. Zinoviev has not held a remunerative post since he came to the West. A combination of circumstances, including perhaps his own personality, has contributed to the fact that his earnings come exclusively from his writing, lecturing and radio and television appearances.

Zinoviev and his wife Olga worked hard when they were in Moscow, but there the proportion of work which was directly linked to income was much smaller. Zinoviev's books on logic, for instance, were not written in order to make money. In the West the pressure to earn has been great, and Zinoviev confesses to having had to work even harder than he did in Moscow (Zinoviev, 1989a:336). This effort has led to a steady stream, indeed a torrent, of books and articles which shows no sign of abating. Books written after *Ziiaiushchie vysoty* appeared in 1978 and 1979, together with the first collection of lectures he had given since arriving in the West (*Svetloe budushchee* (*The Radiant Future*) (1978), *Zapiski nochnogo storozha* (*Notes of a Night Watchman*), *V preddverii raia* (*On the Threshold of Paradise*), *Bez illiuzii* (*Without Illusions*) (1979)). The two-volume *Zheltyi dom* appeared in 1980. In 1981 he published another collection of lectures and interviews under the title *My i zapad* (*We and the West*) and *Kommunizm kak real'nost'* (*The Reality of Communism*), a collection of theoretical essays on the nature of Communism. Two more books appeared in 1982 and another two in 1983. One appeared in 1984. No less than twelve appeared between 1985 and 1991. More books are in the pipeline. There has also been a play and many articles, lectures and interviews. In addition he has continued with his painting and drawing and has had exhibitions in Geneva, Lausanne and Milan. His wife Olga Mironovna has played an enormous role in his success, not only typing his vast output but also contributing to the family income by teaching Russian to units of the American armed forces, acting as his agent and latterly by working full-time for Radio Liberty. As if that were not enough, Olga Mironovna gave birth on 24 April 1990 to their second daughter, Ksenia.

Throughout the 1980s, his reputation as a writer, acquired instantly after publication of *Ziiaiushchie vysoty*, continued to grow. His notoriety, however, grew perhaps even faster. Never a friend of the 'third wave' of emigration, Zinoviev lampooned Soviet émigrés mercilessly in his books *Gomo sovetikus* (*Homo Sovieticus*) and *Moi dom – moia chuzhbina* (*My home – my exile*), accusing them virtually of being little more than the Soviet advance guard in the West and of creating a Soviet system in microcosm. At the same time, he succeeded in alienating almost everyone in the field of Soviet studies by tirelessly asserting that Western experts did not understand how the Soviet system worked, and accusing them of doing as much to misinform the West about the true nature of Soviet Communism as the KGB. Finally, his views on Stalin and Stalinism, set out in his book *Nashei iunosti polet* (*The Flight of Our Youth*), caused great offence among those who interpreted his utterances as nothing less than approbation of both Stalin and his policies.

But throughout most of the 1980s his notoriety was confined to émigré circles and disgruntled Western academics. He had been a non-person in the Soviet Union ever since his exile in 1978. However, in 1989 things began to change. In February of that year, the Soviet publication *Inostrannaia literatura* (*Foreign Literature*) published the replies of exiled Soviet writers, including Zinoviev, to a questionnaire about their attitude to Russian literature. In addition, Zinoviev published a short article in the same issue.[4] In August *Moskovskie novosti* (*Moscow News*) published an interview with Zinoviev conducted by his old friend Evgenii Ambartsumov, which was reprinted in December in *Gorizont*.[5]

In 1990 his 'newsworthiness' increased considerably. On 9 March a televised debate between Zinoviev and Boris Yeltsin was shown on a French television programme.[6] On 6 June *Pravda* published an interview with Zinoviev which produced a reader response of some 700 letters.[7] Zinoviev replied in an article entitled '*Ia ostaius' russkim pisatelem*' ('I remain a Russian writer'), published in *Pravda* on 9 September.[8] In June *Moskovskii literator* published an abridged version of an interview with Zinoviev conducted by Georges Nivat for *L'Expresse* five years previously[9] and in July *Komsomol'skaia pravda* published an article on Zinoviev by his oldest and possibly closest friend Karl Kantor, together with excerpts from Zinoviev's *Idi na Golgofu*.[10] In that month, too, *Izvestiia* reported the return to Alexander Zinoviev of his Soviet citizenship.[11] In September *Komsomol'skaia pravda* published a long article by Zinoviev entitled '*Ia khochu rasskazat' vam o zapade*' ('I want to tell you about the West'), which generated a debate which was still continuing in March 1991.[12] Articles on Zinoviev also appeared in a number of Leningrad and Moscow journals, the details of which need not concern us here. That year also saw the publication of some of Zinoviev's original works. An Estonian publishing house brought out an Estonian version of Zinoviev *Gorbachevizm*, a series of articles on perestroika. In November and December *Sovetskaia literatura* serialised Zinoviev's hilarious *Moi dom-moia chuzhbina*, a work written entirely in verse.[13]

The year 1991 saw the publication of *Ziiaiushchie vysoty* in 250,000 copies, an event which eclipsed the publication of other works, including *Katastroika: Povest' o perestroike v Partgrade* (*Katastroika: A Tale of Perestroika in Partgrad*) which appeared in an Estonian translation, a volume containing *Gomo sovetikus* and *Para bellum* published by Moskovskii rabochii and the serialisation in *Smena* of his *Idi na Golgofu*.[14]

However, he also continued with his publicistic writing. The journal *Zhurnalist*, organ of the Union of Journalists of the USSR, published a long article by Zinoviev entitled '*Kuda my idem?*' ('Where are we going?'), much of which is in fact 'lifted' from his book which we analyse in Chapter 9.[15] This article was prefaced by a long introduction by the editor, who clearly wished to soften the impact it was bound to have and who promised an extensive critique in a forthcoming issue. Already the next issue carried a strong rebuttal, written by the editor of the journal *Politicheskie issledovaniia*.[16]

There is no doubt that Zinoviev has been accepted back into the literary fold. Moreover, such is the pattern of the publication of his work that he has already provided ample ammunition for both extremes of the political spectrum, already reflected in several articles which have appeared in publications as diverse as the Trans-Baikal Military District newspaper and the newspaper of Leningrad writers.[17]

It is fair to say that Zinoviev did not expect that his work would be published in the Soviet Union in his lifetime. The events of the last two years have been truly remarkable. It is clear that his controversial image among the *cognoscenti* in the West is about to be eclipsed by his controversial image in his native land. His early work will be used by the radicals to criticise the nature of the Soviet state, his later work by those who seek to preserve it.

The increasingly stormy nature of Zinoviev's professional life is balanced by the relative tranquillity of his private one. The Zinovievs live today in a modest but comfortable apartment on the outskirts of Munich. Zinoviev's own paintings decorate the walls of their living-room, although they are beginning to make way for some of his daughter Polina's. In the basement of the building he has a room which he uses for his writing. It is simply furnished, spare, ordered. Olga Mironovna now works full-time for Radio Liberty. Their elder daughter Polina hopes to follow a career in stage design. Their younger daughter Ksenia is already displaying the energy and mobility which one would expect in the offspring of such active parents. The fifth member of their family is their dog Sharik, who, according to his master, is endowed with human qualities. In the West, Zinoviev the arch-individualist has found privacy. It is perhaps typical of him that he should profess a yearning for his old collective!

2 Zinoviev's Style and Language

In this chapter we analyse the way in which Zinoviev constructs his works. We examine his 'generative device' and his use of language. This is a necessary preliminary to the examination of individual works in the chapters forming the remainder of this book. Zinoviev is a difficult writer in some respects and demands effort on the part of his readers. He himself has spoken of his work as 'littérature synthétique' (Zinoviev, 1990a:373), by which he means a new form of synthesised literature which is adequate for the task he has set himself, namely the description of Communist society. Such a society is an immensely complex phenomenon, riddled with contradictions and paradoxes. A 'linear' description would fail to capture the way in which the many separate strands of the Communist leviathan interweave and influence each other. What is required is a synthetic approach. He has likened his works to symphonies (Zinoviev, 1990a:388–9), arguing that the only way to understand what he is trying to do is to keep in the foreground of one's mind *simultaneously* the many different angles from which he approaches his subject. This is where effort on the part of the reader is required, for he or she must work hard to share Zinoviev's symphonic vision of Communist society. The insight to be gained, however, is well worth that effort, and it is to facilitate the reader's task that the following discussion is offered.

ZINOVIEV'S 'GENERATIVE DEVICE'

For the purposes of this discussion a Zinoviev 'text' is a passage of continuous writing which is associated with a title. It is distinguished by the following characteristics: (a) brevity; (b) clarity; (c) logical well-formedness; (d) completeness; (e) humour (although not always); (f) a remarkably restricted lexis; (g) the presence of a title. A Zinoviev 'work' is therefore a given number of 'texts' with a corresponding number of titles. *Ziiaiushchie vysoty* (*The Yawning Heights*), for example, can be seen as a 'collection' or 'compendium' of six hundred texts, *Zheltyi dom* (*The Madhouse*) as a compendium of eight hundred and twenty-four, and so on. Since every Zinoviev work is constituted in exactly the same fashion, one can consider his output as the continuous generation of compendia of texts. But why describe *Ziiaiushchie vysoty* as a 'compendium' of six hundred 'texts' rather than as a single 'text' divided into six hundred 'segments' or 'parts'?

The main reason is that Zinoviev's 'texts' are self-contained. When Zinoviev began to write clandestinely, he was worried that he might be arrested or that his manuscript might be confiscated at any time. He thus wrote in a discontinuous, kaleidoscopic fashion, striving to set out the outlines of his socio-political philosophy in all its aspects with the intention of developing them later. Each separate 'text' could, if necessary, stand on its own. This was a very good solution to a pressing problem. However, it is noteworthy that, even after leaving the Soviet Union, Zinoviev has continued to employ the same approach, convinced that it offers the best way of dealing with his subject matter. The texts need not necessarily always be read in the order in which they appear (although some critics tend to exaggerate the extent to which that is true). Many of them are interchangeable in the sense, for example, that certain texts in *Ziiaiushchie vysoty* could be interchanged with certain texts from *V preddverii raia*. Moreover, certain texts could feature in more than one work. Indeed, some do![1]

Zinoviev's 'generative device' for the production of his works is not only remarkably simple, it is also remarkably powerful. The title announces the topic to be treated in a particular text and several texts can be grouped under the same title. Texts, however, can also vary stylistically; prose, poetry, dramatic dialogue are only three of the literary styles which Zinoviev employs. He can therefore discuss a topic in varying degrees of depth (by allocating a varying number of texts to that topic) and in various stylistic modes (narrative, poetic, scientific, etc.). Let us see how this system works in practice.

A typical Zinoviev work is a tightly woven fabric containing a variable number of individual strands of different length. These strands are interwoven as follows. Let us suppose that strand A consists of texts A, A_1, A_2 ... A_n, strand B of texts B_1, B_2, ... B_n, strand C of texts C_1, C_2, ... C_n, and so on. A typical sequence would then be A, B, C, A_1, B_1, C_1, A_2, B_2, C_2 ... A_n, B_n, C_n. If one then adds a 'style system', symbolised by, say, roman numerals, the fabric of a Zinoviev work is further enriched. If I = 'verse', II = 'prose narrative', III = 'dramatic dialogue', and so on, the combinatorial possibilities are vast: AI, BII, CIII, AIV, BI, CII, ... And, of course, a Zinoviev text often reflects more than one style: AI/II, BI, CII/III ... The addition of a title provides a further dimension. Titles can be used to link different texts, for example '*Krysy*' ('Rats'), '*Stranichka geroicheskoi istorii*' ('A Page of Heroic History') in *Ziiaiushchie vysoty*, or they can indicate the topic of an individual text.

Stylistic variation provides Zinoviev with a wide range of ways of discussing an issue. He will typically juxtapose a serious passage of sociological exposition with an intellectual discussion of the same topic by several of his literary characters, followed by a bitingly funny satirical verse. He thus bombards an issue from many angles and with an impressive variety of ammunition, ranging from the scientifically analytical to the mercilessly satirical.

It is now perhaps clear why it is preferable to think of Zinoviev's works as compendia of 'texts' rather than as single texts in their own right. On the other hand, one might argue that he is engaged in the constant production of text as such, various segments of which constitute his individual works. I have discussed this question in some detail elsewhere (Kirkwood, 1990b:216–28), but we may note here that such an approach is consistent with recent theories of text associated with writers like Barthes and Foucault.

There is some merit in considering Zinoviev's writing as 'écriture' as defined by Barthes, i.e. as a process rather than a product, since in fact Zinoviev can be seen as a kind of generative device producing an unending wave of writing composed of an unending stream of particles. One might continue this metaphor and speak of these particles as particles which receive a particular type of charge. These charges may carry various labels specifying topic, stylistic mode, genre type, and so on. This wave can then be divided into segments consisting of various numbers of particles and these segments can themselves be labelled. Zinoviev's text to date, therefore, can be regarded as a chronological list of the 'works' he has published since 1978.

If this preoccupation with the question of how to define a Zinoviev work is at the centre of our attention, it is because Zinoviev himself has a remarkably pragmatic solution to this question, a solution, moreover, which lends some (unwitting, I am sure) support to Foucault's view of what constitutes a 'work'.

In practical terms, a 'work' for Zinoviev is a segment of his ongoing text which a publisher will publish. Increasingly the language in which a particular 'work' appears is also determined by practicalities. For instance, at the time of writing, some of his works have only appeared in Italian or in French or in German. A published Russian version is unobtainable. Such a situation is unusual, to say the least. Nowadays, to read the complete Zinoviev *oeuvre* one must have a good reading knowledge of Russian, German and Italian. Indeed, if one includes his newspaper articles, one would have to add French and Spanish as well as several of the East European and Scandinavian languages.

Zinoviev's earlier works are notable for their length and diversity (*Ziiaiushchie vysoty, V preddverii raia, Zheltyi dom*), although they also include the relatively short *Svetloe budushchee* (*The Radiant Future*), *Zapiski nochnogo storozha* (*Notes of a Night Watchman*), *My i Zapad* (*We and the West*). Later works (those written after 1980) are much shorter and tend to be stylistically more uniform, although they remain structurally kaleidoscopic. Two works entirely in verse are *Evangelie dlia Ivana* (*A Gospel for Ivan*), *Moi dom – moia chuzhbina* (*My Home – My Exile*). A third – on the subject of drink – consists of poems in four languages, interspersed with reproductions of some of his paintings.[2] There is a play: *Ruka Kremlia* (*The Hand/Arm [?] of the Kremlin*). There are collections of essays: *Ni svoboda ni ravenstva ni bratstva* (*Neither Freedom, nor Equality nor Fraternity*), *Gorbachevizm* (*Gorbachevism*), *Die Macht des Unglaubens* (*The Power of Disbelief*), *Die Diktatur der Logik* (*The Dictatorship of Logic*), *Katastroika. Gorbachevs Potemkinsche Dör-*

fer (*Katastroika. Gorbachev's Potemkin Villages*). Finally, there are 'novels': *Para Bellum, Idi na Golgofu, Zhivi! (Live!)*, *Katastroika. Povest' o perestroike v Partgrade* (*Katastroika – A Tale of Perestroika in Partgrad*). It should be remembered, however, that such a segmentation of Zinoviev's ongoing output is at least partly a result of pragmatic factors relating to the 'juridical and institutional' systems (Foucault, 1988:205) within which Zinoviev has had to operate.

ZINOVIEV'S USE OF LANGUAGE

We noted above that one of the features of a Zinoviev text is its relatively restricted lexis. In a sense it is easy to account for this phenomenon. Zinoviev is a descriptive minimalist. Unlike more conventional writers, he ignores vast tracts of context such as time, place, dress, physical description, the weather, psychological states, to list but a few. Lexical items associated with these domains are correspondingly absent. In addition, his characters almost without exception belong to the intelligentsia. They tend therefore to speak in similar fashion, their idiolects devoid of regional variation or dialectal influence.

Speech is not the same thing as language, of course. Speech is text. It has content. It has 'topic' and 'comment'. If the topics are restricted, the speech will be restricted correspondingly, at least in the sense that certain lexical-items relating to the topics will recur, even although the number of possible 'comments' may be infinite. Zinoviev's 'universe of discourse' is Soviet society, which, for him, is Communist society in its purest form to date. Much of the 'Stoff', therefore, of a Zinoviev text is composed of descriptions of various aspects of Soviet realia and of people's reactions to them. The result is a kind of grey uniformity, intensified by the fact that most of Zinoviev's characters have titles rather than names. They are known as 'Teacher' or 'Sociologist' or 'Careerist'.

The expression 'grey uniformity' does not conjure up a vision of great art, and indeed the first comment I ever heard from a Soviet citizen who had read a *samizdat* version of *Ziiaiushchie vysoty* contained the phrase *tam nichego khud-*

ozhestvennogo net (there is nothing of art in it).[3] But in the opinion of this writer Zinoviev's blend of high intelligence, clarity of vision and sense of the grotesque has enabled him to portray the grey uniformity of Soviet reality with conviction, while revealing the underlying complexity of that society in a manner which is artistic, even though one is reminded perhaps more of caricature than of classicism. Perhaps the most important point about Zinoviev's portrait of Soviet society is that it rings true. For instance, one is almost tempted to assert that his description of life on a collective farm in Part Three of *Zheltyi dom* gives one a more realistic picture of what Soviet country life is like than the combined output of the so-called 'Derevenshchiki'. Zinoviev does not describe countryside as such, he describes what makes the countryside in the Soviet Union 'Soviet'. In the words of the Soviet linguist T.G. Vinokur: 'Real art is first and foremost truth. Truth in things big and small. Truth in details.'[4]

Lexical simplicity in Zinoviev's writing is more than compensated by connotative complexity. There are several types of meaning, the 'dictionary' meaning of a word or phrase being but one of them. Zinoviev's language is often richly allusive, never more so than when exposing the insidiousness of the Soviet cliché. The titles of his first two books illustrate the point well. *Ziiaiushchie vysoty* is a pun on the Soviet cliché *siiaiushchie vysoty* (the gleaming heights), which was supposed to signify the longed-for ideals of Communism as mountain peaks illumined by the shining light of Marxism-Leninism. By replacing *siiaiushchie* (gleaming) with *Ziiaiushchie* (yawning) Zinoviev at a stroke simultaneously ridicules the emptiness of the original cliché and, more importantly, captures one of the most characteristic features of Soviet reality, namely the excruciating tedium of Soviet everyday ritual. With the title *Svetloe budushchee* he accomplishes something similar. The full cliché is the following: '*Da zdravstvuet kommunizm – svetloe budushchee vsego chelovechestva*' ('Long Live Communism – the radiant future of all mankind'). It is not just that the title of the book is in stark contrast to the depiction within it of the grey tedium of present-day Soviet reality. The point is that the radiant future has already arrived. The system has set in its mould.

There will be no fundamental change. The radiant future is the grey monotonous present.

We have already noted the range of styles which Zinoviev employs in his work and these styles, of course, are linguistically marked. Formal registers are employed alongside other registers. It is in fact consideration of register that enables us to differentiate among the following types of text: academic treatise, ideological tract, political pamphlet, lecture, dramatic dialogue, memoir, diary, song, poem, polylogue, all of which are to be found in close juxtaposition in Zinoviev's work. He uses all of those registers, and in addition resorts to parody. He shows particular skill in his ability to handle a topic in one register and then deal with it in another, revealing thereby a completely different facet of the problem in question. For instance, he might treat seriously, in 'academic' mode, the concept of the Soviet 'collective', outlining its specific characteristics. A little later he might give examples of the Soviet collective in action, illustrated by the deeds and conversations of some of his characters in what might be called dramatic mode. Here there is scope for humour, exaggeration, irony. Still later he might treat the topic again in the form of satirical verse. The result is that the reader's appreciation of the concept is much fuller than it would have been had Zinoviev been content to restrict himself to a formal register only.

Perhaps the most important register in Zinoviev's armoury is one which is rarely encountered in print and which I will provisionally define as 'academic-colloquial'. This label designates the mode of speech most often adopted by his characters, a mode which is recognisable by its mix of intelligence, cynicism and vulgarity. One of the great pleasures in reading Zinoviev is 'listening' to bright people discussing their society in an informal setting. The amalgam of intelligent insight, thoughtful question, genuine intellectual enquiry, elegant refutation and ribald comment is exhilarating.

Another great pleasure is to examine how Zinoviev's account of an event resonates against the absent official account of the same event. Given that Soviet publications until very recently were by definition official, or officially sanctioned, the type of language that Zinoviev uses to describe Soviet realia was not available in print. This partly explains the freshness of Zinoviev's treatment. But it is this resonance between 'Zinovievese' and 'officialese' that makes the translation of a Zinoviev work very difficult.

It is probably true to say that there are no good translations of Zinoviev, in the sense that there are no Zinoviev texts in translation which can hope to have the impact on their readers that the originals will have. The reason is basically simple: Soviet experience is unique. Western societies do not operate like Soviet society and consequently Western readers can have no access to the rich connotative vein which runs right through a typical Zinoviev text. Very often, therefore, a translation lacks a truly important dimension. We shall illustrate this point by examining a passage from a Zinoviev text, in the course of which we shall discuss questions of text, subtext and context.

ДА ЗДРАВСТВУЕТ КОММУНИЗМ

(1) На площади Космонавтов при въезде на проспект Марксизма-Ленинизма воздвигли стационарный лозунг Да здравствует коммунизм – светлое будущее всего человечества!' (2) Лозунг построили по просьбе трудящихся. (3) Строили долго, главным образом – зимой, когда расценки выше. (4) И убухали на это уйму средств. (5) По слухам, не меньше, чем вложили во все сельское хозяйство в первую пятилетку. (6) Но мы теперь очень богаты, и подобные затраты для нас сущие пустяки. (7) На арабов потратили впустую, а тут несомненная польза есть.

(SB:9)

Long live Communism

(1) On Cosmonaut Square by the entrance to Marxism–Leninism Avenue [they] erected a permanent slogan 'Long live Communism – the bright future of all mankind!' (2) The slogan was built at the workers' request. (3) They built it slowly, mainly in winter when the rates are higher. (4) And spent a bomb on it. (5) According to rumour, not less than the total investment in agriculture

during the first Five-Year Plan. (6) But now we are rich and expenditure like that is a mere bagatelle. (7) We squandered on the Arabs for nothing, but this [the slogan] is of some use at least.

The title of the passage is part of the slogan which features in sentence 1. 'Long live Communism', a phrase which reflects what is officially deemed to be the fervent desire of every progressive Soviet citizen, introduces a description of what Communism is like in reality, only part of which is reproduced above, a description which is the antithesis of an official description and which presents a state of affairs in which graft, corruption, stupidity, careerism seem to be the chief characteristics. The implication that sensible people would be mad to desire such a system is clear.

Let us now consider the seven sentences which begin the text in question. There is a clear and steady progression from an objective reporting style in sentence 1 to pure sarcasm in sentence 7. The first sentence could almost have appeared in a Soviet newspaper, but for the fact that there is no Cosmonaut Square in Moscow, nor an Avenue of Marxism–Leninism. Yet the information that municipal authorities are prepared to spend scarce resources on the construction of a permanent slogan invites the reader to make judgements about priorities. One might imagine the reaction of the average British citizen, for instance, to the appearance of a large ferro-concrete slogan somewhere in central London which said: 'Long live Thatcherism – the bright future of all mankind', especially if the funding of it had entailed the closing down of a school or a wing of a hospital. Sentence 2, therefore, is particularly striking. On the one hand it is stylistically 'official' and could have appeared in the official press. The phrase *po pros'be trudiashchikhsia* is another cliché, which, however, in this context invites the reader to wonder just how likely it is that workers would genuinely want the authorities to erect such a slogan. It loses in translation, however, because the phrase 'at the request of the workers' is not a cliché in English, it does not feature as an everyday occurrence in our press, television or radio.

The humour in sentences 1 and 2 rely on context and subtext. The language is neutral bordering on official and is reminiscent of the official Soviet press. The next sentence is not, and for that reason its impact is striking. If sentence 2 rings hollow – no one believes that workers want permanent slogans – sentence 3 rings absolutely true – and at the same time could not possibly appear in the Soviet press of the time (1976). An official equivalent would stress the enthusiasm and dynamism of the workforce and emphasise the consequent savings in time, wastage, materials, etc. Sentence 3, therefore, resonates against this unwritten Soviet equivalent, which every Soviet reader would have in mind, given the official colouring of sentences 1 and 2. This effect is untranslatable since it derives from a Soviet context which is unknown to the English reader. The language, however, continues to be formal.

This is not the case in sentence 4. Here there is a quite marked stylistic change. The words *ubukhali* and *uima* are colloquial and belong entirely in an informal register. So, whereas the style of sentence 3, if not its content, could still be associated with the official Soviet media, sentence 4 is beyond the pale, both in terms of form *and* content. Sentence 4 thus introduces a commentary on the part of the narrator. Sentences 5–7 expand this commentary in which there is progressively admixed hyperbole and sarcasm.

Again one has to be aware of the Soviet context. Sentence 5, for instance, refers to an especially hallowed period in official Soviet history, the time of the first Five-Year Plan and the collectivisation of agriculture, a time of great sacrifice but also a time of great endeavour. By comparing the sums invested in an essential enterprise like agriculture and an inessential object like a slogan, the narrator juxtaposes the romantic era of self-sacrifice with the humdrum greyness of life under Brezhnev, indicating at the same time that the slogan costs an enormous amount of money. Sentence 6 underlines the cost by its sarcastic assertion that the Soviet Union is rich enough to be able to afford such expenditure. The subtext here is the constant reiteration in the Soviet media of the great achievements of the Soviet people, of the success of its burgeoning economy, despite 'temporary difficulties', of the extent to which people are now so much better off than they were. As an example of this, the narrator informs us in sentence 6 that even more was spent on the Arabs without impoverishing the Soviet Union.

In the final sentence the narrator expands this point and at the same time takes a side-swipe at the whole of Soviet foreign policy in the Middle East since the Arab–Israeli war of 1967, which included the expenditure of vast sums of money on the supply of arms to, and the financial support of, various Arab regimes – all for nothing, in the opinion of the narrator, since the Soviets in the end were kicked out of Egypt and their influence in the Middle East reduced virtually to zero. All that money was entirely wasted, whereas at least the slogan will be of some use. Since we can assume that the narrator believes the slogan to be of very little use whatsoever, the force of the narrator's jibe at Soviet Middle Eastern policy is thereby enhanced. For the Soviet reader it is further enhanced by the fact that for years the Soviet media had promoted the Arab cause, but in a fashion which was heavily biased.

If we now review the passage briefly as a whole we can see that Zinoviev has managed to achieve quite a lot in the space of a few short sentences. He has alluded to the untruthfulness of the Soviet press, ridiculed Soviet ideology by his deadpan reference to the assertion that the slogan was built at the request of the workers, ridiculed Soviet foreign policy in the Middle East, drawn attention to the squandering of resources and the absence on the part of the authorities of concern about matters of efficient economic management. At the same time he skilfully tells us quite a lot about the narrator via his choice of language. We know that he is a Soviet citizen (see sentence 5), that he has a sense of humour with a penchant for irony, sarcasm and hyperbole. It is safe to assume that he is not a shining-eyed idealist who accepts the Communist system uncritically. He is in fact, as becomes clear from the very next 'text', a Professor, Doctor of Philosophical Sciences, Head of the Department of Methodological Problems of Scientific Communism in a prestigious research institute, almost a corresponding member of the Soviet Academy of Sciences, in other words not some kind of disaffected dissident but a respected member of the Soviet establishment, someone whose outward behaviour will be a model of orthodoxy and Soviet respectability.

These remarks on the difficulty of translating Zinoviev
can serve as an introduction to a more general discussion of
Zinoviev's skill in his use of language. In the remainder of
this chapter we shall look at various examples of his verbal
art, with the aim of providing a set of guidelines for those
who have not yet encountered his work and debating points
for those who have.

A theory of language which is useful for our purposes
posits levels of language in ascending order of complexity:
word, phrase, clause, sentence. Each of these levels can
fulfil various speech functions. 'Silence!', for example, or
'Silence?' or 'Silence.' are examples of 'speech' making use
of 'language' at the level of the word 'silence'. The functions thereby fulfilled are respectively 'exclamation', 'question' and 'statement'. Zinoviev's use of language can be
analysed at all four levels, although we shall limit ourselves
to three, namely the levels of word, phrase and sentence.

ZINOVIEV'S USE OF WORDS [5]

We have noted above that Zinoviev's lexical range is restricted compared with most writers of 'belles lettres', yet it
is also true that he uses many words which are not to be
found in any dictionary. This point is perhaps best illustrated
with reference to *Ziiaiushchie vysoty*. The setting for the
novel is Ibansk, a fictitious territory which sounds, nevertheless, Slavic, mainly because of the *–nsk* ending (cf.
Briansk, Minsk). The apparently innocuous *Iba–*, however,
is in any Russian's mind immediately associated with *eba–*
(pronounced *iba–*), which is the stem of the Russian verb
ebat' (to fuck). *Ibansk*, therefore, suggests a placed where
everything is 'fucked up', or 'cocked up'.

The Russian equivalent of 'John Smith' is 'Ivan Ivanovich
Ivanov', which Zinoviev replaces in *Ziiaiushchie vysoty* with
'Iban Ibanovich Ibanov', a universal personage who both
'fucks up' and is 'fucked up'. But Zinoviev goes on to coin
many more neologisms based on the same root *iba–*, of
which Moskovitch cites twenty-four. These neologisms can
be classified under various grammatical categories, includ-

ing *noun*, *adjective*, *adverb* (the verb is already extant in Russian), thus allowing Zinoviev a wide range of application. Examples of nouns: *ibanizm* (cf. 'communism', 'Leninism', 'Marxism'), *ibanologiia* (cf. Sovietology); examples of adjectives: *obshcheibanskii* (cf. *obshcherusskii* (common Russian)), *'drevneibanskii* (cf. *drevnerusskii* (medieval Russian)); examples of adverbs: *po–ibanskomu* (cf. *po–russkomu* (in the Russian manner)). Many aspects of Soviet life are easily and very effectively ridiculed by this ingenious word-formational device.

His neologisms, however, extend much further. One of his most frequent targets is pseudo-scientific terminological precision, and the coining of spurious technical terms is frequently encountered in his work. Many of these terms are richly allusive, often involve an element of punning, and are consequently untranslatable. Examples include the following: *kibenematika* (cf. *kibernetika* (cybernetics)); *idiotologiia* (cf. *idiologiia* (ideology)). The first term reminds every Russian of the phrase *k ebinoi materi*, a particularly foul-mouthed oath. It is, however, very funny, since the 'Russian' word *kibernetika* is unknown to many Russians and Zinoviev's coinage is a very plausible 'folk-Russian etymology'. More sinister examples are: *soznatoriia* (cf. *soznanie* (consciousness) and *sanatoriia* (sanatorium) and *guboterapiia* (cf. *guba* (military prison) and *terapiia* (therapy)).

Another area in which he is energetically inventive is that of proper names and toponyms. Many of his characters are simply given labels instead of names: Teacher, Sociologist, Toady, Creep, Party Member, etc. The word for 'member' in Russian (*chlen*) can also refer to the male sexual organ, thus the 'titles' *Chlen* and the diminutive form *Chlenik* carry an obvious connotation. Sometimes real people are satirised by allusion to their names. Thus Raspashonka, clearly recalls Evtushenko, while Tvarzhinskaia a composite containing the root *tvar'* (creature), refers to a former colleague of Zinoviev's, Professor Modrzhinskaia. Other characters have allusive surnames such as Suslikov (a reference to Suslov, but of inferior stature, denoted by the diminutive infix *–ik–*), or Poluportiantsev, with connotations of 'puttees' (*portianki*) and 'incompleteness', 'half-ness' (*polu-*). Sometimes he is offensive to other Soviet nationalities by coining proper names with linguistic elements from Georgian or Turkic. Good examples quoted by Moskovitch are *Sheiavyiarazve* for Shevardnadze, or *Lomai-Sarai-Kirpichi-Guly* for Azeri names ending in *–ogly*. A particularly fine example is *Sun'khuimuliukov*.

He does the same thing with placenames. The very first text of *V preddverii raia* contains no less than twenty coinages based on the word *vozhd'* (leader, *Führer*), a satirical allusion to the former Soviet practice of naming places and towns after political leaders, notably Stalin. Particularly fine examples are *Vozhdekyzylogly, Vozhdekurulkhurarly, Vozhdegadan* (cf. Magadan), *Vozhdelyma* (cf. Kolyma). Magadan and Kolyma, of course, are famous for their labour camps. At the end of that text is a short 'poem' written by the great folk poet of the 'Vozhdeiasykskaia Autonomous Oblast' highlighting the fact that no matter where one roams in the Soviet Union,

> *Ty vsegda priidesh'*
> *V gorod Vozhshsh.*

> You will always arrive
> In a town called Vozhd'.

The spelling of 'Vozhshsh' is noteworthy. First, it is an approximate phonetic rendering of the folk poet's non-Russian accent. (Zinoviev very often mocks so-called national poets who nevertheless write in Russian rather than in their own language, mainly for career reasons). Secondly, it recalls the Russian word *vosh'* ('louse'), and thereby underlines the total insignificance of provincial Soviet towns, yet simultaneously links this image to that of 'leader'. This duality of reference conjures up the pathetic spectacle of provincial backwaters seeking to curry favour by naming themselves after whichever Party boss is number one and the equally pathetic spectacle of Party leaders deriving an ego-boost from such a practice. Such examples of word-play abound in Zinoviev's works, making them at once richly allusive for 'those in the know' and rather elusive for those who are not.

ZINOVIEV'S USE OF PHRASES

We use the term 'phrase' to denote a string of words which does not contain a finite form of a verb. There are three notable ways in which Zinoviev employs phrases. First, phrases make up the vast majority of the thousands of titles which accompany his texts. Many of them are stylistically neutral and fulfil no other but an explanatory function. Some of them are well-known, or allude to phrases which are well-known. For instance, the title *Zhelat' ili ne zhelat'* (to want or not to want) recalls *byt' ili ne byt'* (to be or not to be), *sochetat' nepriiatnoe s bespoleznym* (combine the unpleasant with the useless) (ZhD I:75) is a neat parody of the Russian (Soviet?) cliché *sochetat' priiatnoe s poleznym* (combine the pleasant with the useful), *sotsial'no-postel'nye otnosheniia* (socio-carnal relations) (VPR:74) is a refashioning of the common *sotsial'no-bytovye otnosheniia* (everyday social relations). Others, however, are reminiscent of Soviet newspaper headlines: *rabotat' po udarnomy* (to work in a Stakhanovite spirit) (ZhD I:92), *v tvorcheskom poiske* (in creative search) (ZhD I:108), *uverennoi postup'iu* (with confident step) (ZhD I:109). Such headlines accompanied articles in the Soviet press which were long on ideology and short on truth. The accompanying texts in Zinoviev's work are usually highly revealing. Again one must emphasise how refreshing, how novel this was when his earlier works first appeared.

There are two words in Russian, *shablon* and *shtamp*, both of which in one of their meanings refer to clichés and mechanical speech. *Govorit' shablonami* means 'to speak in clichés'. Official Soviet speech consists to a large extent of clichés and when this fact is related to the highly routine, yet essentially ritualistic behaviour of Soviet citizens at work in their primary collectives, an important aspect of Soviet life is revealed: responses to events are verbalised in a code which is hermetically sealed and essentially theatrical. A typical Soviet response to a problem is to call a Party meeting and discuss that problem – but only in ways permitted by the rules of Soviet intercourse: often the 'solution' would be expressed in a row of clichés: *rabotat' po udarnomy v tvorcheskom poiske i s uverennoi postup'iu* (work in a Stakhanovite fashion in a spirit of creative search and with confident step). If the English translation sounds stilted, the Russian is not much better.

The situation is actually more serious than that, however. People can get their way by means of invocation of these clichés, to which there is no legitimate response. If some chore is presented as a '*vazhnaia obshchestvennaia rabota*' (business of great social importance or significance), it is very difficult to find a legitimate reason for not carrying it out. This situation has not changed under *perestroika*, if anything it has intensified. No one in the Soviet Union is officially against *perestroika*, for instance. Debate, while considerably freer, is still to a great extent hamstrung by the need to use Soviet clichés. Gorbachev's speeches in this respect differ not a whit from Brezhnev's. Notice, however, another consequence of clichés. They are devoid of genuine communicative content. Thus when Gorbachev urges people to support *perestroika*, his exhortations are often clothed in the same old clichés.

Clichés, however, are not confined to Russian. What makes the Soviet cliché special is the accompanying ritualistic behaviour. In times of crisis, collectives 'volunteer' to 'take on increased responsibilities', 'to become vigilant', 'to take measures', and so on, while everyone knows that most of the ensuing effort will go into making it appear *as if* new responsibilities, etc. are being taken on.

Zinoviev is masterly in his use of Soviet clichés to expose the reality of Soviet experience which exists behind the façade of Soviet rhetoric. That reality, in his depiction, is a mixture of incompetence, cynicism, skulduggery, careerism, mutual back-scratching and oppression, the poverty in which the vast majority of the population have to live and the affluence of the successful few. It is largely true to say that, in Zinoviev's works, the number of clichés uttered per character increases with that character's position in the social hierarchy. None of Zinoviev's positive characters, intellectuals who seek to understand their society, uses clichés. Those who do are the successful professors, Doctors of Science, Directors of Institutes, Higher Party Officials, and the like. And, of course, Party activists, whatever their niche in society.

Zinoviev's most effective device is to truncate the Soviet cliché, thereby exposing its vacuity – the bit missed out is totally predictable, e.g. *'Aktual'nye problemy marksistsko— leninskoi teorii v svete...'* ('Topical problems of Marxist-Leninist theory in the light of...') (ZhD I:116). Since the implication is that Marxist–Leninist theory is applicable to every phenomenon on this earth, what comes after 'in the light of...' is irrelevant. A more esoteric example (but only for the Western reader) is the following. A junior colleague in an institute has been charged with reading the manuscript of a died-in-the-wool Stalinist – who, however, is an old Party member who at one time held important posts. His boss therefore stresses the need for caution: *'On staryi chlen partii, posty zanimal. I voobshche vremia seichas ne takoe, chtoby. Tak chto esli v sluchae chego, to bylo by razumno.'* ('He's an old Party member, held important posts. And generally speaking, it isn't a propitious time to. So that if anything happens, it would be sensible.') (ZhD I:197.)

These remarks are largely incomprehensible as they stand, yet are totally intelligible in a Soviet context. First, the excuse that the time is not propitious is a well-worn Soviet excuse for doing nothing. Secondly, since that is the case, if anything were to happen it would be sensible not to have done anything which could land him in trouble. The junior colleague replies in similar vein. What is being asked of him is perfectly clear, as long as his department is informed that he has been so instructed *'...Tak chtoby oni ne ochen' i voobshche'* ('So that they don't too and in general'). Deciphered, this means: that his department doesn't ask too many questions, or gives him a hard time for not doing all his other duties and in general that he's covered in the event of something untoward happening by being able to prove that he was instructed to carry out his assignment by the appropriate authority.

Finally, Zinoviev makes fun of Soviet clichés by punning and other forms of word play. There is a marvellous example in *Ziiaiushchie vysoty*. On the basis of *udarniki kommunisti-cheskogo truda* ('shock-workers of Communist labour' – an appellation of high distinction in the Soviet Union) he coins *ibarniki izmaticheskogo truda*. The juxtaposition *udarniki /ibarniki* invokes the juxtaposition of 'shock-worker' and

'ambitious fucker(-up)'. The subtext is that shock workers
are not necessarily the best workers, but those who for
various reasons are officially recognised as such. The juxtaposition *kommunisticheskogo/izmaticheskogo* invokes a similar
contrast. The word 'Communism' is (or was in 1976) one of
the most hallowed in the Soviet vocabulary. Zinoviev's view
is that the concept has been so emptied of meaningful
content during decades of ideological waffle that *izm* is all
that is left. 'Communist labour' is therefore 'empty labour'.

Another hallowed concept is *dialekticheskii materializm* (dialectical materialism – a scientific theory for the 'explication'
of the material world). A character in *Zheltyi dom*, one
'Matrena-Dura', a peasant woman full of (Soviet) folk-
wisdom whom Zinoviev has created as an antithesis of Solzhenitsyn's Matrena, is noted for her pithy comments about
life in the Soviet village, as well as everything else of which she
has no immediate experience, including *abasraktsionisty* ('ab-
stractionists', i.e. abstract artists). She is so free with her
interpretations of the world that the intellectuals who are
staying in her barn during the 'battle for the harvest' (a
reference to the autumn campaign to get the harvest in with
the help of urban labour) define her philosophy as *izvorotlivyi
matrenalizm* (resourceful/shrewd 'Matrenalism'). The in-
tended contrast here is between a discredited philosophical
approach which tries to fit everything into the procrustean
bed of its own categories and an apparently straightforward,
'common sense' interpretation of the world. In fact the
contrast is more subtle than that, since Zinoviev believes that
the dialectical method has much to offer on the one hand,
and on the other he is suspicious of the so-called 'folk-
wisdom' of the unsophisticated, uneducated peasant.

He also uses malapropisms and spoonerisms to make fun
of uneducated Party hacks who often occupy academic posts.
One character in *Zheltyi dom* (ZhD I:19) speaks of the *bedro
dialektiki* (the *crotch* of dialectics) rather than the *rebro
dialektiki* (the *crux* of dialectics).[6] Another uses the expression *ideia fikus* (idea ficus), instead of *ideia fiks* (*idée fixe*)
(ZhD II:316); a third inverts a well-known saying *v"edennoe
iaitso i lomanyi grosh* (an eaten away egg and a broken
farthing) and produces *lomanoe iaitso i v"edennyi grosh* (a
broken egg and an eaten away farthing) (ZhD I:34).

ZINOVIEV'S USE OF SENTENCES

The most characteristic feature of a Zinoviev sentence is its brevity. His books are collections of various numbers of short texts composed of short sentences. Part of the explanation is that much of his text reflects the rhythms of the spoken language rather than the written. Either his characters are debating a particular issue or one of them is recounting some anecdote or episode to illustrate or emphasise a point. Brevity and relative syntactic simplicity are characteristic of the units of speech. There is, however, another factor which comes into play, namely Zinoviev's penchant for clarity, unfussiness, elimination of unnecessary detail. He has the cartoonist's eye for detail and nuance and his gift for accurate delineation.

The multitudinous conversations conducted by his characters, however, are not set out in conventional form with indents and inverted commas (in Russian the convention is a dash (–)), but in the form of prose narrative, no doubt originally for reasons of economy. Moreover, many of his works, especially the earlier, large ones like *Ziiaiushchie vysoty*, *V preddverii raia*, *Zheltyi dom*, are set in very small print. The effect, paradoxically, is that the reader is confronted with large slabs of apparently dense prose, often with very little paragraphing. This is part of the reason why some readers find Zinoviev hard going.

As might be expected, the mean length of Zinoviev's sentences increases in his collections of articles and his theoretical works such as *Kommunizm kak real'nost'*, reflecting the characteristics of written language. The corresponding increase in the syntactic complexity of his sentences, however, is accompanied by transparent clarity of thought. His utterances are occasionally complex, but always logically well formed. One always knows what he is saying.

In this respect, no doubt, his training as a logician has influenced his literary style. It has certainly coloured his approach to various historical and sociological problems, many of which he treats from a logical point of view. This makes him at once formidable and vulnerable. He is formidable in that he is often difficult to refute logically and vulnerable in that he is prepared to be explicit about what he thinks and therefore presents clear targets. If it is sometimes easy to agree with him, it is equally easy to disagree with him.

These remarks on Zinoviev's use of language at various levels lead naturally to Zinoviev's use of register. Register is slightly different from style in the sense that, whereas the latter can be discussed in terms of 'good' and 'bad', register designates the use of a particular variety of the language which is appropriate for a particular domain. One may define 'register', for example, as 'the language of legal documents', 'the language of advertising', 'business language', 'scientific language', 'philosophical language'. There are other varieties of language, not tied to any one domain, which can be characterised respectively as 'formal', 'informal', 'colloquial', 'officialese', 'bureaucratese', 'obscene', etc. A variety of Russian which has been associated with Soviet officialdom has been variously designated as 'Redspeak', 'Sovspeak', or *langue de bois*' (F. Thom, Wolf Moskovitch, O. Reboul).

If one had to choose one register above all which characterises Zinoviev's writing it would be the one which I have called above 'academic-colloquial'. It is a manner of speaking adopted by intellectuals while discussing subject matter relating to one or another academic discipline, usually a social science. The content of utterances is often quite complex and requires effort on the part of the reader to comprehend it, but the style is also colloquial so that the effect is often that of intelligent people 'taking the mickey'. Here is an example from *Ziiaiushchie vysoty*:

(1) По дороге в сортир Интеллигент изложил свой метод измерения интеллектуального потенциала отдельных людей и целых социальных коллективов. (2) Для этого надо умственную деятельность разложить на элементарные операции примерно одинаковой силы и подсчитать среднее число таких операций за единицу времени. (3) Готов держать пари, сказал Интеллигент, что при этом умственный потенциал Старшины, которого мы несправедливо считаем дегенератом, будет во много раз выше такового у самого Начальника Штаба, которого все считают гением. (4) Мерин сказал, что распре-

деление людей по социальной иерархии не имеет ничего общего с умственными спосбностями. (5) Он это заметил еще в детстве. (6) Его отец был очень крупной шишкой. (7) Правда, его потом за что-то шлепнули. (8) Но он от этого умнее не стал. (9) Даже мать временами удивлялась, как могут таким болванам доверять управление. (ZV:64)

(1) On the way to the shithouse Intellectual set out his method for the measurement of intellectual potential in individuals and entire social groups. (2) This involved the division of mental activities into elementary operations of roughly equal strength, and calculating the number of such operations per unit of time. (3) 'I am prepared to bet,' said Intellectual, 'that using this criterion, we shall see that the mental potential of Sergeant, whom we unjustly consider to be a degenerate, is many times higher than that of the Chief of the General Staff, whom everyone regards as a genius.' (4) Gelding said that the positions allocated to people on the social ladder bore no relation to their intellectual capabilities. (5) He had noticed this when he was a child. (6) His father was a very big wheel indeed. (7) It's true that he was taken down a peg for something, but this didn't make him any more intelligent. (8) Even Gelding's mother used to express her surprise that a fool like that could be trusted with responsibilities.[7]
(YH:93)[7]

It is typical of Zinoviev that the setting should be on the way to the shithouse. Many of his characters discuss lofty subjects of philosophy and art on rubbish dumps or in sleazy bars or on smoke-filled staircase landings. It is rare for the setting to match the subject matter. Apart from the reference to the shithouse, however, the register of sentences 1 and 2 is formal, appropriate to the subject matter. Sentence 3, which follows directly on sentence 2, slips swiftly into informal mode, characterised by *gotov derzhat' pari* ('ready to bet') and *degenerat* ('degenerate', a strong word in Russian). Sentences 6, 7 and 9 contain the colloquialisms *krupnaia shishka* ('a big wheel'), *shlepnuli* (literally, 'spanked' or 'smacked') and *bolvan* ('idiot').

It has to be said that this particular register, the 'academic–colloquial', is particularly difficult to capture in
translation. Partly that is because the 'dictionary' equivalent
of many of the colloquial words and expressions which
Zinoviev puts into the mouths of his characters sound odd
in the mouths of characters speaking English. Attempts to
find 'real' equivalents often founder on the fact that in
English they often sound 'wet' or have a milk-and-water
flavour.

This is particularly true of obscenities. Critics accuse
Zinoviev of overdoing it in this domain (Moskovich, 1988:92;
Rubinshteyn, 1977:14). Certainly he introduces unneces-
sarily whole sequences of texts under the rubric of 'sex and
ideology', for example, which in my view are laboured and
unfunny.[8] Moskovich states that he uses 'unprintable' words
far more often than most modern Russian writers, which is
possibly true. On the other hand, his view that Zinoviev uses
them 'as a protest against the restrictions of Soviet life and
an appeal for more freedom' is debatable. It seems to me
rather that his use of a very varied and rich vocabulary of
'unprintable' words is more often than not motivated by the
circumstances in which his characters use them. Whether
he overdoes the use of obscenities or not, however, they
form a rich vein running through most of his work, im-
parting a quality to the conversations of his characters
which if anything lends them authenticity.

We noted earlier on in this chapter that the style of his
texts varies. We are now in a position to be more specific. He
makes use of a wide range of registers which, in various
combinations, coloured often by the introduction of colloquialisms or even obscenities, highlights the kaleidoscopic
nature of his handling of the realia of Soviet society. His
works are made up of a range of registers which we associate
with: a lecture, treatise, learned article, political tract,
academic textbook. There are examples of all of these in his
works, all of them genuine examples of their kind. Their
doppelgänger exist as well: pastiches of all of these genres in
'Sovspeak'. Then there are ballads, lyrics, poems, doggerel.
There are dramaturgical 'scenes' involving characters and
dramatic dialogue,[9] not forgetting his play *Ruka Kremlia*.
There are jokes, anecdotes, tales. It is hard to think of a

literary genre which is not represented.

It is this sort of stylistic 'mishmash' together with the alleged 'formlessness' of his works which have allowed people to compare him to writers such as Apuleius, Rabelais, Sterne. The comparison is only partly valid. As we shall see, Zinoviev's works are actually constructed rather intricately and the 'formlessness' is much more apparent than real. It is also true to say that he is more a logician writing as an artist than an artist writing as a logician. But he is a logician with a splendid sense of humour. We shall end this chapter by offering examples of three of his poems.

Жалоба неудачника

О судьба! Молю тебя, будь ко мне милее!
Для чего ты мне дала опыт Галилея?!
Для чего мне Канта ум, Свифтова сатира?!
Для чего размах Данта, глубина Шекспира?!
Забери обратно! Дай лучше мне нахальства,
Чтоб вертеться на виду высшего начальства.
Еще лучше, если ты вдаришь прямо в точку,
То есть выдашь в жены мне высшей сферы дочку.
А за это я тебе, силы не жалея,
Если надо, помогу срезать Галилея;
Научу, как засорить чистый разум Канта;
Узкой щелкой обернуть взгляд широкий Данта;
Как до пошлости свести Свифтову сатиру;
К нам на службу привести самого Шекспира.

(ZhD I:168)

The Loser's Lament

Oh, Providence, I pray you, why not give me better breaks?!
What use to me is Galileo, for all the difference that it
    makes?
What do I need with Kantian wisdom or the satire of
    J. Swift?
Or with Dante's breadth and Shakespeare's depth, or
    don't you get my drift?
Take them back again and give me what I need to get
    a grip.
Upon the levers or the strings to reach the higher
    leadership.

Even better, why not have a go at scoring a bull's eye?
Marry me off with a daughter fair of one of Them on high.
And if you do that for me then here's what I will do for you:
I'll tear up Galileo and I'll flush him down the loo;
And on Kantian wisdom pure I'll gladly pour a pail of slop;
Attack the breadth of Dante's vision till you tell me
　　when to stop;
And the satire of J. Swift I'll very gladly trivialise,
And get Shakespeare to work for us! Well, now, try that one
　　on for size!

(TM:104–5)

This is vintage Zinoviev. The 'loser' is a bright young Soviet philosopher, not a dissident, but short of 'what it takes' to be a successful academic careerist. In a moment of depression he asks fate why he was not granted the cynicism, intellectual barbarism and absence of scruple necessary for making a career rather than the intellectual gifts which allow him to enjoy the works of the great philosophers and writers, gifts which by implication in Soviet academe are totally worthless attributes. Ability to press world literature into the service of Soviet ideology is what will enable the bright young careerist to progress up the ladder, not intellectual integrity.

In similar fashion the same young man lampoons two hallowed totems of the Soviet system, the great Russian people and the collective. Let us look briefly at each lampoon in turn.

Послание Русскому народу

Меж гор, лесов, полей, морей,
Меж необъятных океанов,
Без буржуев и без царей
4　　Расти и ширься, страна Иванов!
Не мясом – лозунгом питай
Свою первичную натуру!
И в тесном транспорте читай
8　　Про рай земной макулатуру!
Не в шелк – в газетный треп одень
Свое проверенное тело!

И помни, дан текущий день,
12 Чтоб выть Да здрасьте оголтело!
Славь мудрость партии вождей!
И все житейские прорехи
Вали на дефицит дождей,
16 На объективные помехи.
Чтоб даром хлеб не продают
За океаном сионисты.
Покоя сзади не дают
20 Мао... их мать!... цзедуинисты.
Напоминай, что мы должны
Кормить задаром пол-Европы,
И жрут из нашей же мошны
24 Свободолюбы-эфиопы.
Но ты достигнешь все равно,
И, верный Ленина завету,
Всепобеждающим говном
28 Засрешь по уши всю планету.

(ZhD I:124)

An epistle to the Russian people
'Tween mountain, forest, field and sea
And oceans to the north and east,
Without the tsars and bourgeoisie,
Oh, Russia thrive! Your past has ceased!
With slogans rather than red meat
Your nature primary sustain!
And crushed in tramcar without seat
Read how it's all so good, again!
In newsprint hogwash, not in silk,
Your tested flesh and bones attire
And 'Hip hooray' (stuff of that ilk)
Shout all day long and never tire!
To Party leaders sing their praise
And blame deficiencies upon
The lack of really rainy days
And brass hats in the Pentagon.
And zionists who keep their wheat
Instead of selling it for free,
And Mao brethren who would eat
Us all for breakfast, lunch or tea.

Remember that we have to feed
The half of Europe from our store
And Ethiop's fighters also need
To be supplied by us, what's more.
But in the end you'll get your way,
And true to Lenin's testament,
Your bullshit's bound to win the day
And bury Earth in excrement.

                                              (TM:80–1)

Russians make up half the population of the Soviet
Union. Together with Ukrainians and Belorussians (who
count as no different from Russians for many Soviet citizens)
they constitute nearly 70 per cent. Numerically they vastly
outnumber any other ethnic group. As if that were not
enough, under Stalin, Khrushchev and Brezhnev they were
hailed as the 'great' Russian people, the 'elder brother' in
the sibling nationalities that make up the Soviet Union.
Rightly or wrongly, for many Soviet citizens the Russians are
primarily responsible for the Soviet state. The 'epistle' is a
marvellously condensed view of the essential characteristics
of that state.
    Lines 1–4 refer obliquely to Russia's great size and its
bright future after the yoke of tsarism. Lines 4–8 develop
the propaganda theme with simultaneous references to
Marxist ideological shibboleths like 'nature (matter) is
primary, consciousness secondary', the inability of the system to provide enough food, especially meat, the dreadfully
overcrowded public transport system and the 'pulp' of
Soviet propaganda generally. The next four lines refer to
one of the main Communist rituals – the need for praise of
the leadership, not only in the daily press but also by the
population itself, hinted at by the generalised '*Da zdraste*'
('Long live'). One of the most tedious aspects of Soviet
reality was the performance of ritualistic acts of praise,
enthusiasm and approbation. At the same time, problems
are never the fault of the leadership or the population,
always the fault of circumstances beyond control, and the
rest of the poem constitutes a list of hilariously sarcastic
examples of the 'objective' difficulties with which the people, under the glorious leadership of its Party, has to

grapple. The final quatrain contains one of Zinoviev's gloomiest predictions: in the struggle between Communist and capitalist propaganda, Communist propaganda will win in the long run – because it allows the communalist tendencies of man in society to flourish. Finally, the language is robust, colloquial, spiced with the occasional 'unprintable' expression (line 20 should be understood as something like 'Mother-fucking Maoists'), but not gratuitously so since the disrespectful tone of the language matches the disrespectful content of the poem.

The young man's attitude to collectivism and the collective is similarly disrespectful. Soviet society is above all a collectivist society. People work in collectives and these collectives are instrumental in perpetuating the Soviet system. In Zinoviev's view, the collective monitors the behaviour of its individual members and it will ensure that no individual steps too far out of line, either in a positive or a negative sense. That is, it will try to ensure that no individual member obtains 'more' than is his or her due, for instance an early promotion. It will seek to restrain individual initiative, if it appears excessive. On the other hand, it will intervene if the behaviour of the individual falls below a standard which might threaten the interests of the collective and take steps to make that individual fall into line. Above all, the individual is lost without the collective since the benefits of society are available only through the collective. An individual outside a collective is in an important sense outside society.

The essential characteristics of the collective are stated pithily in the following 'epistle':

Послание коллективу

Хоть расшибись, хоть лезь из кожи,
Хоть лбом о стенку колоти,
Ничто тебе уж не поможет,
Коль отвернется коллектив.
Не минет бдительного глаза,
Что ты вчера был пьяный в дым.
С отчетов за год ни разу
Не выйдешь цел и невредим.

Брось о защите мысль лелеять.
Надбавку – в памяти сотри.
В день торжества и юбилея
Лист премий больше не смотри.
С уходом старые уловки
Теперь уж болше не пройдут.
И уж со скидкою путевки
Тебе в месткоме не дадут.
Лечь будешь вынужден в кровать,
Никто на яблоки не будет
Тебе копейки собирать.
Неровен час, прокол случится,
И захотят тебя изъять, –
Никто с работы не примчится
На перевоспитанье взять.
Итог? Он априори ясен,
Фундаментальный примитив.
Ты омерзительно прекрасен,
О, нелюбимый коллектнв!
Ко мне лицом оборотися,
Объятья жаркие раскрой!
Меня обнюхай, приглядися!
Не видишь разве – я весь твой?

(ZhD I:180)

An Epistle to the Collective

You can plead on bended knee or
You can tear your hair all day.
I assure you that you're done for
If 't Collective turns away.
You won't escape its watchful eye
If you've been pissed as fabled newt,
And for a long time then they'll try
To show that you're in bad repute.
Forget about your dissertation,
A rise in salary as well,
And of a prize-day celebration
You've not a snowball's chance in hell.
Your old tricks for skiving off
Will never ever work again

And there'll be no more hiving off
Cheap tickets for you now and then.
If you catch the 'flu and end up
Staying home all day in bed,
There'll be no one who will send up
Flowers and fruit, or stroke your head.
If the time comes when it suits Them
To remove you from the throng,
If you think workmates won't help 'em
Then you are simply very wrong.
So what's the score? It's very clear,
It's even somewhat *primitiv,*
You are obnox-i-ously dear,
Oh unbeloved *kollektiv!*
Oh, let me once more see your face!
Stretch out once more your arms to me!
Keep me no longer in disgrace!
Henceforth I'm all yours, don't you see?!

                                        (TM:111–12)

Zinoviev himself has said more than once that his own attitude to the collective is ambivalent. On the one hand he finds the 'intimacy' of it repellant; on the other, he consistently claims to be nostalgic for it, even after fifteen years of freedom from it. The poem captures these contradictory feelings as well, especially in the last eight lines. It is a relatively succinct statement of the relations of mutual dependence which operate within the collective.

We end our survey of Zinoviev's use of language at this point. We have touched on elements of text structure, his use of various levels of language and his use of register and genre in an attempt to give some idea of his stylistic range. It encompasses virtually every mode of writing and the combinatorial possibilities, as we noted, are endless. It allows him maximum flexibility in the treatment of his themes and to be in turn serious, funny, thoughtful, provocative, but also, it must be admitted, on occasion tedious and boring. Not all his puns work, not all his paradoxes are successful, not all his perceptions are novel, or even interesting. He has written too much for all of the immense corpus to be uniformly brilliant. But enough of it is to warrant our attention and the works to be treated in ensuing chapters are important landmarks in his evolution both as a writer and as a commentator on Soviet reality.

Part Two
The Brezhnev Era

3 Ziiaiushchie vysoty

THE RECEPTION OF *ZIIAIUSHCHIE VYSOTY* IN THE WEST

Ziiaiushchie vysoty was published in 1976, although Zinoviev claims that he thought of the title as long ago as 1945 (Zinoviev, 1990a:366). Apparently one of the prime motives for writing this huge book was the desire to 'do something' after the Soviet invasion of Czechoslovakia. Zinoviev regarded Poland and Czechoslovakia as two socialist countries who sought by various means to resist the crushing effects of Soviet domination, and the abrupt ending of the 'Prague Spring' was a deeply disappointing event for him as for many others.

Most of the book he wrote in the summer months of 1974, working on it for up to twenty hours a day. He would write in longhand and his wife Olga would then type up what he had written, using paper as economically as possible by typing on both sides and foregoing lay-out conventions such as paragraphing and the use of dashes to indicate dialogue. Since they were under KGB supervision, they had to invent various ways of putting them off the scent. Finally they hit on the idea of renting a dacha outside Moscow. Even there, they were under surveillance, but Zinoviev, by the simple ruse of leaving pages of his manuscript in full view on his desk while throwing drafts of complicated work on logic in his waste-paper basket, convinced the snoopers that he was working on a legitimate academic project (Zinoviev, 1990a:-369). As each chapter was finished, it was smuggled out to the West.

The book was completed in a remarkably short time. Zinoviev, however, had been collecting material in various ways for years. We have noted his long career as the writer of satirical articles and verse for various wall–newspapers. In 1971 and 1973 he had written a series of articles on Soviet current affairs for publication in Poland and Czechoslovakia. In 1973 a Polish journalist published an interview in a Catholic journal in Cracow. Parts of that were published in 1975 in an Italian journal. In effect it was an excerpt from *Ziiaiushchie vysoty*. There were also his public lectures on a variety of topics to a variety of audiences, including the military, many of which went into the book almost in the form in which they were delivered. He had also written an essay on the work of Ernst Neizvestny, apparently at the latter's request, which was incorporated into the book in the form of Chatterer's 'notes'. Consequently, when he finally took the decision to write a book which would do justice to his conception of Communist society, it more or less wrote itself.

Its success when it appeared in August 1976 was instant and dramatic. The Paris-based Russian language journal *Kontinent* described it as a book that was destined to occupy a special place in literature.[1] Helen von Ssachno called it 'the wittiest and most abstruse protest yet directed by the Russian spirit at the *Condition humaine* in the world and in its own country' (von Ssachno, 1977:83). Michael Heller wrote: 'A marvellous book has come out of Moscow, one of the most marvellous to appear for several decades... The *Yawning Heights* sustains the reader's interest right up to the end' (Heller, 1978:11). Vail' and Genis praised its revolutionary nature while acknowledging its undoubted right to be considered as a work of artistic literature (Vail' and Genis, 1979:147). Geoffrey Hosking referred to Zinoviev as a 'superb satirist' (Hosking, 1980:571). V.S. Pritchett in *The New Yorker* called the book a 'rich and devastating satire'. Boris Sorokin noted that '[with] his larger than life satire of the Soviet Union [Zinoviev] has won the praise of Western critics throughout the world' (Sorokin, 1980:303–4). Soviet readers I have met are even more fulsome in their praise, not least because there is a rich vein of Moscow 'subtext' running through the whole book which escapes the Western reader.

The enthusiastic reception of the book was underscored by frequent comparisons of Zinoviev to great writers of the past. Vail' and Genis compared him to Rabelais, Swift and Voltaire (Vail' and Genis, 1979:151). This was echoed by a reviewer writing in *The Chicago Tribune*: 'The brilliance of Zinoviev's satire in this monumental novel ranks him with

Orwell, Swift, and especially Voltaire.' Deming Brown in *The Washington Post* referred to the novel as a 'Soviet Satyricon' (Brown, 1979:11). Peter Petro quotes Alexander Nekritch as placing Zinoviev's satire 'in the tradition of Hobbes, Voltaire, George Orwell, Anatole France, and of Mikhail Saltykov-Schedrin' (Petro, 1981:70). There are also comparisons with Kafka. Zinoviev's rather sardonic response is that he is not a second Rabelais or Swift but the first Zinoviev (Zinoviev, 1990a:371). We may note, also, Claude Schwab's remark (Schwab, 1984:103) in which he implies that Anglo-Saxon inability to resist comparing Zinoviev to so many classical writers bears witness more to the enthusiasm and surprise with which his book was received than to literary-critical acumen.

The praise, however, was not unadulterated. Right from the beginning cautionary, even discordant, notes were to be detected in the general symphony of adulation. Thus Helen von Ssachno thought that 'in its raw, i.e., unrevised abundance [it] makes too many rather than too few demands on the receptivity of a reading public' (von Ssachno, 1977:85). Vail' and Genis, while recognising the literary qualities of *Ziiaiushchie vysoty*, were less sure that Zinoviev could be counted as a writer. Indeed, they went so far as to state that he was obviously *not* a writer, but that he might yet become one (Vail' and Genis, 1979:150). Deming Brown, having hailed *The Yawning Heights* as a 'Soviet Satyricon', went on to say: 'As a work of literature it is in many respects a disaster' (Brown, 1979:1) Boris Sorokin called it a 'turgid extravaganza of wit and crudity which is likely to try the patience of at least some readers' and added: 'Herein lies the book's most aggravating weakness' (Sorokin, 1980:306). More recently, Edward J. Brown wrote: 'Only a very small minority, one to which the present writer belongs, agree that it is a magnificent book. Of every five readers about four are baffled, disgusted, repelled or bored, and only one is charmed and delighted. They complain that it is long and repititious, and that an excessive amount of ore must be removed to receever the fragments of metal that it offers' (Brown, 1987:308).

How does one account for this disparity of view? How can the same book arouse feelings of delight and dismay? There are several possible explanations. First, much is lost in translation. We have already considered this point in Chapter 2, but it is worth stating again. In English, for instance, much of what makes the Russian version exhilarating is missing. In the case of this book the medium really is the message. There had never been anything quite like it in Russian before, certainly not in the Soviet period. The Russian language was used to utter things in print which had never been expressed before. The intoxicating mixture of registers, the exuberant mickey-take of Soviet rhetoric, the merciless lampooning of Soviet officialdom using its own time-worn, empty clichés cannot be reproduced in English or French or Italian, mainly because these languages have not been hijacked in the service of a bankrupt political system. In the Soviet Union the only permissible printed Russian was what was officially sanctioned. The endless turgid nonsense spouted by Brezhnev and his ilk, the ghastly, mind-numbing mixture of vacuity and untruth, had spread though the Soviet media to the point where it had drowned out any alternative. Bookshops were filled with volumes of speeches, empty of works of literature. Suddenly *Ziiaiushchie vysoty* appeared (in the West, of course) and the contrast was absolutely electric. None of this comes across in translation.[2] Secondly, there is the sheer amount of work which Zinoviev expects of his reader. Without commitment, stamina, a delight in verbal games and paradoxes, an ability and desire to wade through complex issues, the reader is likely to falter, perhaps even to give up. Thirdly, it is not literature in any conventional sense of the term. It appears to be a hotch-potch of bits and pieces which do not fit together, a patchwork of forty shades of grey. Moreover, it contains passages which some people may well find offensively coarse and unfunny. Fourthly, it makes fun of much that goes on in the world of academe, particularly in the field of the social sciences. Sociologists, historians, political scientists have much to be annoyed about. On the other hand, there is so much intelligence, erudition, eloquence, wit and wisdom in the book that the reader who perseveres is richly rewarded. Some passages are absolutely hilarious in Russian, like the '*Gimn ocheredi*' (Hymn to the Queue')

(ZV:511–2; YH:757–8) or the '*Bezobraznyi gimn*' ('The Monstrous Hymn') (ZV:293; YH:428–9), to give but two examples.

STRUCTURE AND CONTENT

Let us now consider the structure of this remarkable work. There have been several attempts to assign *Ziiaiushchie vysoty* to a particular genre. The task is a difficult one since the work is an amalgam of elements of many genres: novel, short story, social science tract, poem, anecdote, philosophical disquisition, farce. Zinoviev himself calls it a sociological novel. Geoffrey Hosking (1980:571) calls it a 'four million word expletive'. Vail' and Genis (1979) and Petro (1981) have discussed *Ziiaiushchie vysoty* in the context of Bakhtin's remarks on Menippean satire and locate Zinoviev at the end of a literary tradition stretching from Hesiod via Lucian, Rabelais, Swift, Gogol', Dostoevsky and Bulgakov. Petro (1981:70–1) argues that the work can be seen as an anatomy in the sense in which that term is used by Northrop Frye, i.e. as a kind of 'encyclopaedic parody'. Remi Roche (1982, pp. 136–44) discusses the structure of *Ziiaiushchie vysoty* in a structuralist/deconstructionist framework, as an example of Levi-Straussian '*bricolage*'. Norbert Franz (1986) attempts to establish a functional connection between the structure and style of the book and Zinoviev's critique of ideology and society. Gerry Smith (1988) has discussed the structure in the context of an analysis of the poems in the book. The present writer (Kirkwood:1987) has attempted the more mundane task of keeping track of all 600 texts and showing how they interrelate.

There is no doubt that one of the most difficult tasks facing the reader of *Ziiaiushchie vysoty* is knowing at any one time what is going on. Such is the kaleidoscopic nature of the work that the reader can easily be stunned into a state of bewilderment. It is to mitigate that effect that we shall discuss in outline some of the main themes in the book, associating them with particular texts.[3] We shall not discuss them all, but simply those which constitute the foundations of 'Zinovievism'.

Before we embark on this task, however, we should say a few words about the work as a whole. The setting is Ibansk, an indeterminate territory located indeterminately in time. The reader meets a great number of its citizens, who fall broadly into two categories: those belonging to the establishment, and renegades or intellectual drop-outs. Much of the 'action', which in Ibansk takes the form of endless chatter, takes place in a few locations, such as a rubbish dump, a beer-bar, Dauber's studio. The establishment figures have titles such as 'Sotsiolog'/'Sociologist', 'Myslitel''/'Thinker', 'Literator'/'Writer', 'Supruga'/'Wife', whereas the renegades have nicknames such as 'Shizofrenik'/'Schizophrenic', 'Boltun'/'Chatterer', 'Mazila'/'Dauber', 'Nevrastenik'/'Neuraesthenic', 'Krikun'/'Bawler', etc. The formerare careerists. The latter have been marginalised, since Ibanskian society can find no use for them. They are the ones, however, who have discovered how it works, whereasthe former intuitively know how to operate within it to their best advantage. Dauber's studio acts as a kind of 'no man's land', where members of the establishment feel it is safe to meet the renegades and perhaps steal some of their ideas. None of them is worth a proper name, since individual worth in Ibansk is not something which is recognised, and in any case Ibanskian society produces such sterotyped citizens that there is little point in differentiating between them, other than by the function they fulfil as anonymous cogs in the machine.

The work is made up of approximately 600 segments, each with its own title. The independent structure of these segments allows us to give them the status of individual texts, as we noted in Chapter 2. The 591 pages contain 600 texts which vary in length from a few sentences to a maximum of five pages. They are grouped into five sections, each with its own title. The title of the first section comprises the initials of some of the leading characters who participate in the 'enterprise' to which the book is dedicated. The aim of the enterprise is to find out who does not approve of the enterprise and to take measures. The nature of Ibanskian logic is thus revealed in the very first text.[4]

There are 93 texts in this first section, most of which can be grouped round four main themes: excerpts from Schizophrenic's tract on the laws which govern the behaviour of people in society;[5] texts associated with that tract in the form of commentary and discussions by other Ibanskians;[6] texts centring round the Kiosk or rubbish dump where many of Schizophrenic's colleagues and friends meet to drink and chat;[7] excerpts from another tract written by Schizophrenic many years before and which describes life in a pilot-training school during the war.[8] The first three strands are set in contemporary Ibansk, the fourth is set in the past. Zinoviev thus constructs a very simple synchronic/diachronic framework, replicated in other sections of the work, which allows him to develop one of his most powerful ideas, namely the evolution of Communism from the abstract ideals to their concrete realisation and the discovery that the Communist paradise has turned out to be hell on earth. The simplicity of this framework is admittedly rendered more complex by the fact that these strands are shuffled and mingled and set out in discontinuous order.

Schizophrenic's tract on the laws which govern social behaviour contains some of Zinoviev's fundamental ideas on the nature of Communism. These include (a) the nature of scientific laws (pp. 27–9); (b) the nature of social laws (pp. 37–40); (c) the relationship between social awareness and official awareness (pp. 57–8); (d) the nature of the 'social individual' (pp. 66–8); (e) the nature of the 'social act' (pp. 81–3); (f) social groups (pp. 89–93); (g) the individual and the cause he serves (pp. 96–7); (h) social relations (pp. 99–103); (i) the bosses (pp. 104–9).

These discussions are at once complex, revealing and funny. Schizophrenic begins by demonstrating that the laws which govern people's behaviour are derived from scientific laws of the type 'A if B'. Social laws are universal and begin to operate when a sufficiently large number of people interact for a sufficiently long period of time. These laws take the form of particular rules of behaviour which include the following: grab as much as you can while giving as little as possible in return; maximise advantage for yourself while minimising risk; maximise your prestige and minimise your responsibility; minimise your dependency on others, maximise their dependency on you, etc. In short they reduce to the formula: dog eat dog.

These rules are not written down, unlike moral codes and the like, yet people discover them for themselves. On the other hand, the consequences of these rules, were they not held in check, would be catastrophic for the functioning of society, and so human progress to a large extent can be seen as progress in erecting bulwarks which contain and regulate the effects of these rules. Such bulwarks include morality, the law, art, religion, a free press, *glasnost*(!), public opinion, and so on. Societies differ in the extent to which they have successfully developed such constraints. Needless to say, they are absent in Ibansk. The consequences are profound. These social rules are given full play with the result that they determine the nature of that society.

Schizophrenic gives quite a detailed description which is worth reproducing:

> И тогда сложится особый тип общества, в котором будет процветать лицемерие, коррупция, бесхозяйственность, обезличка, безответственность, халтура, хамство, лень, дезинформация, обман, серость, система служебных привилегий и т.п. Здесь утверждается искаженная оценка личности – превозносятся ничтожества, унижаются значительные личности. Наиболее нравственные граждане подвергаются гонениям, наиболее талантливые и деловые низводятся до уровня посредственности и средней бестолковости. Причем, не обязетельно власти делают это. Сами коллеги, друзья, сослуживцы, соседи прилагают все усилия к тому, чтобы талантливый человек не имел возможности раскрыть свою индивидуальность, а деловой человек: – выдвинуться.

(ZV:40)

And then a special kind of society is brought into being, in which hypocrisy, oppression, corruption, waste, irresponsibility (individual and collective), shoddy work, boorishness, idleness, disinformation, deceitfulness, drabness, bureaucratic privilege, all flourish. These societies betray a distorted evaluation of personality – nonentities are elevated to great heights, exceptional people are debased.

The most moral citizens are subjected to persecution, the most talented and efficient are reduced to the lowest common denominator of mediocrity and muddle. It is not necessarily the authorities that achieve this. A person's own colleagues, friends, workmates and neighbours bend all their efforts to deny a man of talent the possibility of developing his own individuality, or an industrious man the chance of advancement.

(YH:56)

The second section, entitled '*Nadgrobie*' (Gravestone) contains 110 texts and the pattern of interweaving is similar. It includes the following important strands: the history of Ibansk;[9] the battle between the radicals and reactionaries for control of the Journal;[10] the famous 'ratorium' strand[11] and Slanderer's notes on ideology.[12] there is also the strand in which the saga of Mazila's commission to sculpt a gravestone for Khriak/Hog unfolds. This is of interest as a gloss on the Khrushchev/Neizvestnyi incident but is not of particular importance for Zinoviev's model as a whole, save for the many references to 'temporary difficulties' of one sort or another, difficulties which are not so much 'temporary' as 'endemic'.

The section as a whole is an extended allusion to the Khrushchev era in Soviet history. The very title of the section alludes to the issue of Khrushchev's attitude to modern art and his ambivalent attitude to Ernst Neizvestnyi. In the third text reference is made to the disappearance of Khoziain/Boss (Stalin) and the advent of Khriak/Hog (Khrushchev). Zinoviev's contention is that the period of history associated with Khrushchev is a period of uncertainty, of disorientation, of perplexity. Before Khrushchev's famous 'secret speech', Stalinism was still in place. No doubt it was less secure than it had been, no doubt there were forces within the complex politico-administrative structure which threatened its monolithic façade, but to all outward appearances, and certainly in the ideological domain, Stalinism was still very much alive.

One can argue about whether Khrushchev's speech to the 20th Congress of the CPSU in 1956 was the culmination of a process which had already begun (anti-Stalinist pressures within the system) or whether it was the initiator of an overt process of de-Stalinisation. For Zinoviev the important point is that, during the Khrushchev period, and possibly thanks to Khrushchev's speech which initiated the dismantling of the Stalinist cult, people stopped believing in the shining ideals of Communism. The ideology continued to assert that the Soviet people were on the road to Communism – indeed at one point a slogan appeared promising that 'the current generation will live under Communism'. (From a Zinovievan point of view that was a marvellously ambiguous slogan. In the first place it was neither true nor false, although clearly its intention was to encourage the belief that the advent of Communism was very close. In the second place, however, it was true – if you believed, as Zinoviev did, and does, that Communism in structural terms had already arrived.)

But there was a chance that the period of the 'thaw' might have provided the opportunity for genuine change. Perhaps it *could* have been possible to reform agriculture and education, decentralise, allow more freedom of debate, and so on. For a few years there appeared to be that 'window of opportunity', Zinoviev's argument is that the so-called 'radical' elements within the power structure were simply opportunistic careerists, no better than the 'reactionary' Old Guard they purported to challenge. No doubt Zinoviev is being unfair but there is equally no doubt that he deeply believed that to be the case.

This belief underlies the strand in which the 'battle for the Journal' unfolds. Control of an important philosophical journal in the Soviet context is crucial for the promotion of sectional interests, whatever ideologically sound pretext may be found. The 'liberals' are represented by 'Pretender' and 'Thinker' – who have decided, cynically, that the best way of making a career in the new situation is to appear to campaign for progressive change. As the strand unfolds, we are shown how the liberals are just as wont to stab each other in the back as anyone, to plagiarise each other's ideas and to trim their ideological positions to the prevailing political winds. That the window of opportunity eventually closed, Zinoviev implies, was as much the fault of the liberals as of anyone else, and possibly more, since others were in favour of a continuation of the status quo. This theme was to be explored in more detail in *Svetloe budushchee*, the subject of Chapter 4. We might note at this point, however, that the 'liberals', the '*shestidesiatniki*' or 'sixties people' whom Zinoviev so bitterly criticises, belong to the generation which is now in power today under Gorbachev. A major problem for discussion in future chapters will be the extent to which the revolutionary changes associated with Gorbachev are a consequence of attempts by rep-resentatives of that generation who were thwarted in the 1970s to promote their policies in the 1980s.

The 'ratorium' strand is a sequence of texts about a study of rat behaviour carried out by psychologist, and published in a book which Bawler happens to acquire. It is clear that these texts parallel Schizophrenic's tract on the laws of communalism in the first section so that the equation man = rat is inescapable.[13] The rats, having attained the pinnacle of development, are vanquished by an invasion of fleas. The equation is thus replaced by the formula man > rat > flea. Human society differs from a rat colony only in the extent to which man is prevented from acting like a rat by various sorts of constraint (law, morality, religion, education, art, open government, freedom of speech, etc.).

Slanderer's notes on ideology provide the first statement of one of the fundamental tenets of a Communist society as Zinoviev understands it. A Communist society is above all an ideological society. Ideology is to Communism as monetary relations are to capitalism: it is a defining feature. Slan-derer's principal theses include the following:

(a) An understanding of the workings of ideology can be obtained by examining the sociology of contemporary science, and the nature of methodology in science. Science today is a mass phenomenon and is thus gov-erned by social/communalist laws. There is very little genuine science.

(b) Science influences the ideology of a society via the methodology of science in which all the ideologically important elements of science are gathered together. Methodology, however, is a social phenomenon. Methodological literature is growing at a frightening rate, its terminology becoming ever less precise and open to varying interpretation. Methodology tries to

keep pace with science. Everyone, right down to the
level of the lowliest research assistant, wants his work to
be regarded on the same level as that of Newton,
Galileo, Einstein.

(c) Modern man is subject to influence via many different
channels (radio, cinema, television, popular scientific
literature, etc.) and his ideological manipulation contains a large element of scientific information. In fact,
however, because of methodology, scientific terms which
are used with precise meanings in science acquire im-
precise meanings in the area of methodology and ideology. Ideological terms are indeterminate, multiply ambiguous, unprovable and irrefutable.

(d) A most curious feature of scientific propaganda is the
attempt to pass off concrete scientific discoveries as
discoveries which not only change the ways in which a
given phenomenon has been regarded before but sensa-
tionally change the logical foundations of science. 'Old'
logic is replaced by 'new' logic.

(e) Ideology and science are incompatible. 'Scientific' ideology makes as much sense as 'scientific' art.

(f) Ideology's great enemy is logic.

(g) What is important is the existence of an ideology, not its
content.

(h) Ideological texts are not important in themselves but
only in the context of an environment in which people
are obliged to regard them as such.

Schizophrenic develops these theses in some detail. Zinoviev
will return to them in later works and add to them, hammer-
ing home his conviction that a Communist society is above
all an ideological society. He will also devote much space to
the discussion of scientific and non-scientific language.

The next section is entitled '*Skazanie o Mazile*' ('The Tale
of Dauber'). It contains 101 texts and includes the following
important strands: Chatterer on art and Dauber's work;[14]
life in a penal battalion during the war;[15] discussions between Neuraesthenic and Journalist against a backdrop of
the period in Ibanskian history when Hog was emulating
Peter the Great and attempting to open, if not a window,
then at least a hole to the West.[16]

Chatterer's disquisitions on art are based on Zinoviev's essay on Neizvestnyi (Zinoviev, 1990a:367). Zinoviev tells us that Ernst Neizvestnyi had asked him to write that essay and it is significant that Chatterer writes down his thoughts on art at the request of Dauber. In Chatterer's notes, Dauber is referred to as EN, which might refer to the letter 'N', but also happen to be the initials of Ernst Neizvestnyi. The central question for Chatterer is the nature of art in Ibanskian conditions. Via a discussion of theories of the sign, he arrives at the conclusion that a work of genuine art is the product of a 'generative grammar' made up of elements which both depict and transform. There is, on the other hand, the context in which art takes place. Ibansk has yet to crystallise into a state where the question 'What?' in relation to a work of art can be answered. This is because there is as yet no clear ideological conception of the state of Ibansk and of the average Ibanskian's place in it. There is no metalanguage for describing Ibansk. Schizophrenic's tract was a beginning, but also a step in the wrong direction, since it was a scientific conception, not an ideological one. Dauber's 'grammar', understood as 'rules of composition', does not emanate from 'art' but from his 'ideological conception'. In other words, Dauber is producing Ibanskian works of art according to his ideological conception of Ibansk, a conception which is his alone and which observers of his works only begin to glimpse. What is interesting is that Chatterer talks about Dauber's visual art in a way which gives us an insight into the structure of *Ziiaiushchie vysoty*:

Интересно, что смысловые фразы у ЭН образуют не обязательно смысловые единицы, расположенные рядом (например в одной комнате, на одном листе бумаги, а рядом расположенные единицы могут быть единицами из разных фраз – основа и скрытый ритм его полифонии. Нужна память и хорошее знание большого комплекса работ ЭН, чтобы читать их именно как фразы и совокупности фраз. Конечно, их можно упорядочить, что облегчит их изучение новичками. Но для этого надо еще построить общие правила идеологической грамматики языка.

(ZV:249)

It is interesting that in EN's work the semantic phrases are not necessarily made up of semantic units set out side by side (e.g. in one room, or on one sheet of paper), and that juxtaposed units may be units from different phrases – the basis and the concealed rhythm of his polyphony. One needs to have a good memory and considerable knowledge of a large number of EN's works before they can be read as sentences and collections of sentences. Of course, they could be set in order, which would make it easier for non-initiates to study them. But to do this, one would have first to construct general rules for the ideological grammar of the language.

(YH:363)

Zinoviev has argued that the official Soviet claim that Communism was far in the future and that Marxism–Leninism was a truly scientific ideology which accounted for the history of the world to date needs to be stood on its head. In his view Communism, seen as an organisational structure, has already arrived but what has been missing is a truly scientific theory of Communism. He regards himself as having made a start in that direction and consequently as having acquired an 'ideological conception' of Communism which allows him to produce 'Communist' works of art. The polyphonic structure of *Ziiaiushchie vysoty* exactly matches the structure of Dauber's art.

The penal battalion strand in this section links up with the pilot-training school strand in the first section, thus allowing Zinoviev to continue his description of wartime Ibansk. The texts recount the fortunes of members of a penal battalion, who are given the most dangerous assignments since they are the most expendable troops. We see them up to their knees in November mud in the trenches, and listen to their anecdotes about army life and conversations about their children, about women, about their hopes for the future. In connection with a forthcoming Ibanskian red-letter day, the penal battalion is instructed to capture N, a place of no strategic importance whatsoever. The soldiers are granted a general amnesty before they attack, since they are not expected to survive. Many do not, but a few miraculously do – to see advancing towards them, pens at the ready, the well-fed and warmly-clothed league of bureaucrats who have sat out the war in relative safety and who are destined to be the careerists of the future: Troglodite, Thinker, Secretary, Sociologist, Pretender and many others, pillars of contemporary Ibanskian society. Zinoviev's '*pointilliste*' approach to description allows him to present a remarkably detailed picture of army life with the minimum of exposition. His basic theme is that the social laws of Ibansk operate in wartime also, only more so.

We now come to the strand in which Neuraesthenic, Chatterer and others attempt to explain the workings of Ibansk to a foreign Journalist who has come to Ibansk to experience Ibanskian life. The theme of the naive Westerner is one which Zinoviev has never tired of developing, and indeed we shall see that since his arrival in the West it has become predominant. Long before he was exiled, however, he had decided that the West was incapable of understanding the Soviet mentality. His formula is very simple. Journalist makes an observation on some aspect of Ibanskian life which seems eminently reasonable but turns out to be entirely wrong, because rational explanations do not work in irrational Ibansk. Some of the issues touched upon include the social structure of Ibansk, art, the absence of fixed parameters in Ibanskian society by which an individual can orient himself, power, the nature of Ibanskian problems, what Ibanskians are like. The source of Journalist's confusion is indicated succinctly by Neuraesthenic:

> Мы Вам кажемся загадкой не потому, что мы неизмеримо сложнее амебы, говорит Неврастеник. С точки зрения способа понимания мы даже проще. А потому, что Вы к нам пробиваетесь через систему собственных предрассудков, нашего официального камуфляжа и всеобщего желания скрыть от посторонних, кто мы на самом деле.
>
> (ZV:278)

'We may seem an enigma to you but we're not in fact much more complex than an amoeba,' said Neuraesthenic. 'Indeed, as far as ease of comprehension goes we're a good deal simpler. It's because you approach us through this whole system of your prejudices, our official

camouflage, and our general desire to conceal from
foreigners what we really are.'

(YH:405)

This may sound familiar, yet there is an interesting
corollary: Journalist is despised because he is taken in by
Ibanskian propaganda. Were he, however, to break through
the propaganda and learn to live like an Ibanskian, he
would be despised as an Ibanskian.

The next section is entitled '*Reshenie*' ('The Decision')
and contains some 267 texts. A new character Bawler
(Krikun) is introduced and an important strand deals with
his life-story from his birth on a collective farm sometime in
the Ibansk equivalent of the 1930s to his incarceration in a
mental hospital for having tried to smuggle out to the West
an important book by Pravdets/Truth-teller. Zinoviev charts
the transition of Bawler, born and raised during the worst
period of Boss's reign, from an honest, forthright citizen
who believes in Ibanskian ideals, into a disillusioned critic
of the regime who, as a last act of desperation, decides to try
to do something useful. Like the strand dealing with the
pilot–training school and the penal battalion, it depicts the
sweep of Ibanskian history as it affects individuals. The
theme of the disenchanted idealist is to be found in several
works by Zinoviev and illustrates his view that the nature of
Communist society is such that even good Communists are
rejected.

Two other important strands reveal the thoughts of
Klevetnik/Slanderer[18] and Uchitel'/Teacher.[19] The former
writes a series of lectures on the State, government and
'Brotherhood', i.e. the Ibansk equivalent of the Party. These
encapsulate Zinoviev's firm views about the nature of power
in a Communist society: (a) the administration of power
requires the involvement of about one fifth of the adult
population; (b) the vast majority are in low-paid jobs which
tends to encourage a compensatory misuse of power for
personal gain; (c) Communist power is both all-powerful
and powerless in the sense that it has tremendous power to
destroy and very little power to create; (d) it is powerless to
carry through the smallest reform (what price *perestroika*?)
and is in principle unreliable; (e) its promises are never

fulfilled and at the same time there is an absence of responsibility for the running of the affairs of state (ZV:329–30;
YH:482–5); (f) the backbone of the power structure is the
'Brotherhood'; (g) entry into the Brotherhood is voluntary
(although far from every aspirant succeeds) (ZV:346–8;
YH:508–11); (h) it is not the case that a Communist leadership oppresses the masses, the masses are voluntarily implic-
ated (ZV:360; YH:529).

Teacher was for a time the leader of a 'progressive' group
within an unnamed institute, whose ideas were plagiarised
and later undermined by the members of that group when
the political climate changed. Little was left except for a few
scraps of writing on social systems (ZV:328–9; YH:481–2).
The strand containing Teacher's thoughts on the working
of social systems is short, but contains some of Zinoviev's
most important ideas on the nature of social behaviour in a
Communist society. He begins by arguing that repressions,
labour camps, purges and the like are the sensational
aspects of Ibansk society, aspects which have been revealed
in the works of Truth-teller. What is equally, indeed arguably
more, important is an understanding of the workings of
society at the level of the mundane day-to-day. What characterises Ibansk society is the behaviour of its citizens, as they
act out their social roles in various combinations (ZV:337–8;
YH:494–5).

Teacher advocates a systems approach to the analysis of
society, differentiating between the components or building
blocks of society, and how that society functions, or to be
more precise, how behaviour within a society is conditioned
by the workings of that society. He gives as an example a
decision to raise the quality of science in Ibansk. Quality is
determined, among other things, by the number of Doctors
of Science, publications, scientific conferences, learned
journals, etc. Among the measures proposed naturally is the
need to increase the number of Doctors of Science and
scientific publications. Now, if Ibansk functioned as it is
officially supposed to function, a simple numerical increase
in cadres and publications would equal an increase in the
level of science, since officially Ibansk science is the most
progressive, the best, etc., etc. However, in Ibansk things
work differently. Were there to be a campaign to raise the

level of science, the number of Doctors would be increased by lowering the entry qualifications for postgraduate work, publications of lower quality would be accepted, thus opening the door to mediocrities of all sorts, who, once they gained entrance to the world of science, would begin to repress real scientists by virtue of their superior numbers, lack of scruple, and so on. Any increase in the quality of science in absolute terms is more than cancelled out by a decrease in the level of science, since the insurge of mediocrity lowers the mean level of science as a whole (ZV:378–9; YH:556–7).

Having determined the nature of social behaviour as a general phenomenon, Teacher then proceeds to analyse how individuals behave in terms of goals, strategies and tactics. Typically, he chooses a rather depressing example: Goal – A wants B's job; strategy – A will try to get B fired; tactics – A will endeavour to get B drunk in circumstances where it will be noticed by B's boss, A will try to get B involved with some woman to stimulate gossip, and so on (ZV:405–6; YH:598–9).

A systems approach to the study of Ibansk would reveal that its structure is that of a nesting-doll. At the lowest level there are individuals who combine into units forming more complex 'individuals' right up to the level of governments and individual countries. Social behaviour, whether at the level of the individual citizen or the government, is governed by the same tendencies, which in turn are determined by the nature of the social structure and its functioning. Teacher shows how it is subject to constraints within the system by means of simple formulae: individual A desires outcome C which depends on the free will of individual B (B can help or hinder, accelerate the process of realisation of C or slow it down, permit it or forbid it, etc.). This simple formula establishes the basic link in the system from which all others can be derived. For example, A depends on B^1, ..., B^n in relation to C where $n > 2$; Individuals A^1, ..., A^n depend on B in relation to C; A depends on B in relation to C and B depends on A relative to D. If A and B can help each other to realise C and D, there is equivalence. Usually, however, there is not, in so far as one individual or individuals may depend to a greater extent on other individuals than the latter do on the former. Oppression in society, argues Teacher, is the coercion brought to bear on individuals or groups to render a particular service, or to enter into an unequal relationship of dependency. (ZV:416–17; YH: 614–16)

These two strands parallel those of Schizophrenic's tracts and Chatterer's notes on art in previous sections. There are also other parallels. Bawler's life-story is intermeshed with the pilot–training school and the penal battalion. The 'battle for the Journal' is paralleled in the section under discussion by the plans of Teacher and Pochvoed/Soilophagist, representing the liberal intelligentsia – Zinoviev's pet hate – to 'introduce improvements' under Zaveduiushchii/Leader.[20] Subsequently they decide not to introduce improvements since to do so might jeopardise their careers.

A key text is entitled '*Zhizn' nachinaetsia*' ('Life begins') (ZV:462–3; YH:684–6), since here many threads are combined and tied off. Soilophagist suddenly dies of a heart attack and Dauber is commissioned to sculpt his gravestone. In this text Dauber also gets permission to go abroad for two years. Chatterer goes off, this being a symbolic flight of Dauber's soul. Shortly afterwards (ZV:464–5; YH:687) Dauber is interviewed in Paris and is asked about the leading intellectuals in Ibansk. He names a row of establishment figures like Brat/Brother, Rezhisser/Director, Thinker, Sociologist, etc., *not* renegades like his friends Slanderer, Schizophrenic, Chatterer, etc. This is significant because we suddenly see that Dauber has lost his innocence and that he is thinking in a calculated fashion, just like any ordinary Ibanskian citizen.

The final section is entitled '*Poema o skuke*' ('A Poem on Boredom') and contains 87 texts making up eight important strands, not all of which we shall discuss here. The first is composed of texts devoted to the theme of 'return'.[21] Dauber has returned from the West, where he has learned much, including cynicism. He and Chatterer have a long series of talks about various aspects of the relationship between art and life, the role of the artist in society, talks which link up with Chatterer's notes on art in a previous section. The second strand deals with the emergence of Sub-Ibanskian society,[22] a society which lives underground and has gone on a path of separate development after being abandoned by Ibansk proper. The inhabitants of Sub-Ibansk are the offspring of former scientific, technical and government staff who had manned underground installations at times of crisis. The link between Sub-Ibansk and the ratorium strand is implicit. It is an important strand since it allows Zinoviev to expand on the question of foreign relations between Ibansk and other countries, a topic to which he returns again and again in his later work. Another important strand contains more Ibanskian history.[23] A diachronic strand which links up with those in previous sections contains the twelve texts entitled '*Legenda*'.[24] The narrator is Teacher and the setting is once more the war.

Two other strands which are important for Zinoviev's model of Communism are made up of the texts devoted respectively to the queue as an endemic feature of Communism[25] and to the nature of political opposition in Ibansk.[26] The queue epitomises the permanent nature of shortages under Communism which, Zinoviev argues, are permanent features of that system, not the result of 'temporary difficulties'.

What seems to be a spontaneous attempt to form an opposition in Ibansk turns out to be a ploy of the Organs under the supervision of Colleague. He is commissioned to set up an opposition onto whose shoulders the authorities will be able to transfer the responsibility for the shortcomings of Ibanskian life. Unfortunately, since it is Ibansk citizens who are involved, the setting up of a genuine opposition founders on such rocks as the propensity of Ibanskians to inform on their fellows, their inability to get things done, etc. The social laws strike again!

It is of course impossible in the space of a single chapter to reproduce the detail of Zinoviev's arguments as they emerge from the 561 pages of *Ziiaiushchie vysoty*. What we can do, however, is list the important issues which together reflect Zinoviev's theory of Communism as it appears in camouflaged form in Ibansk. There is first of all the importance which he attaches to what he calls universal rules of human behaviour in society. The history of civilisation is in large measure the history of attempts to harness the effect of these rules. Secondly, there is the role which ideology plays, a role which is great enought to allow us to designate a Communist society as above all an ideological society. Notice that ideological texts only become such in the context of an environment which attributes that property to them. There is no such thing as 'scientific ideology'. Thirdly, there is the important question of the distinction between appearance and reality. Several texts in *Ziiaiushchie vysoty* deal with that theme (ZV:191–3, 216, 267–8, 333; YH:280–2, 316–17, 390–2, 487–8).

Much of *Ziiaiushchie vysoty* is a description of the consequences of the operation of the social laws in an ideological environment, but the book also contains a disguised account of Soviet history from the Revolution to the era of Brezhnev centring round the figures of Khoziain/Boss (Stalin), Khriak (Khrushchev) and Zaveduiushchii/Leader (Brezhnev). Themes which are introduced in *Ziiaiushchie vysoty* and which will be developed in later works include the following: the role of the 'liberal intelligentsia', the naiveté of the West, the nature of power in a Communist society, the stability of Communism. (This 'stability' would appear to have been a mirage, judging by the events in Europe and in the Soviet Union since 1989, but it is too early to say that Communism, particularly in the Soviet Union has been destroyed. Zinoviev currently refers to its period of 'crisis', but believes it still has a long future.)

We have endeavoured to isolate the main strands in *Ziiaiushchie vysoty*, but we have not given an indication of the linear structure of the work. To give the reader some idea of the kaleidoscopic nature of a Zinoviev work we shall comment briefly on the first twenty texts. Texts 1–2 are linked by the theme of the enterprise. Text 3 locates Ibansk in space and time with references to new leaders (who are as old as the old leaders) and the construction of modern tenth–century churches for tourists to look at in the time they have left over from visiting 'model enterprises'. Text 4 is linked to 3, 5 is linked to 1, 2 and 3 via references to Schizophrenic's sociological tract (1) and the Laboratory (2). Text 6 contains the first mention of the famous 'social laws'. Text 7 contains Sociologist's commentary. Text 8 is linked to previous texts via Schizophrenic's tract and also to texts 10–15 and 17–20 by virtue of the reference in 8 to a second

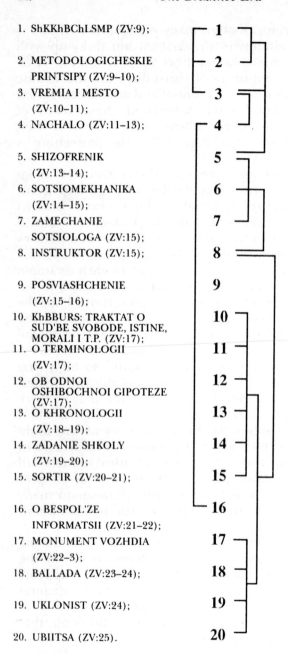

1. ShKKhBChLSMP (ZV:9);

2. METODOLOGICHESKIE PRINTSIPY (ZV:9–10);

3. VREMIA I MESTO (ZV:10–11);

4. NACHALO (ZV:11–13);

5. SHIZOFRENIK (ZV:13–14);

6. SOTSIOMEKHANIKA (ZV:14–15);

7. ZAMECHANIE SOTSIOLOGA (ZV:15);

8. INSTRUKTOR (ZV:15);

9. POSVIASHCHENIE (ZV:15–16);

10. KhBBURS: TRAKTAT O SUD'BE SVOBODE, ISTINE, MORALI I T.P. (ZV:17);

11. O TERMINOLOGII (ZV:17);

12. OB ODNOI OSHIBOCHNOI GIPOTEZE (ZV:17);

13. O KHRONOLOGII (ZV:18–19);

14. ZADANIE SHKOLY (ZV:19–20);

15. SORTIR (ZV:20–21);

16. O BESPOL'ZE INFORMATSII (ZV:21–22);

17. MONUMENT VOZHDIA (ZV:22–3);

18. BALLADA (ZV:23–24);

19. UKLONIST (ZV:24);

20. UBIITSA (ZV:25).

Figure 3.1

tract by Schizophrenic, written many years before. Text 9 is free-standing in relation to the first 20 but links up with Chatterer's notes on Dauber and his art in section 3. Texts 10–20, with the exception of 16, introduce the diachronic strand about the pilot-training school and are excerpts from Schizophrenic's second tract. Several of these texts, of course, link up with others which occur after the first twenty. As we can see from Figure 3.1, the patterning is rather complex.

The kaleidoscopic approach also allows Zinoviev to indulge in a veritable fireworks display of gags and puns, humorous asides and general mickey-taking. Text 2 contains a witty exposition of Ibanskian 'practical ideology'. Text 5 contains a reference to free time left over from compulsory time-wasting, Zinoviev's view of the average Soviet's time spent at the workplace. In text 11 we find an early example of Zinoviev's view that the educational level of the bureaucrat is in inverse proportion to his official position. Thus the technical term '*perespektivy*' has the same referent as the term '*perspektivy*' but is distinguished from the latter by the higher social position of the person using it. The term '*prespektivy*' belongs to an even higher rank, so high that permission to use it has to be obtained from the authorities. Text 13 contains a side–swipe at the level of scientific work done in Ibansk with titles of dissertations such as 'A timid introduction (and only with the permission of the authorities) to so-called non–abstract sociology', 'Informers in the service of social cybernetics', 'Mathematical models and theories of informer classification'. As we noted in Chapter 2, Zinoviev's text is densely packed with allusions to many facets of Soviet life and this is *a fortiori* true of *Ziiaiushchie vysoty*.

We have already given some idea of the reception of the novel when it first appeared. We now need to survey the criticisms of Zinoviev's 'model' of Communism as it appears in *Ziiaiushchie vysoty*. Hanson (1982:30) makes the general point that, for a large book, it is surprising how much it does not contain. In particular, it gives the impression that Ibansk is populated exclusively by intellectuals, a point made also by Panin (1980:76). However, whereas Hanson notes that the novel is mostly about intellectuals and not about most of the Soviet population, Panin argues that Zinoviev, as a 'devotee' of the Soviet regime, is describing the views of that stratum of the population which supports the Ibansk regime. One might counter these criticisms with the observation that, since Zinoviev's 'social laws' are universal, especially in Ibansk, intellectuals are as likely to be representative of the Ibanskian population as any other stratum. Panin's criticism also fails to acknowledge that many of the characters in *Ziiaiushchie vysoty* are *not* devotees of the regime.

Critics have varied in their opinion of Zinoviev's 'social-laws'. Berelowitch wonders about their scientific status (Berelowitch, 1985:20). Do they have the force of a scientific law like the law of gravity? Hanson (1982:32) regards Zinoviev's contention that Ibansk is a normal society in which 'normal social laws operate' as a novel idea, whereas Panin wonders whether Zinoviev has not simply rediscovered the wheel. Zinoviev himself, or rather Schizophrenic, defines these social laws as 'rules of behaviour', the basis of which has been determined by the natural tendency of people and groups of people to protect themselves, and if possible improve their standard of living, in the environment of a given society. Valerii Valius (1986:184–5), however, makes an interesting comparison between Zinoviev's social laws and M.L. Tsetlin's theory of the behaviour of automata in varying environments. In outline the theory is simple. An automaton moves in a particular direction from a point of departure, say point A, according to the 'stick/carrot' principle. Its 'memory' is measured by the number of 'carrots', i.e. steps it takes from point A. A 'stick' deducts one notch of memory, inducing the automaton to take one step back towards point A. Its environment is conceived of as a 'mix' of 'sticks' and 'carrots'. Interaction with other automata leads to patterns of reciprocal behaviour which Tsetlin labelled 'behavioural stereotypes'. Valius does not accuse Zinoviev of plagiarism but points out that he has managed to dress up Tsetlin's theory in human form, indicating the following parallels: the principles of behaviour are similar; mass individuals have a few stereotypical forms of behaviour (instead of convictions, beliefs, thoughts, feelings, etc.); mass individuals are similar, i.e. resemble each other. On the other hand, Fabrice Fassio (1989) essays a formal, rigorous representation of Zinoviev's 'dog eat dog' communal laws as they apply to human beings.

One of Zinoviev's key claims about Communist society is that the primary collective is the environment in which his social laws are most in evidence, irrespective of the activity of that collective or its slot in the socio-economic structure. Panin (1980:78) accuses Zinoviev of ignoring everyone (engineers, doctors, workers, etc.) except the 'devotees' of the regime, and asserts that how they behave is very different from the way in which ordinary people behave. He argues that Zinoviev wishes to disguise the pyramidical structure of Soviet oppression and that he refuses to acknowledge the existence of millions of 'micro-brotherhoods' (*mikrobratstva*). Valius (1986:187–8) argues that Zinoviev leaves out of his scheme the 'non-mass individual' (*ne massovyi individ*) who would upset it. He quotes adults' treatment of children as an example of the non-application of Zinoviev's laws and asserts that Zinoviev's scheme fails to account for 'intelligence', a quality to which Valius seems to attach moral significance.

One might point out in Zinoviev's defence that he does not deny the existence of groups outside the primary collective. What he asserts is that the primary collective is the environment in which the social laws operate. It is the environment in which the social individual most often finds himself. The private lives of individuals are of no concern to Zinoviev since they are not important for his description of Communist society. Zinoviev does not deny the existence of Panin's 'micro-brotherhoods', they simply do not impinge.

Valius's remark about adults' treatment of children needs to be set in the context of Soviet youth organisations which accept children from a very early age into kindergartens, followed by the October Children, Pioneers, Komsomol. As for 'intelligence', Zinoviev does not state that Communist society does not contain individuals of high moral standing, he states that there are not enough of them to form a critical mass.

In *Ziiaiushchie vysoty* Zinoviev sets out, via Neuraesthenic's notes, his preliminary ideas on the importance of ideology in Communist society. He will have much more to say on

this subject in later books and articles. In *Ziiaiushchie vysoty*
he primarily attacks the claim that Marxism–Leninism is
scientific. Science has been hijacked in the service of ideology, and scientific terms have been ideologised, i.e. denuded of scientific content. A 'scientific' ideology is deemed
by the authorities to be superior to any other. Hanson
(1982:31) notes that few people are prepared to claim that
Marxist doctrine is both powerful *and* idiotic, and acknowledges that Zinoviev in this respect has made a novel contribution to our understanding of the workings of ideology in the
Soviet Union. Panin (1980:79–80), on the other hand,
attacks Zinoviev for not exposing to the Western reader the
extent to which Marxism failed to keep up with modern
science. Here he is simply being unfair, since Zinoviev is
very insistent that the tenets of ideology are unimportant, as
compared with the existence of ideology itself. Hence his
'Ism' without a prefix.

Chatterer, during a conversation with Dauber (ZV:234),
alleges that the Ibansk system suits the population and that
it would not change it for any other. This notion is at odds
with the widespread assumption that the Soviet population
is oppressed and would change its social system tomorrow if
it could. Panin (1980:81–4) takes particular exception to
this assertion by Chatterer (which he equates correctly with
a belief of Zinoviev's) and mounts a blistering attack, citing
the many millions of lives which have been sacrificed at
various stages of Soviet history, and the all-encompassing
power of the KGB, as evidence that the Soviet population is
anything but content with its social system. Zinoviev's view is
that the Soviet system, for all its disadvantages, offers people
a guaranteed job without much responsibility, a roof over
their heads and three meals a day. The resistance to his
reforms which Gorbachev is encountering, particularly in
the economic sphere, seems to support Zinoviev rather than
Panin.

Related to this question is Zinoviev's position on '*narodo-
vlastie*' ('people power'). His view is that the administration
of power in the Soviet system requires the involvement of so
many people that it is possible to speak of a kind of
symbiosis between the leadership and the population, en-
capsulated in a phrase used by Chatterer (ZV:281): '*nachal'-*

stvo narodno a narod nachal'stvenen'. This phrase is untranslatable but means roughly the following: those in positions
of authority are drawn from the people as a whole and the
people as a whole exercise authority.

We need to be clear about what Zinoviev means. Critics
like Panin (1980:84–5) and Valius (1986:190–1) tend to
accuse Zinoviev of alleging that the population as a whole
participates in the decision-making, as opposed to the
administration of power. We shall see later on that per-
ceptive critics like Hanson and Hosking tend to make the
same point. It seems to me, however, that Zinoviev is in fact
drawing attention to something else, namely to the fact that
(a) the Soviet bureaucracy is very large and (b) everyone
who has a little bit of power, from the lift-operator and
cloakroom–attendant onwards, will exercise it. In sum we
have a society where everyone is dependent on the will of
others at every turn, a situation which is exacerbated by the
widespread shortages of goods and services. The exercise of
power is thus mainly negative. People have the power to say
'no'. Other people therefore have to spend a great deal of
effort and time, and often money, to get them to say 'yes'.
No doubt this is true of bureaucracies everywhere, but the
point is that the administration of power in the Soviet
system maximises the size of the bureaucracy, not in the
interests of 'efficiency' but for various ideological reasons to
do with 'democracy', 'dictatorship of the proletariat', the
need for 'vigilance', the citizen's right to guaranteed employment, and so on.

A consideration of the responses to *Ziiaiushchie vysoty*
would be incomplete without reference to the work of the
philosopher Jon Elster, who has written about Ibansk in
relation to the concept of irrational politics (Elster, 1980:
11–13; 1984:44). He has shown convincingly how Zinoviev
has made good use of his training in logic in writing
Ziiaiushchie vysoty. Elster discusses the concept of an irrational law, and then makes the fundamental distinction
between active and passive negation to show that Ibansk is
irrational and oppressive. In particular, he draws attention
to the difference between non-obligation and interdiction,
and then illustrates how Ibansk thrives on the confusion
of these two phenomena. Take for instance a law which pro-

hibits emigration and permits enforced exile. That is an irrational law (Elster 1988:130). An example of active and passive negation is the following. The negation of the statement 'I believe that God exists' can be either (a) 'I do not believe that God exists' (passive) or (b) 'I believe that God does not exist' (active). Elster finds many examples in *Ziiaiushchie vysoty* which illustrate the confusion between these concepts. For instance, how should Ibansk handle opposition? By ignoring it, or oppressing it? If it ignores it, that might be taken as a sign of weakness. If it oppresses it, it draws attention to it. Another example is careerism. In Ibansk the successful careerist is one who does not actively pursue a career, since what counts is mediocrity. Striving to make a career is likely to ensure failure.

Ziiaiushchie vysoty contains the general schema of Zinoviev's view of Communism, structured according to an approach which Zinoviev will use in all his other works. Themes which are first set out in *Ziiaiushchie vysoty* will recur and will be explored in greater detail, receiving the emphasis which Zinoviev considers to be appropriate at the time. We shall begin our analysis of some of these themes with a study of *Svetloe budushchee.*

4 *Svetloe budushchee*

We have seen in the previous chapter that Zinoviev's analysis of Ibansk was wide-ranging and thorough. In *Ziiaiushchie vysoty* we are given a panoramic view of the issues with which the author is concerned. In *Svetloe budushchee* (*The Radiant Future*) Zinoviev alters the focus radically in order to give us a close-up of a micro-world in which the workings of his social laws are seen in more detail. As he himself might have put it, he zooms in from a view of the ants' nest as a whole to consider the machinations of a few of the actual ants.

Zinoviev has always maintained that two parts of the original manuscript of *Ziiaiushchie vysoty* were lost in transit, namely '*Zapiski nochnogo storozha*' ('Notes of a Night Watchman') and *Svetloe budushchee*. The former, set in Ibansk, was published in 1979 as a kind of appendix to *Ziiaiushchie vysoty. Svetloe budushchee*, however, was rewritten as a separate book in 1976 (Zinoviev, 1978:43; 1990a:374), the setting being switched from Ibansk to Moscow. It was published in 1978 and an English translation appeared in 1981.

Given the apparent collapse of Communism in Eastern Europe and the current unfashionability of socialism, it is perhaps worth outlining briefly the political situation at the time the book was written, both in the Soviet Union and in Great Britain. In the Soviet Union, Brezhnevism was at its height. Conservatism had triumphed over reformism. Dissidents were on the defensive. The 'Brezhnev doctrine' and '*détente*' guided Soviet foreign policy. Western scholars wrote admiringly about the stability of the regime and the notable increase in egalitarianism which had been achieved. The Soviet Union seemed impervious to the troubles besieging the West as a result of student protests connected with the Vietnam war and the colossal increase in commodity prices associated with the oil-price rises in 1973. This was to lead to a situation in the mid–1970s which one historian has called 'the worst economic depression since the 1930s' (Warner, 1981:333). The second half of the 1960s and all of the 1970s in Britain was a period of high unemployment, strikes, wage increases of up to 30 per cent and inflation peaking at 24.2

per cent. There were landmarks like the six-week merchant seamen's strike in 1966, the defeat of Labour policy as set out in Barbara Castle's blueprint *In Place of Strife* in 1969, the 1972 miners' strike, the 'three-day week' which began in January 1974, the Lib-Lab pact, the 'Social Contract' in 1974, which read like a socialist's charter, the intervention, at Britain's request, of the International Monetary Fund in 1976, and so on. One government adviser wrote about the 1972 miners' strike thus: 'Many of those in positions of influence looked into the abyss and saw only a few days away the possibility of the country being plunged into a state of chaos not so very far removed from that which might prevail after a minor nuclear attack' (quoted in Warner, 1981:317). The contrast between Soviet *stability* and Western *turmoil* could scarcely have been sharper.

When *Svetloe budushchee* appeared in 1978, it did not make anything like the impact of *Ziiaiushchie vysoty*, yet it was well received. Bernard Levin thought that Zinoviev had accomplished with this book a more difficult task more successfully than the task he had set himself in *Ziiaiushchie vysoty* (Levin, 1981:43). Geoffrey Hosking called it an 'excellent introduction to Zinoviev's work' (Hosking 1981). In 1979 it received the Prix Medicis étranger.

Svetloe budushchee is much more recognisably a work of 'literature' than *Ziiaiushchie vysoty*. The characters have proper names, the place is Moscow and the time is not long after the 25th Party Congress. The plot is simple. The narrator is a Moscow 'liberal' academic who is desperate to be elected a corresponding member of the Academy of Sciences, not for reasons of academic honour but for the access membership will give him to the Academy's special shops and services. His campaign for election is conducted at the institute where he works, and forms one important strand in the book. His family life, however, is at odds with his official persona. His two children no longer believe in the official ideology, although both of them are exemplary members of the Komsomol and academically very gifted. The narrator is continually worried by the anti-Soviet tone of the conversations round his table, lest his family attract unwelcome attention. He is even more worried by the activities of his old friend Anton Zimin, who has written a

book about the true nature of Communist society and is
trying to get it published in the West. The narrator offers his
help in order to delay publication, at least until after the
Academy elections are over. In the end, the narrator's
campaign is unsuccessful, and his daughter commits suicide
when she discovers that Anton had spent many years in the
camps, having been secretly reported to the authorities by
her father. The plot, however, in a Zinoviev work is seldom
of outstanding importance, and *Svetloe budushchee* is no
exception. What *is* important is the insight Zinoviev offers
into the workings of Communist society at the 'micro' level.

Before we examine that insight in detail, it will be useful
to say something about the literary quality of the work.
Several critics have condemned it as a 'bad novel'. Bar-Sella
(1982) argues that the purpose of the novel is to show the
development of human character, and since there is no
character development in *Svetloe budushchee*, that work is
therefore a bad example of the genre. This point is echoed
by Natalia Rubinshteyn (1978:248) and Horst Koepke
(1979:8). Zinoviev himself, however, has never claimed the
status of novel for *Svetloe budushchee*, and if the work does
not contain the defining characteristic (character development) it is hardly fair to criticise it as a bad example of
something it does not aspire to be.

In the view of this writer, *Svetloe budushchee*'s claim to the
title of 'work of literature' is perfectly justified. As we shall
see, it is an intricately constructed network of current and
past events within which various dramas are played out.
While it is generally true that there is no character development, we have to make an exception in the case of the
narrator to the extent that his character comes through in
his mode of discourse. We learn a lot about the narrator
from the way he narrates. He is intelligent, humorous,
cynical, devious yet relatively honest about himself. He is
capable of acts of treachery but is by no means wholly bad.
The important point to make, however, is this. For Zinoviev,
the individual in a Communist society is unimportant *qua*
individual. Individuals lose their individuality and become
members of collectives. The uniformity of life is such that
individual differences are relatively unimportant. The narrator and his family are representative of the Soviet intelli-

gentsia, and it is as representatives of that stratum of society
that they are interesting, not as 'Sasha', 'Lenka', 'Tamurka',
or 'mother-in-law'. Anton, of course, is an exception, but
even he has a representative role to play, that of 'decent
human being'. According to Zinoviev, such a creature is
rarely to be found in a Communist society and if it is, it is
likely to be suppressed.

We should also note the timescale of the work. The
framework is the narrator's campaign for election to the
Academy, a few weeks at most. There is also the matter of
'distance'. The reader is accorded the status of 'acquaintance', rather than 'close friend'. What we learn about the
various people in the book is appropriate to that status.
Thus we do not learn about their inner, private lives, we do
not share their intimacies, we are not invited to examine
how their lives have developed over the years. The news of
the narrator's treachery or the suicide of his daughter
affects us no more than we might be affected by similar
events in the lives of people with whom we are barely
acquainted. The 'distance' chosen by Zinoviev is a matter of
conscious choice, it seems to me, not a consequence of any
absence of literary talent.

We noted above that *Svetloe budushchee* is important for
the insight it provides into the workings of Soviet Communism at the 'micro' level. The wealth of detail which
Zinoviev provides is most easily revealed via a discussion of
the structure of the work in question. *Svetloe budushchee*
contains 113 texts grouped into ten separate strands which
are interwoven to produce the fabric of the work as a whole.
If we number these texts from 1 to 113, we can associate
particular texts with strands as follows:

Strand 1 – The Slogan: 1, 15, 20, 32, 54, 68, 88.
Strand 2 –The Institute: 3, 7, 8, 13, 19, 47, 53, 61, 69,
          73, 78, 84, 89, 91, 95, 104, 108, 110, 111.
Strand 3 – The Family: 2, 4, 9, 11, 14, 21, 22, 23, 24, 25,
          26, 34, 40, 41, 43, 46, 49, 50, 51, 52, 55, 63, 70,
          71, 75, 77, 83, 90, 97, 100, 105, 106.
Strand 4 – Anton's book: 12, 16, 58, 74, 86.
Strand 5 – The Narrator's 'collective' book: 10, 31, 47.
Strand 6 – Publication of Anton's book: 18, 28, 33, 48, 62,
          113.

Strand 7 – Discussions between the Narrator and Anton
about the usefulness/uselessness of Marxism
as a theory of society: 5, 25, 29, 36, 44, 60, 67,
81, 85, 94, 98, 101, 107.

Strand 8 – Scenes in the pub: 27, 30, 42, 45, 59, 66, 92,
102, 103, 112.

Strand 9 – Liberalism in the Soviet Union and what it
means: 10, 36, 44, 47, 50, 56, 57, 78, 80, 82, 84,
87, 109.

Strand 10 –The Old Woman: 38, 42, 64, 72, 113.

The sum total of these texts comes to more than 113,
since a few texts can be allocated to more than one strand.
Also, a few texts have been omitted as not obviously belonging to any strand. Nonetheless it can be seen that the
overwhelming majority of the texts can be grouped one way
or another. It is also noteworthy that the numbering of the
texts in any strand is largely discontinuous. This approach
allows Zinoviev to change subject with remarkable economy
without having to provide motivation, the space thus saved
being available for other purposes, notably the inclusion of
further detail about Soviet society as he sees it. This point is
well illustrated by the distribution of texts 1–20 among the
various strands:

Text no.	Strand	Topic
1	The Slogan	Its unveiling
2	The Family	Introduction to the Narrator (N)
3	The Institute	Description of N's place of work
4	The Family	Family mockery of Communism
5	Not allocable	Anton's view of Communism
6	Not allocable	Brief portrait of Anton
7	The Institute	Long poem on marxist ideology/ Tvarzhinskaia's ode to the Slogan
8	The Institute	Description of mediocrities who work in the Institute
9	The Family	N's daughter Lenka and her opinion of her father's literary 'talent'

10	N's 'collective book'	N on the need to write (collectively) a book about the 'liberal' period between the 20th and 25th Congresses of the CPSU; on 'liberalism' and what it means
11	The Family	Children of leaders of the regime are dissidents
12	Anton's book	Anton's views on Communism
13	The Institute	Portrait of the Institute Director, Academician Kanareikin
14	The Family	Anti-Soviet conversations in N's apartment
15	The Slogan	On how the Slogan was vandalised and on the measures taken
16	Anton's book	Anton on the 'period of perplexity', i.e. the period between the 20th and 25th Congresses
17	Not allocable	N on the death of Stalin and its significance
18	Publication of Anton's book	N agrees to help Anton find a Western publisher for his book, in order to be able to make sure it is not published before the elections to the Academy of Sciences
19	The Institute	On '*prisposoblenchestvo*'
20	The Slogan	On its degradation and its attraction for all sorts of riff-raff

A closer study of the strands reveals that they can be grouped under various headings. Three of them are *contextual* (strands 2, 3 and 8). Two of them serve as *leitmotivs* (strands 1 and 10). Three of them contain elements of '*plot*' (strands 4, 5 and 6). The remaining two (strands 7 and 9) are devoted in the main to the *analysis of philosophical questions* (the usefulness/uselessness of Marxism; the nature of Soviet 'liberalism').

The strands in the contextual group are distinct and discrete. The strand devoted to the Institute allows Zinoviev to describe the ways in which Soviet intellectuals have to operate in their work milieu. As we shall see, the 'successful' Soviet academic has to command a range of skills which are by no means purely intellectual. As a counterpoint to the context of the workplace, Zinoviev devotes much space to the milieu of the family. This setting allows him to demonstrate the extent to which unofficial, *private dissidence can coexist with apparent public conformism*. Finally, there is the setting of the 'pub', a kind of political 'no man's land' where, under certain conditions, it is safe to meet and discuss openly questions which are either taboo at the workplace or which, if they are discussed, can land the discussants in trouble. These three separate contexts allow Zinoviev to introduce us to a large cross-section of the Soviet intelligentsia, both 'at work' and 'at play'. The simplicity with which he thus underlines what might be uncharitably called the 'duplicity' of Soviet citizens is impressive. It is those three strands together with the 'philosophical' strands which are of most interest, and we shall now consider each briefly in turn.

THE INSTITUTE

In this strand are grouped all the texts which relate to Institute matters, Institute staff, Institute work practices, office politics and so on. The topics discussed include the following, with the number of the text in question given in brackets: the Institute as 'madhouse' and its occupants (3); the long poem on Marxist ideology which appeared in the wall–newspaper during the 'thaw' and the impossibility of its appearance now, contrasted with Tvarzhinskaia's 'ode' to the Slogan (7); the concept of the 'good Soviet person' (8); a portrait of Academician Kanareikin and reference to the paradox of Marxist teaching being taught by 'cretins'; Soviet science as 'imitation' (13); on Vas'kin and the question of unprincipled 'sail-trimming' (19); difficulties encountered when trying to write a book 'collectively' (20); Agafonov and careerism (53); the meeting with Mitrofan Lukich (only useful in that it actually took place) (61); the international conference and the machinations surrounding the selection of Soviet participants (65); the Korytovs and mutual back-scratching (69); hospitalisation for political reasons (73); on 'cynical idealists', 'unselfish greed', etc. (78); the hospital visit (84); the outcome of the 'international conference' (89); the Communist 'Sabbath' (91); the petty meannesses of colleagues (95); unmotivated nastiness (104); N's failure to be elected, having been bypassed in favour of Vas'kin (108); N's fall from grace (110); his probable nervous break-down (111). These topics taken together, treated with Zinoviev's familiar amalgam of wit, satire and clarity of thought, paint a graphic picture of life in a Soviet research institute, a picture which, however, is by no means unique to that type of Soviet institution.

Zheliagin and Popov (1978:34) claim that Zinoviev has based some of the characters in *Svetloe budushchee* on real people. Indeed, according to those writers, almost half of the then editorial board of the Soviet journal *Voprosy filosofii* (*Questions of Philosophy*) can be identified. Their point is that Zinoviev, as a member of the same board, was in a particularly good position to observe the behaviour of the type of people who make it to the top. They claim to identify the Narrator himself, Kanareikin, Frol Ivanov (assistant to Mitrofan Lukich), Mitrofan Lukich and Agofonov.

According to Zheliagin and Popov, Agofonov is an exact copy of Victor Grigor'evich Afanas'ev, one-time editor of *Pravda*. Agofonov is a successful careerist, for reasons that the Narrator cannot quite understand. He concludes that Agofonov continues to be promoted from one post to another on the grounds that he does not constitute a threat to anyone. As we shall see later on, Afanas'ev seemed to make a favourable impression on several Western scholars during the time of the 'scientific-technical revolution' associated with the Brezhnev era around the time of the 25th Congress.

Given the importance attached to 'science' in connection with the Brezhnev era, it is worth bearing in mind Zinoviev's distinction between science and the imitation of science.

Anton, complaining that those selected for training as theorists of Marxism are usually untalented careerists or lead–swingers, puts it like this:

> Раз наука есть массовое социальное явление, в ней наверняка греют руки бездарности и карьеристы. Но если она вынуждена сохранять статус науки, в ней обязатеьно есть некоторое ядро способных, грамотных, добросовестных людей. Иначе это не наука. Иначе это имитация науки. Каких теперь много. Нет, дорогой мой, выход тут есть. И очень простой. Твоя теория [marxism – MK] вовсе не наука в собственном смысле слова. И сама ее претензия быть 'самой, самой...' есть претензия чисто идеологическая. И атмосфера лжи есть нормальная среда.

(SB: 35)

> Once science becomes a social phenomenon of the mass, certainly there will be inept careerists who will milk it for all its worth. But if it is obliged to preserve its status as a science, it must necessarily contain a certain nucleus of able, literate and conscientious people. If not, it is not a science but an imitation of a science, of which today there are many. No, my friend, there's quite a simple solution. Your theory [Marxism – MK] is in no way a science in the proper sense of the word. Even its pretensions to be 'the most what-have-you', are purely ideological pretensions. And the atmosphere of lies is its natural milieu.

(TRF:40)

Science, according to Zinoviev, has become a mass phenomenon and is thus subject to the workings of his social laws. In the Soviet context, much of what passes for science is pseudo-science or imitation. It is almost certainly the case that the mushrooming of scientific research institutes, especially in the social sciences, during the Brezhnev years led to the production of much pseudo-science, with consequent adverse effects on the quality of the 'input' into the problem area of 'management'. We shall return to this point below.

THE FAMILY

In the following texts, most of which are accounts of family conversations, Zinoviev offers us a picture of intellectual Soviet family life: N's family and its irreverent attitude to Soviet ideology (4); Lenka's hilarious mockery of her father's article on the materials of the 25th Congress of the CPSU (9); the first of Lenka's irreverent poems (11); a poem on the Jewish emigration, a reference to Solzhenitsyn and Sakharov, a reference to the 'Golden Age' (i.e. the period between the 20th and 25th Party Congresses) (14); genuine versus counterfeit history and the relationship between outer conformism and inner irreverence (21); generational differences in relation to careerism (22); religion (23); wartime (24); real Communism, the inability of Marxism to give straight answers, the threat of Communism for all mankind (25); N's mother-in-law and the power of pensioners (26); morality (34); Anton's anti-Russian toast (in verse), for which he was sent to the camps (40); toilet-paper, nastiness, envy, Schadenfreude (41); Lenka as an exemplary member of the Komsomol (43); Lenka's 'The Careerist's Dream' poem (46); Anton tells Sasha how he ended up in the camps (49); art (50); the Jewish question (51); Lenka's sarcastic poem on Brezhnev (52); Lenka's poem on the cretin/careerist (55); family mockery of the whole system (63); Sasha and Anton on the Communist system (70); mockery of the electoral system, another Lenka poem (71); Sasha and the cynicism of youth (75); Lenka finishes a poem begin in text 11 on the immorality of constructing the Bright Future on the corpses of others (77); the future of Soviet youth and the question of what they are to believe in, given the bankruptcy of Marxism-Leninism (83); Lenka's poem on the romantic dream – of being First Secretary (90); Lenka's poem on the significance of everything; Ilych the Second (97); on social laws in wartime, 'depersonification' (99); on how social laws train children to be 'real Soviet people' (100); N's brother and the need for *perestroika* (105); on friendship and betrayal (106).

Despite the disparaging criticisms of people like Bar-Sella and Rubinshteyn, the picture of Soviet family life which is revealed by these texts is both credible and familiar. The present writer has had the privilege of dining with many Soviet families over the years and can testify to the authenticity of Zinoviev's portrayal. Private dissidence among intellectuals is a familiar and widespread phenomenon. Its juxtaposition with public conformism in this book, however, underlines the basic irrationality, and consequent inefficiency, of a social system in which a mode of public discourse is developed which guarantees that what people say will not be believed, or if it is, that their motives will be suspect.

What is particularly refreshing about the family scene is the vitriolic wit with which issues are discussed. An example is provided by the following excerpt of an impromptu poem composed by a friend of the family during a discussion of the Jewish emigration:

Теперь-то я понял, какой был болван,
Родившись на свет, как посконный Иван.
Теперя хоть яйца отрежешь к херам,
Не станешь ни Хайм, ни Исаак, ни Абрам.
Теперя хоть тресни, теперь хоть убей,
В пункт пятый не выпишешь стыдливо: еврей.
И в первом отделе не скажут: он – жид,
Возьмешь как Ивана, а он, блядь, сбежит.

(SB:37)

Now I can see what an idiot I was
To appear on this earth as an Ivan, because
I could top-slice my dick, things would still be the same,
It's too late to change now to an Isaac or Chaim.
You can curse your bad luck, but that's all you can do,
In the space number 5 you can never write: 'Jew'.
And in Dept. No. 1 no one'll say: 'He's a yid!
He was "Ivan" for years. Will he go? He just did!'

Another example is Lenka's poem on the cretin/careerist:

Мне душонку лишь одна сжигает страсть
Не припомню даже, с коих давних пор:
Жажду-стражду в академики попасть:
И согласен для начала на член-кор
Не скрываю, академиком зазря
Привилегий всяких кучу отхвачу.
Но не ради них, по чести говоря,
В академики я сызмальства хочу.
Я мечтаю хоть бы в жизни раз один
Ощутить в чужих глазах немой вопрос:
Как же этакий подонок и кретин
До высот таких немыслимых дорос?

(SB:119)

One passion burns alone within my breast,
I don't remember when it first began.
An Academician's rank is my unending quest.
To get it I'll do anything I can.
I won't deny the title's worth a lot
In terms of perks, and privileges, too.
But that is not the only reason that I've got,
It's also worth it from another point of view.
I'd like just once to get the chance, however slim,
To see the question lurk in someone else's eyes:
'How come a cretin and a jerk like him
Could to the heights of Academe thus rise?'

Apart from Lenka's poems, there are many examples of a less than reverent attitude to Marxism and the person of Lenin. Anecdotes and jokes come from many sources: school, the University, the Academy of Sciences, the Central Committee, even the KGB. Typical is the neat anti-Marxist anecdote about the cave-man sitting outside his cave with a slogan which says: 'Long live slavery! The bright future of all mankind!'

THE 'PUB'

The word 'pub' is the nearest English equivalent for the word *zabegalovka*. It is a place where one can drink alcoholic beverages, usually standing up and usually in rather dreadful surroundings. In that respect a *zabegalovka* is a much less pleasant place than the average English public house. Zinoviev uses it as a setting where people can meet anonymously and discuss controversial questions in relative safety. It fulfils much the same role as Dauber's studio in *Ziiaiushchie vysoty*.

The topics associated with this strand include the following: the 'uneventfulness' of Soviet life (27); the long-term future of Communism and the types of people bred by the 'social laws' (30); the impossibility of equality (42); the monotony, boredom and unscientific nature of Marxist ideology (45); the difference between reality and abstract theory, Marxism as untruth, the high coefficient of parasitism alongside the low coefficient of exploitation of talent (59); the need for someone to oppress and for individual opposition (66); the power of history to restrain, the great service rendered by Solzhenitsyn's *Gulag* (92); nationalism (102).

These contextual strands give some idea of the *range* of topics which are covered in *Svetloe budushchee*. The two strands on Marxism and liberalism respectively deal with two very important questions in some depth. This depth, however, is achieved by Zinoviev's usual 'scatter-gun' approach to the discussion of issues. That is, he peppers his target from a variety of angles.

MARXISM

The texts in this strand are mainly composed of conversations between the Narrator (N) and Anton (A) on the relevance of Marxism as an ideology. They do not contain a critique of Marxist texts. Topics discussed include the following: A's classically simple outline of Communism (5); the reality of Communism and the absence of a theory of Communism (25); science and ideology (29); the end of the liberal era, ideology and science, the 'greatness' of Marxism and its absence of spirituality (36); conscience (44); how to analyse Soviet society and the uselessness of Marxism for that purpose (60); alternatives to Marxism, A's feeling that Communism really *is* the future of mankind (67); A on what

N would see if N adopted A's 'model', checklist of all the
failings of Soviet society (81); A on Soviet literature as
'*vran'e*' (falsehood) (85); how the upper strata are not
required to live by the rules of Communism (94); cynicism
as the real ideology of the ruling classes (97); the uselessness of N's (Marxist) 'theory' (101); A's desire to emulate
Marx in respect of Communism, the desire of Communism
to *conceal* the mechanisms by which it operates (107).

LIBERALISM

In an important sense 'liberalism' as it manifested itself in
the Khrushchev years is the central theme of the book. We
shall discuss below the extent to which a 'liberal' epoch can
be said to have existed since the death of Stalin and, if it
did, for how long. Zinoviev's view is that the majority of
Soviet 'liberals' were opportunists, rather than idealists,
who bet on 'liberalism' as the vehicle by which they would
propel themselves up the career ladder. Uncharitable as
this view is, his views on dissidents are in the main even
more so. The 'liberal's strand is represented by the following texts and topics: N on the need for his sector to write a
'collective' book on why the liberal epoch failed (but in
circumspect fashion, of course!) (10); the end of the liberal
epoch (36); liberalism and its opposite (44); N on the
liberal epoch and on the signs that the liberal intelligentsia
is going to have to watch its step (47); liberals and their
'shady little deals' (50); the beginning, middle and end of
the liberal period (56); the liberal intelligentsia and its
familiarity with dissident literature (Solzhenitsyn etc.) (57);
N on how the post-Stalinist break with the past has left
everyone unaffected except his generation (78); liberalism
and liberals in the Soviet Union (80); dissidents as hardly
better than liberals (82); the demolition of the traditions of
the 1960s (84); on voting patterns (at meetings) and how
they have changed (87); N's admission that he was a '*shesti-
desiatnik*' – a 'man of the 1960s' – and that the 1960s were a
mistake (109).

It will be recalled that the theme of 'liberalism' was an
important strand in *Ziiaiushchie vysoty,* reflected in the battle

for control of the Journal. It was, however, only one of a large number of themes. In *Svetloe budushchee* this particular theme receives more intensive treatment and, given the importance of the 'reformers/conservatives' debates of the 1970s in Western studies of Soviet politics, it is worthwhile examining this treatment in some detail.

As usual Zinoviev's approach is kaleidoscopic. Individual texts deal with individual facets of the problem. The Narrator discusses with a colleague the idea of writing a collective book about the liberal era and why it came to an end. His colleague's response is that it *has* come to an end and that therefore liberals face a difficult future and they should do all they can to prolong the writing of the book and above all write something 'safe' (pp. 26–8). However, since it is no longer possible to write books and articles of a type which were published just three years before, what is the way forward? Anton points out to the Narrator that there are two options. Either he becomes a 'jackal' like Vas'kin, i.e. he trims his sails to the prevailing political wind, or he tries to 'innovate' in his field of Marxist theory. He is not capable of taking the first option, and the second is doomed to failure since it will be the Vas'kins who judge whether the 'innovations' are legitimate or not (pp. 83–6). He tries to convince himself that the higher up the ladder someone 'decent' like himself (as opposed to 'dregs' like Vas'kin) can climb, the more good he can do for other people, but cannot shake off a vague feeling of guilt. He concludes that the antithesis of liberalism in the Soviet context is not Stalinism but dissidence and opposition. Liberalism is merely a softer form of Stalinism (pp. 101–2). Again the Narrator pleads that liberals were right to take as much as they could get, climb as high as they could up the career ladder in order to maximise their influence. Where would Anton be and what would Solzhenitsyn have achieved without people like himself?

So far we have a picture of a Soviet academic who tries to convince himself that his behaviour has been motivated by a morally defensible combination of altruism and self-interest, proclaiming views which are cautiously reformist, but only in so far as it is safe. Personal gain is a by-product of behaviour dedicated to a furtherance of the cause of

Communism by 'softening' it. In a sense, however, liberals
like the Narrator are compromised like liberals elsewhere –
their radicalism falls short of action which will decisively
change the system within which they operate, and is no
match for the conservative opposition, whose interest is in
the preservation of the status quo. A 'softening' of Stalinism
is still a defence of Stalinism. Paradoxically, therefore, the
antithesis of liberalism in the Soviet system is not Stalinism
but dissidence and opposition. Two examples illustrate why,
in the Narrator's opinion, the liberal epoch did not endure.

The first concerns the publication, with 'liberal' help, of
two books on modern art, one taking an orthodox Marxist
line, the other an uncompromising non-Marxist line
(110–11). The author of the first compromised herself by
taking the path of least resistance – writing an orthodox
Marxist critique of modern painting as a way of including in
the book some reproductions of actual paintings. The
author of the second did not compromise, fought to get his
way, and did, in the end, manage to have his book published. The book was an outstanding success, but in the
West. In Moscow it was ignored because it showed too much
talent and too much freedom of spirit. The Marxist book
was lauded to the skies. Mediocrity was preferred to talent.

The second example is similar (120–3). At the beginning
of the 'liberal' era an original thinker is brave enough to
ridicule in public Lenin's contribution to logic. He is not
arrested but simply transferred. At the height of the liberal
era he is invited to take part in a scientific conference. His
paper is one of the most interesting and generates the most
discussion, yet cannot be published because it 'goes too far'.
At the end of the liberal era he applies successfully for
permission to emigrate. Henceforth he will be a non-person
and his genuine contribution to science will be ignored.
One is reminded of a whole host of scholars and artists who
left the Soviet Union during the 1970s for exactly those
reasons.

Zinoviev's point is that the liberals were too faint-hearted
and too self-centred to achieve a critical breakthrough.
Their self-interest was stronger than their altruism, although
they had sufficient of the latter to feel superior to the
unreconstructed conservatives who favoured a return to

Stalinism, but without the terror. The liberals, however, according to the Narrator, had a sufficient sense of altruism to be affected by the climate in a way that no other generation was. The older generation (Petin, Tvarzhinskaia, *et al.*) was set in its ways and unashamedly Stalinist. The younger generation (Lena, Sasha) had rejected the ideology and did not believe in any of its ideals. Only the Narrator's generation thought for a while that perhaps a reformed 'Communism with a human face' was possible, and that generation produced moral deformities like himself – 'cynical idealists', 'greedy altruists', 'honourable careerists', etc. Such people were unable to break the Stalinist mould, and were by no means a match for those who did not believe in liberalism anyway. To that extent, they shared responsibility for the increasing conservatism of the Brezhnev era.

We have thus far seen the period between the 20th and 25th Congresses of the CPSU through the eyes of what Zinoviev conceives to be an average member of the Soviet liberal intelligentsia. The Narrator's interpretation of the changing atmosphere between 1956 and 1976 is very different from those offered by Western scholars. Solzhenitsyn in his famous essay 'The Mortal Danger' sharply criticised what he believed to be serious Western misconceptions about Russia and the Soviet Union, and it might be instructive to attempt to see Western accounts of the period under review written at, or about the time of, the appearance of *Svetloe budushchee* through the Narrator's eyes.

He would probably be disparaging about Western debates about whether the Soviet system was best seen as an example of 'institutional pluralism' or whether a 'systems approach' would not offer a more appropriate insight into the 'complexity' of the politico-administrative structure.[1] He would be disparaging because such debates are based on the assumption that Soviet bureaucracy can be seen as a relatively 'inefficient' type of Western bureaucracy. They tend not to address questions such as 'What makes the Soviet bureaucracy "Soviet"?' The assumption that 'bureaucrats are the same everywhere' would be rejected by the Narrator as totally erroneous. He would agree with his friend Edik:

У нас нормой являются самые отвратительные качества человеческой натуры, только обладание которыми обеспечивает выживаемость в социальных условиях. И прикрыта вся эта мерзость самой грандиозной и самой лживой идеологией. Рядовой советский человек на голову выше любого западного чинуши, интеллигентика и т.п. !

(SB:72)

Our norm comprises the most repugnant qualities of human nature without which it is impossible to survive in Soviet social conditions. And all this filth is veiled by the most grandiose and the most mendacious of ideologies. The rank and file Soviet man is a whole head higher than any Western official or intellectual!

(TRF:85)

and with his friend Anton: 'U nas atmosfera lzhi est' normal'naia sreda' (SB:35). ('Our natural medium is an atmosphere of lies.') Falsehood and imitation, theatricality and deception, creating a yawning chasm between appearance and reality, form a constant theme of Zinoviev's. It is present in *Ziiaiushchie vysoty* and it recurs in *Svetloe budushchee*. The '*atmosfera lzhi*' is constant and all-pervasive. As a contributory factor to Soviet inefficiency it is hard to overestimate, and it should not be left out of account.

The Narrator would be even more critical of Western debates about the 'scientific-technical revolution' associated with the Brezhnev years and particularly with the 25th Congress. For a start, one of the Soviet management science experts who is often quoted with approval by Western scholars is none other than V.G. Afanas'ev. Robert Miller (1976:146) quotes Afanas'ev with approval:

Administration in its most general sense is the ordering and regulation of a system under the conditions of a continuously changing internal and external environment, and the bringing of the system into conformity with the requirements of its characteristic objective laws.

Miller (1976:147) refers to this definition as 'a curious

blend of modern systems concepts and historical materialism'. One imagines that Anton and the Narrator would be
considerably less polite. The point is that Miller dismisses
the 'objective laws' component of the definition as being
unimportant, whereas in fact Afanas'ev is really engaging in
pseudo-scientific discourse, in imitation. The pseudo-scientific quality of Miller's next quotation from a Soviet source
(Miller, 1976:147) is even more striking:

> Leadership and administration in principle coincide only
> in socialist society. Now the task obviously consists in
> maximally approximating the contents of leadership to
> the objective tendencies of social administration and self-
> regulation... The object of leadership is controlled (*uprav-
> liaetsia*) in its development by certain laws, independently
> of the subject of leadership. And this subject will be really
> leading (*deistvitel'no rukovodiashchim*) when its conscious,
> volitional activity is determined by these laws of 'self-
> regulation' in the object'.

Even allowing for the difficulty of translating such gobblede-
gook, one can be confident that the level of generality and
woolliness renders it useless as science but useful as a kind
of ideological pseudo-scientific contribution to an apparently important debate. Useful, that is, as a 'publication' that
one can add to one's list. It is the sort of stuff that people in
the Narrator's institute write. One can thus have some
sympathy for Brezhnev when he described the main task
facing political leaders at the 24th Congress. It was:

> To *combine organically* the achievements of the scientific
> and technological revolution with the advantages of the
> socialist economic system, to unfold more broadly *our own,
> intrinsically socialist forms* of fusing science with production.
> (Cocks 1976:177)

From the Narrator's perspective, such a formulation will
stimulate the production of even more pseudo-scientific
research, most of it stolen from the West under the pretext
of 'adapting' it to Soviet conditions. Cocks (1976:176) makes
the same point more politely:

At the same time the systems movement in the Soviet Union should not be seen as simply a campaign to replicate Western methods, to transplant them wholesale into Russian soil... Though such terms as 'systems analysis', 'management science' and 'network planning' are becoming more and more a part of the Soviet managerial idiom, they necessarily acquire different meanings in Russian translation and practice.

Fedor Burlatsky, quoted by Cocks (1976:177), is closer to the Narrator:

A fashion has set in... to make a show with a whole mass of words, which, when translated into the Russian language prove to be fairly trivial.

Jerry Hough (1976) was perhaps more sceptical than some of his Western colleagues about the scientific-technological revolution in Soviet conditions:

It is quite possible that the discussion of 'scientific decision-making' is little more than an 'ideology'... – a doctrine that has consciously or unconsciously been developed to forestall attacks upon the status quo and the policies emanating from the current leadership.

(1976:14)

He goes on to note that 'in the new fascination with "science" many... fail to recognise that specialists have interests and that their judgement may be affected by those interests' (1976:15).

The scope for 'scientific research' of the type that Anton and the Narrator despise would certainly have been extended as a direct result of a meeting of the USSR Academy of Sciences called at the end of May 1976 to hear a report on 'The Decisions of the Twenty-Fifth CPSU Congress and the Tasks of the USSR Academy of Sciences' (Cocks 1977:44). According to Cocks, the congress 'had added an important dimension to the draft guidelines for the economy, noting the need to raise the role of the Academy of Sciences as the center for theoretical research and coordinator of all scientific work in the country.' One can almost see Academician Kanareikin wondering how he can turn that directive to his advantage: more staff, more research projects, more post-graduate students, more influence, more prestige, etc.

Before we come to discuss the 'reformers versus con-servers' question we should underscore an important point concerning the question of ideology. We have already noted a Western tendency to discount 'ideological' components of Soviet scholarly writing on the grounds that ideological trimming is of little importance. Indeed, most Western scholars would probably agree with Reddaway (1978:122) that 'Soviet Marxism–Leninism has become ossified, ritual-ised and almost universally – except within the party apparatus, where it is the obligatory language – discredited or ignored.' This is largely true (it is also discredited within the Party apparatus), but Reddaway fails to make the correct inference. One of the key contrasts in *Svetloe budushchee* is the juxtaposition of family life and life at the Institute. Clearly the official ideology is ridiculed – by the very people who enact it in their daily lives! Zinoviev has shown con-vincingly that belief in the ideology is not important. Accept-ance will suffice, manifested in the ritual already noted. Ideology, however, permeates the whole of Soviet life, notably the educational system. Children from an early age are 'brought up in the Communist spirit', i.e. learn to operate like Soviet people in the '*atmosfera lzhi*'. Private ridicule and public acceptance of the ideology results in public behaviour which everyone takes to be false. That is the great Soviet tragedy – as has become clear even after the advent of *glasnost'*.

The period associated with *glasnost'*, however, is outside the context of our present discussion and we must turn now to consider Western assessments of the 'reformers/con-servers' battles during the period under review, again from the perspective of the Narrator.

The essence of the issue is best put by Stephen Cohen:

Reformism is that outlook, and those policies, which seek through measured change to improve the existing order without fundamentally transforming existing social, politi-cal, and economic foundations or going beyond pre-

vailing ideological values... Conservatism is often little
more than the sum total of inertia, habit, and vested
interests.

(Cohen 1984:87,88)

That is a very neat formulation, one with which Anton and
the Narrator could agree, except that they would add that
Soviet reformism is vitiated by the self-interest of the
reformers, which prevents them fighting hard enough for
the reforms they allegedly support or believe in. Cohen,
however, is one of that very small number of Western
experts on the Soviet Union who even acknowledges the
existence of Alexander Zinoviev and he is familiar with that
line of argument. His own view is compelling:

[But] reform from above everywhere is always limited in
substance and duration, and it is usually followed by a
conservative backlash. This circumstance is partly a result
of the nature of reformism, which struggles against the
natural inertia of people and institutions on behalf of
limited goals. Many adherents of reform are quickly
satisfied, many allies are easily unnerved, and many who
only tolerated reform are soon driven to oppose further
change. All become part of a neo-conservative consensus,
defenders of the new, reformed status quo, and critics of
reformist 'excesses'.

(1984:91)

No doubt both Zinoviev and Cohen would agree that
there is a dialectical opposition between the forces of
reformism and conservatism, and that the balance can swing
from one to the other. Where they might disagree is over
the question of motivation. Cohen's view is more charitable
than Zinoviev's in that his definition applies to all political
systems, whereas Zinoviev seems to accuse Soviet liberals of
self-interest and moral cowardice on the one hand, and an
acceptance of the Stalinist system on the other. Cohen
eschews the word 'liberal', and indeed stresses that it is 'a
serious analytical mistake... to insist that real change or
reform in the Soviet Union must mean *liberalisation* or
democratisation in our sense of these words' (1984:87).

More, perhaps than others writing at the time, Cohen stresses the deep conservatism of the Brezhnev period, especially after the Soviet invasion of Czechoslovakia, which he regards as running right through the system from top to bottom, both 'downstairs and upstairs' (1984:95). His emphasis is interesting, since it helps to offset the rather misleading image, hinted at by others, of a politico-administrative system vibrant with the desire to introduce the fruits of the scientific-technical revolution into government. On balance, it seems likely that much of the 'desire' for such innovation was good old-fashioned Soviet eyewash, which does not mean that there was no genuine desire.

Not only was there conservatism 'downstairs and upstairs'. This conservatism seemed to be present across generations. It was *not* the case that the younger generation (the Sashas and Lenkas) wanted to change the system. One study (Connor, 1975) attributes to Soviet youth a kind of apolitical conformism which would probably be reflected by the public behaviour of young people like the Narrator's children. We should bear in mind, however, that their 'apoliticism' does not mean political unawareness, but a sense of political impotence neutralised by a determination to make a successful career.

Western writers seem not to have considered the moral dilemma of the Narrator's generation in the same terms as Zinoviev. A non-conformist himself, he quite clearly has difficulty giving his conformist peers the benefit of any moral doubt. Conservatives were Stalinists. Liberals were also Stalinists, but almost worse because they wanted to 'improve' Stalinism by getting rid of its excesses. Dissidents operated outside the system and could be ignored or despised. In *Svetloe budushchee* he still shows much respect for Solzhenitsyn, as he did in *Ziiaiushchie vysoty* via the figure of Pravdets. Yet already his respect is tinged with criticism. The conversations in both these works refer to Solzhenitzyn's courage, and above all, his honesty, but in *Svetloe budushchee* we begin to notice criticism of Solzhenitsyn's 'understanding' of the Soviet system. Later we shall see Zinoviev's criticism harden and deepen, and his attitude to dissidents change from a kind of paternalistic tolerance in *Svetloe budushchee* to something reminiscent of contempt. Real contempt, however, he will reserve for the Soviet 'liberals'. In *Svetloe budushchee* they are moral degenerates, 'cynical idealists', etc., but they are only at the beginning of their careers. How they develop will be one of the themes in the remainder of this book.

It would be wrong, however, to give the impression (as Zinoviev does constantly!) that you have to be Soviet *really* to understand the Soviet system. Surveying Western literature on the Soviet Union written in the 1970s, one is impressed by the prescience of some of the scholars who contributed to it. Jerry Hough (1976:16–17), for instance, made three predictions which have proved to be remarkably accurate: (a) the system under Brezhnev was moving towards a state of sluggishness and inflexibility 'that courts the possibility of explosion'; (b) 'we should at least consider the possibility that the succession to [Brezhnev] may in fact involve a genuine crisis... If Brezhnev has been following an "after me the deluge" line instead of trying to guarantee his policies after he has gone (a distinct possibility in this observer's opinion), some type of deluge cannot be ruled out'; (c) 'there is a major problem of controlling a successor who has every excuse to rejuvenate the political adminis-trative elite'. Connor (1975:31) argued that one of the sources of the stability of the Brezhnev years was a sterile political culture, serviced by producing enough goods to keep the population happy and went on to say: 'A regime which rests on the apoliticality of the masses in "good" times cannot be confident of apolitical masses in bad times.' Other observers have pointed to the vulnerability of the regime to national unrest in a variety of republics (Redd-away, 1978:136); Brown, 1978:229; Carrère–d'Encausse, 1978:280).

There is little of such prediction to be found in *Svetloe budushchee*. One gets the impression that the regime is here to stay, that the period between the 20th and 25th Con-gresses was both a 'Golden Age' and a 'mistake'. Under Brezhnev, Communism as a social system has set in its mould and may last for many centuries. Communism, moreover, is likely to spread and engulf the West. In 1978, one suspects, Zinoviev's gloomy prediction probably had more adherents than the predictions of scholars like Jerry

Hough. On the other hand, the events of 1989 in Europe were foreseen by no one, and the current situation in the Soviet Union is one of near-total chaos. One development which at first sight confirms the view that Soviet ideology was moribund has been the virtual disappearance of what one might call the 'textual' features of Communism. A counter-argument, which will be developed in the next chapter, is that ideology is not just 'doctrine' but also a 'guide to action', and that, while Soviet people can easily slough off the slogans associated with Communism, they cannot so readily change the way they think or act.

5 *Zheltyi dom*

Of all the books that Zinoviev has written, *Zheltyi dom* (*The Madhouse*) is his favourite. In the view of this writer it is also one of his best, if not *the* best. It is a tragedy that it has not been available to a Soviet readership. Were one to provide annotations revealing the subtext of this gigantic work, they would require many volumes. The translations which are available constitute varyingly successful attempts to produce equivalent texts at the linguistic level, but they founder on the rock of non-Soviet ignorance of Soviet reality. Once more we have to repeat that non-Soviet cultures (and therefore their languages) lack the connotational equivalences which are necessary for a rendering of the subtextual complexity of Zinoviev's writing. It is for that reason more than any other that the book has had a disappointing reception in the West. Part of the aim of this chapter is to endeavour to bring to light the book's many qualities, qualities which more than compensate for its undeniable defects.

We shall begin by drawing attention to the importance of *Zheltyi dom* not only in terms of Zinoviev's biography but also in terms of its place in his *oeuvre* as a whole. It was published in two volumes in 1980, and thus appeared two years after *Svetloe budushchee*. He had begun writing it in 1978, completing about half of it before his enforced exile in August of that year. He finished it in 1979. In one account of the genesis of the 'novel' (his own term) he states that he wrote both halves simultaneously (Zinoviev, 1981b:99), whereas in another (Zinoviev, 1990a:441) he affirms that he wrote the 'first' half in Moscow. Since the book is in four parts, it is not clear whether he means 'half' in terms of 'amount' only, or, which is more likely, that he wrote parts of all four sections in Moscow, finishing these in Munich. It will be clear from our later discussion of the structure of the work that such an approach is entirely plausible.

There are strong links between *Zheltyi dom* and *Svetloe budushchee*. For a start, the setting is identical. As the Narrator in *Svetloe budushchee* points out (SB:12): 'Nash

114

Institut zanimaet verkhnie etazhi Zheltogo doma' (*'Our Institute
occupies the upper floors of the Madhouse'*). The Institute
in *Svetloe budushchee* is not named as such but the Narrator
works in the Department of Theoretical Problems in the
Methodology of Scientific Communism. In *Zheltyi dom* we
are told (ZhD: I:29): 'Zheltyi dom, esli khotite znat', eto
zdanie gumanitarnykh institutov Akademii nauk' ('The Madhouse, if you want to know, is the building containing the
Academy of Sciences Institutes of the Humanities'). The
hero of *Zheltyi dom* (JRF) works in one of those institutes,
namely the Institute of Ideology, which could well be the
Institute containing the above-mentioned department. The
Narrator from *Svetloe budushchee* and JRF, therefore, could
well be colleagues. Moreover, many of the characters in
Zheltyi dom figure in *Svetloe budushchee*: Kanareikin, Tvarzhinskaia, Tormoshilkina. Academician Kanareikin, however, has been promoted in the intervening two years
between the publication of the two works. In *Svetloe
budushchee* he is the Director of the Narrator's institute,
whereas in *Zheltyi dom* he has moved on, and his post of
Director has been taken over by Petin. There is also a
passing mention in *Zheltyi dom* of Anton Zimin (ZhD: I:271).

There can be no doubt that the Madhouse refers to a real
institution. Indeed, Zinoviev explicitly says that the Institute
of Ideology in *Zheltyi dom* is in fact the institute in which he
himself worked for twenty-two years, i.e. the Academy of
Sciences Institute of Philosophy (Zinoviev, 1990a:441). He
also affirms that most of the characters in the book are
based on real people, namely colleagues at the Institute and
various Soviet philosophers.

Zinoviev must have enjoyed writing *Zheltyi dom*. Life when
he began writing it had become very difficult. Friends and
colleagues of long-standing had turned against him. He had
been dismissed from his academic posts. His scientific work
had been publicly declared to be worthless. He and his
family were in grave financial straits. It is thus not surprising
that he decided to write a book about the place where he
worked for so long, and which had turned against him. A
comparison of his account of his life as a young researcher
at the Institute of Philosophy in his autobiography (Zinoviev, 1990a) and that of young JRF at the Institute of

Ideology reveals many parallels. For instance, both were required as part of their duties to read the manuscripts of various 'psychologically disturbed' people which were sent to the Institute either directly or via the KGB. In addition, they were required to interview these people and provide a preliminary assessment of their mental health, on the basis of which a decision would be taken as to whether they required psychiatric 'help'. Both of them occasionally drew the attention of the KGB on the basis of 'denunciations' by the cranks they were interviewing.

If *Svetloe budushchee*, although set in the Brezhnev period, looks back from the vantage point of 1976 to the battle between liberals and conservatives during the period of 'perplexity' between 1956 and the 25th Congress of the CPSU, *Zheltyi dom* is largely (but not exclusively) devoted to a depiction of the later Brezhnev era from 1976 to 1980. As Zinoviev says in his memoirs, the main hero of *Zheltyi dom* is only partly based on Zinoviev himself. Much of what he experiences is based on Zinoviev's biography, while his character and psychology apparently derive from those of Zinoviev's friend Dmitrii Khanov, a graduate of the Institute of Foreign Languages (Zinoviev, 1990a:383).

The major theme of this work is one which, more than any other, has preoccupied Zinoviev for most of his adult life: the individual versus the collective in the context of a Communist society. Zinoviev from an early age realised that he had been endowed with exceptional ability. His childhood, moreover, had trained him to work hard with others for the common good. As he says himself, he was a model member of a model Communist society. What he could never stand, however, was the injustice of a system in which acclaim and recognition were routinely divorced from real talent. To recall Jon Elster's distinction between active and passive negation, Zinoviev was equally contemptuous of those who passively accepted the disjunction between talent and recognition and those who were in a position actively to suffocate the spirit of creativity, to undermine the achievements of gifted people and to block the promotion of people whose talents could have been put to the service of society.

Zinoviev has been accused by his critics of confounding

the Communist system with life in a Soviet institute of higher education, staffed by careerists and Party members drawn exclusively from the intelligentsia. However, while it is true that Zinoviev regards life in a Soviet institute as typical of life in any Soviet collective, and therefore representative of Soviet society as a whole, in *Zheltyi dom* he makes room for representatives of both the officially recognised classes of workers and peasants, in addition to representatives of the 'stratum' of the intelligentsia. The setting is not exlusively the Institute of Ideology, although much of the 'action' is located there, but includes also a typical Soviet village and a typical Soviet rest-home (*dom otdykha*).

The 'story' in *Zheltyi dom* is soon told. A young Junior Research Fellow wishes to become fully integrated into his collective in the Institute of Ideology, but is incapable of doing so, for reasons which have more to to with genetics than ideology. In other words, he is congenitally incapable of being an ordinary member of the collective because of his individual character. On the one hand he wants to make an academic career, but on the other is incapable of mastering the rules of the game. To put the same point another way, he does not possess the collective instinct which guides unerringly the behaviour of those who do. Perhaps the best example of his attitude is the public lecture he gives in his Institute during which he demonstrates formidable talent in the field of mathematical logic which results, however, in a conclusion which is at once logically inexorable and ideologically unsound (ZhD: I:311). One of the mental patients with whom JRF has to work discusses with him the formation of a 'workers' group' to overthrow Brezhnev. The KGB finds out and institutes an investigation into the reliability of JRF. Needless to say, he is betrayed by everyone and is eventually removed from society, an entirely innocent man but a thorn in the side of the body politic nonetheless. The 'plot', which, as we see, can be described in a paragraph, is buried in no less than 760 pages of small print, and it is time now to move to a consideration of the structure of the work as a whole.

In common with all of Zinoviev's works, the basic constituents of *Zheltyi dom* are the title and the short text, of which there are no less than 824. These are grouped in

various strands which, as usual, interweave in complex ways.
Unusually, however, there are levels of narration, not all of
which are artistically motivated. Given the complexity of the
work, it will be convenient to focus our analysis on two basic
levels of structure, which we may label respectively 'macro'
and 'micro'.[1]

The interrelationship of title and text operates at both
the macro and micro levels. The complete title of the work
is *Zheltyi dom, Romanticheskaia povest' v chetyrekh chastiakh s
predosterezheniem i nazidaniem* (*The Madhouse. A Romantic Tale
in Four Parts with a cautionary foreword and exhortatory epilogue*)
and relates to the work as a whole. This we may term level 1.
The 'tale' or 'novel' (Zinoviev has used both terms) consists
therefore of six parts, each of which has a title and which
together form level 2: *Predosterezhenie* (*Cautionary Foreword*),
Propadevtika (*Propadeutics*), *Apologiia nechistogo razuma* (*A
Defence of Pure Reason*), *Apologiia prakticheskogo bezumiia* (*A
Defence of Practical Unreason*), *Vechnyi mir* (*Eternal Peace*),
Nazidanie (*Exhortatory Epilogue*) These titles recall the philo-
sophical work of Emmanuel Kant.

In his foreword Zinoviev explains why he has chosen
these titles. *Propadevtika* contains the theoretical prelim-
inaries which are required for what comes later. It is written
from the point of view of the central hero, JRF. *Apologiia
nechistogo razuma* is so-called because, after Kant's *Kritik der
reinen Vernunft*, it is only possible to offer a defence of
'unreine Vernunft'. Similarly, after Kant's *Kritik der prak-
tischen Vernunft*, one can only attempt a defence of 'prak-
tische Unvernunft'. Zinoviev's aim is to show in *Apologiia
nechistogo razuma* an attempt on the part of JRF to understand Soviet society, using the tools of education and culture, and a particular method of thinking. By contrast, in
Apologiia prakticheskogo bezumiia, he offers examples of ways
of living in Soviet society and adapting oneself to the
circumstances of one's environment by non-intellectual
means. *Vechnyi mir* is set in a rest-home (*dom otdykha*) outside
Moscow. Zinoviev uses this setting as a symbol for full
Communism, in which all the conditions of abundance are
met, and proceeds to demonstrate that it is a totally undesir-
able goal, not least because of the crucifying boredom of it.

We may consider levels 1 and 2 as the macro levels of

structure. Level 3 is the micro level, containing the individual titles and texts which are grouped under the headings of level 2. We shall examine level 3 in some detail below, but first we need to say a bit more about level 2.

Two questions which require discussion are the issues of 'setting' and 'narrative perspective'. In *Propadevtika* and *Apologiia nechistogo rezuma* the setting is Moscow, and more particularly, the Institute of Ideology. In *Apologiia prakticheskogo bezumiia* the setting is partly Moscow, but mainly a collective farm near Moscow. In *Vechnyi mir* the setting is principally a rest-home, which is set, however, in the Soviet countryside. JRF is the main link between the different settings, being sent to a collective farm to help in the 'battle for the harvest' and to a rest-home near Moscow to concentrate on 'editing' a book for Tvarzhinskaia.

Propadevtika is written from the perspective of JRF. We learn about the Institute of Ideology largely through his description of how it works. His mixture of wit, cynicism and intelligence tells us also quite a bit about his character. But the 190 texts in this section are structurally so diverse that it will be helpful to set up a typology.

There are four main types of text: straightforward narrative; narrative with dialogue and/or verse; dialogue only; individual verses or poems.

The narrative texts reveal JRF's opinions of his colleagues, the workings of the Institute and his own thoughts on the nature of Communist society. Much of his thinking is done on his walks to and from work which take him past the statue of Dzerzhinsky on Dzerzhinsky Square and the statue of Karl Marx on Marx Avenue.

Often he stops to engage them in conversation (probably when he is drunk) and they appear to respond, allowing the possibility, therefore, for argument between two of the architects of Soviet society and a citizen who has to live in it. Obviously Dzerzhinsky spends a lot of time justifying the need for terror, while Marx spends an equal amount of time disclaiming responsibility for the mess which has been made of his ideal society in practice.

The second type of text, 'narrative with dialogue', is of course a perfectly standard type of text, so long as it is clear who is actually taking part. In a Zinoviev work it is not always

immediately apparent. In the section under review there are
four types of partner in the dialogues. First, there are JRF's
colleagues and friends (Teacher, Dobronravov, Shubin,
Poet, Herself, and so on). Occasionally the Poet will break
into verse, which will be included in the text. We have
already mentioned JRF's 'conversations' with two statues.
The third set of characters with whom JRF converses are his
various 'egos', of which he has an inordinate number. On
one occasion they insist on taking on individual personalities and decide to be Lenin, Stalin, Marx, Beria,
Dzerzhinsky, etc. A typical text, therefore is partly an account by JRF of an event in his day which is then commented
upon by his egos under their various names. This allows
Zinoviev to explore a whole range of theoretical problems
of Communism in his unique register of bawdy, drunken,
witty erudition. The simplicity of the device is extremely
clever and the 'conversations' are almost invariably hilarious. Finally, there is the mysterious character Himself
(*On*), JRF's mentor. It is never clear whether this is a real
person or a figment of JRF's imagination. The quest for
clarity in this matter is not helped by the occasional ambiguous hint that Himself might indeed be Stalin. The role
of this figure is to offer advice and support to JRF while at
the same time justifying the way the Soviet Union has
developed, and in particular, the need for oppression.

The texts which contain nothing but dialogue divide
mainly into those involving JRF and his colleagues/friends
on the one hand, and JRF and his 'egos' or Himself on the
other. The topics of the conversations are always related to
problems of Communism, whether of a theoretical or practical nature, yet the division between 'external' and 'internal' dialogues allows for a corresponding breadth of
perspective, the link between both being provided by JRF.
What is interesting is that, neither with his friends nor with
his egos, does JRF ever dominate. His forte is the posing of
simple questions which require simple answers, which, however, when they are forthcoming, strip the emperor of his
clothes.

Finally, there are the 32 individual 'poems'. Most of them
(23) are 'epistles' (*poslaniia*), all written by JRF, but attributed to various people. Thus in his own name he sends

epistles to his parents (ZhD I:77), Tvarzhinskaia (ZhD I:70), Barabanov (ZhD I:72), Kirusik (ZhD I:78), Kachurin (ZhD I:81), Tormoshilkina (ZhD I:82), Smirniashchev (ZhD I:85), his neighbour ((ZhD I:87), Zaitsev (ZhD I:90), Ezhov (ZhD I:97), the Russian people (ZhD I:122), Herself ((ZhD I:161), the Collective (ZhD I:180). But his various egos also send epistles: An Epistle from Iron Felix to Everyone ((ZhD I:101), An Epistle from Lenin to Everyone (ZhD I:107), An Epistle from Stalin to Lenin (ZhD I:113), An Epistle from Marx to his Successors (ZhD I:117). These are in the main very funny, succinct summaries of various types. The 'domestic' ones to his parents, his neighbour and Herself relate to information JRF has provided elsewhere and are not intelligible on their own. The same is true of the epistles sent to his senior colleagues. The ones sent by his egos, however, are independent of the rest of the text, apart from the fact that the reader needs to know that they are in fact JRF's egos and not Marx, Lenin, Stalin, etc. In general, however, these free-standing epistles complement much of the discussion to be found in other texts and provide in that respect a summary, like the other epistles mentioned above. All of them might be described as very funny verbal cartoons.[2]

By the end of *Propadevtika* the reader has a rather detailed picture of JRF, as presented by himself. He is a Soviet 'wimp' figure, small, physically not particularly strong, wears a beard and jeans as a token of non-conformity, and a Western-style anorak even in winter, not because he is a dissident, as his neighbours erroneously think, but because he cannot afford a coat. He is highly intelligent but idle, is apparently successful with women (but not the kind of women he would like to be successful with), goes in for regular bouts of heavy drinking, which can land him in serious trouble (forgetting about his girlfriend locked up in his flat, losing important documents on issue from the KGB, etc.). He would very much like to make a successful academic career (as is clear from many hints in the text, but perhaps most wittily expressed in his Loser's Lament (ZhD I:168)). He believes that Communism is the best possible system and that it is the bright future of all Mankind, although he hates it (ZhD I:62). He is also a 'romantic', in the sense that he longs for some alternative to the remorselessly grey present, unalleviated by any sense of adventure, hope, joy, the unknown. He constantly dreams of his childhood heroes like Ivanhoe or the Three Musketeers, the sound of clashing swords and the hooves of foaming steeds, wakening inevitably to a prosaic Marxist-Leninist reality which has a scientific explanation for everything and no room for phenomena which appeal to the soul.

In *Apologiia nechistogo razuma* the setting remains the same, but there is a significant change of narrative perspective. The first person narrative of *Propadevtika* is replaced by third person narrative. This is true, of course, only with regard to those texts which actually contain narrative. Of the 231 texts which make up this section, only 68 are narrative, including 17 with elements of dialogue. A few more contain elements of both verse and dialogue. The remainder comprise: pure dialogue (58), some of which have JRF as a participant, many of which do not; verse (27); texts relating to a manuscript written by one of JRF's mental patients and JRF's commentary (41 and 4 respectively); monologue (7); dramatic dialogue in the form of scenes from a play (12).

The dialogues break down into four types: those involving JRF and his egos Marx, Engels, Stalin, Beria, Marshal Zhukov, etc.; those involving JRF and his colleagues; those involving a series of conversations JRF has in his head with an imaginary dead fighter pilot; those involving the KGB and JRF's friends and colleagues. With the exception of the last group, which is exclusively related to plot development, the perspectives represented in the other three groups are widely differentiated. JRF's conversations with his colleagues and his egos parallel those in *Propadevtika*. The conversations with the dead pilot provide a juxtaposition of two perspectives: the present and the past. Here we have an echo of the diachronic strands in *Ziiaiushchie vysoty*.

It is difficult to establish who is suppose to have composed the 27 free-standing verses, but it is highly likely that all of them were composed by JRF and it is certainly the case that some of them were. There is a short series of poems on the theme of nostalgia, the authorship of which we may safely attribute to JRF, since nostalgia is a theme which he has explored himself (ZhD I:84–5).[3] He is definitely the author of the poems '*My est'* ('We exist') (ZhD I:367), and '*Golosa*' ('Voices') (ZhD I:389–90). We know this because JRF converses with the dead pilot in other texts in the 'Voices' strand, and in '*My est'* there is a reference to the poet falling, as usual, fully dressed into bed – a clear reference to JRF. JRF is equally definitely, if less obviously, the author of the hilarious poems '*Grustnaia ballada o gomoseke*' ('The Ballad of the General Secretary') (ZhD I:334–5). The content of the '*Ballada o pokoleniiakh*' ('The Ballad of the Generations') (ZhD, I:340–1), recounting a drunken conversation beneath a fence between representatives of the younger and older generations, is entirely in keeping with JRF's life-style, thus we may safely attribute the authorship of that ballad to him as well.

The 41 texts in the 'manuscript of the Stalinist scoundrel' series appear to have been written by one of JRF's patients. JRF, however, manages to lose the manuscript after a boozing session (ZhD I:202–3) and has to write it himself. Only the first of the 41 texts in the strand thus belongs to the pen of the Scoundrel, the rest are JRF's. We shall discuss the importance of this in our analysis of the main themes of the novel. For the moment it is important to note that JRF is the author.

We need not tarry over the monologues. They are in the main short texts revealing the thoughts of various characters, but form too small a proportion of the total to merit particular comment. The 'dramatic dialogues', however, do require some comment, since again it is not immediately clear who has composed them. They allegedly belong to a play written by Academician Petin, who has asked JRF to 'edit' it. JRF throws it in the waste-paper bin and rewrites it, in the course of which his egos Marx, Lenin, Stalin, *et al.* attribute the main roles to themselves. Thus when reading these dialogues one has to remember, for instance, that 'Tania' is played by 'Marx'. It has to be said, however, that the motivation behind this role–assignment is obscure. Presumably the play is acted out in JRF's head, but why his egos should play the roles is unclear.

If we now add up the number of texts of which JRF is the author, in one capacity or another, we arrive at a figure of around 100 (18 dialogues (egos and voices), 44 texts of the

Scoundrel's manuscript plus his comments, 12 dramatic dialogues, 27 poems). This is a significant proportion of the total number of texts in this section. Thus, although JRF does not speak in his own voice at any time, we do learn a lot more about his inner world, refracted through the 'personalities' of his egos, his manuscript, his poems and the conversations he has with the 'voices'. This is in contrast to his outer world where he interacts with his colleagues, friends, the occasional chance drinking companion, his girlfriend, the KGB who is investigating him, the KGB 'swallow' who is planted on him to find out about these friends of his who go under the pseudonyms of Marx, Engels, Stalin, *et al.* By the end of Volume I we have as full a picture of JRF's character as we shall get. What is most striking is the contrast between his outward passivity, conformity, 'typical' Russian attitudes to drinking and women, and his inner rebellion, nostalgia, contempt for the system and incisive insight into the workings of the society in which he lives.

In *Apologiia prakticheskogo bezumiia* there is not only a change of setting and perspective, but also a grave disruption of the time sequence of the novel. As so often with a Zinoviev work, the key to a textual problem is buried in another text hundreds of pages before. If the reader has chosen not to read the 'Cautionary Foreword', he or she will not know that the events recounted in this section took place before those in *Propadevtika* and *Apologiia nechistogo razuma. Apologiia prakticheskog bezumiia*, we are told in the 'Foreword', is volume 3 of the KGB file on JRF, which is why it forms Part III of *Zheltyi dom.* From the point of view of 'plot development', it could be excised completely and make no difference whatsoever. The reader who has not read the Foreword will, furthermore, be rather confused. At the end of Part II (Volume I) JRF is preparing to set off for a sojourn in a sanitorium near Moscow, but does not arrive there until Part IV (Volume II).

Although Part III must be regarded as a major structural flaw in the novel as a whole, the work is richer for its inclusion. We shall discuss this point below, but for the moment we should note that in this section Zinoviev operates a kind of 'split screen' technique, in the sense that the action is located partly in the Institute and partly on a collective farm. There is again a major shift of narrative perspective.

The narrator in this section, which comprises some 192 texts, is a Senior Research Fellow (henceforth SRF) in the same Institute as JRF. As usual, the texts are stylistically varied, but to a lesser extent that in Parts I, II and IV. In Part III, for instance, there are very few free-standing poems, and the proportion of verse included in the prose texts is also significantly smaller. The whole section can be seen as a kind of diary, containing the private thoughts of SRF. Much of the content describes life in a brigade of 'volunteers' from the city to help with the harvest, one of whom is JRF. We actually learn very little about JRF from SRF, who in the main corroborates our view of him and underlines his completely nondescript appearance and almost total self-effacement.

In *Vechnyi mir* (206 texts) the narrative persepective is again relatively complex. As in Part II, by no means all of the texts are, strictly speaking, narrative. Indeed, only 88 contain narrative, with or without admixtures of dialogue and/or verse. In these texts, however, the narrator, as in those in Part II, is of the 'omniscient' type. The texts can be further subdivided into those which deal with events in the actual 'story' and those which are digressions of a semi-philosophical nature addressed to the reader.[4] The remainder subdivide as follows: individual poems (27); dialogues between various sets of characters, always including JRF (50); the Stalin 'drama' (12); Il'ych's memoirs (5); excerpts from Tvarzhinskaia's book (19); monologue (2); JRF's notes (3); '*nash chelovek*' (4 'lectures' by JRF).

The poems are written by JRF. Most of them are letters to his girlfriend in Moscow, only two of which reach her, the remainder being diverted into the KGB file on JRF. The dialogues can be subdivided into those involving JRF and his group in the 'ward' in the rest-home and those with his 'New Friend', who is probably an informer. The Stalin drama is supposedly another literary masterpiece by Academician Petin, but in fact JRF has thrown the original away and written a new one. Il'ych's memoirs form a short set of monologues by a stoker in the boiler-room of the rest-home,

blatantly ridiculing Brezhnev's memoirs as recounted in
Malaia zemlia (*The Little Land*). The nineteen excerpts from
Tvarzhinskaia's book are supposedly just that. She had given
her book to JRF so that he can hunt down and supply it with
the necessary quotations from the 'classics' of Marxism–
Leninism. Here Zinoviev is parodying a standard Marxist–
Leninist textbook on Soviet ideology. It is so reminiscent of
the real thing, however, that one wonders if Zinoviev has
not overdone it. There is so little detectable difference that
the effect of parody is lost.

This concludes our analysis of level 2 of the structure of
Zheltyi dom. We have seen that the settings include the
Institute, a collective farm and a rest-home. We have also
noted the complexity of the narrative structure, particularly
in relation to the question of narrative perspective. We have
managed to define the 'authorship' of all 824 texts, not
counting those in the Foreword and Epilogue (these are by
Zinoviev himself). We now turn to a consideration of level 3,
the texts themselves.

It goes without saying that we cannot comment on each of
the 824 individual texts. The vast majority contain much of
interest and contribute to the very detailed picture of the
workings of Soviet society which the novel as a whole
produces. What we must do, however, is indicate the extent
to which individual texts combine to form strands. We have
already given some indication of this in our discussion of
narrative perspective but our classification of texts has been
precisely in terms of perspective and not in terms of the
interrelationship of texts in thematic terms.

By no means all of the texts can be linked into strands,
but we can provide data for those that can. In *Propadevtika*,
fourteen strands account for 68 of the 190 texts. There are
eighteen strands of varying length (from those containing
two texts to the largest containing 40) in *Apologiia nechistogo
razuma*, accounting for a total of 139 out of 231. Of the 192
texts in *Apologiia prakticheskogo bezumiia* eight strands account for 76. Finally, in *Vechnyi mir* fifteen strands account
for 111 texts out of a total of 206. In sum, 394 texts out of
824 are grouped into 55 strands.[5]

What about the remainder? A certain number of individual texts can be associated with particular strands, which might account for a further 20 or so (Kirkwood 1982:-99–101). In other words, very roughly half of the novel is structured, the other half being made up of texts which bear no structural load. This is why, incidentally, it was possible to translate an abridged version of the novel which was 50 per cent shorter than the original, yet retained the overall structure. While the skeleton was kept intact, however, what was lost was a great deal of the 'flesh'.[6] The English version as a result was inevitably an emaciated, pale reflection of the robust original.

It is now time to address some of the themes of the novel. We have already stated that the main theme is the relationship between the individual and the collective in a Communist society. This theme is embodied in JRF's relationship to the members of his collective in the Institute of Ideology. He wants to be one of them but is congenitally incapable of thinking and acting like them. They sense that he is not 'one of them', and in the end he is removed from their midst.

We shall look at various facets of this problem as they are treated in the novel in particular groups of texts. Thus the problem of the individual versus the collective can be examined under the rubric *ideology and behaviour.* It is explored in conversations between JRF and Teacher, the Stalinist Scoundrel's manuscript (written by JRF) and JRF's reflections in *Vechnyi mir* on '*nash chelovek*' (our [new Soviet] man). Secondly, under the rubric of *alienation,* we can look at this problem via a discussion of the texts analysing the issues of '*romantika*' and its absence, nostalgia, loneliness and the search for a way out. Thirdly, we can look at the problem under the rubric *intelligentsia* vs. *narod* (the 'intelligentsia' versus 'the people'). On the other hand, there are issues in the work which are not directly concerned with the main theme, but which are nonetheless important. These are Zinoviev's view of the Soviet countryside, the portrait of Stalin in *Zheltyi dom,* and Western perceptions of the Soviet Union.

IDEOLOGY AND BEHAVIOUR

As we have seen, this is not the first time that Zinoviev discusses ideology. In *Ziiaiushchie vysoty* his main intention was to demonstrate that ideology is by definition not scientific, even if it claims to be. In *Svetloe budushchee* he made a very important point about ideology in the Soviet Union, namely that, while belief in it is not required by the regime, acceptance *is*. Soviet citizens are thus quite capable of ridiculing it in private and performing the rituals of acceptance in public. In *Zheltyi dom* he is at pains to emphasise three further points about ideology: first, that it is important to distinguish between ideological *doctrine* and ideological *practice*, secondly, that ideological practice strongly influences intellectual and moral behaviour, and thirdly, that the ideology must be adequate in relation to what he calls the 'social intellect' (*obshchestvennyi intellekt*).

JRF's friend the Teacher introduces the first point thus:

Ее [идеологию] надо рассматривать не как некое 'учение' ..., а как некий практически действующий аппарат идеологической организации населения... Дело в том, что главное в идеологии – не смысл ее утверждений, а тот способ мышления, какой она прививает людям... Она есть собрание упражнений... Поэтому советские люди не сговариваясь и без подсказок со стороны начальства одинаково реагируют на события, происходящие в стране и за границей, на научные открытия, на явления природы.

(ZhD I:38, 54–5)

You have to regard [ideology] not as some 'doctrine' or other... but as an apparatus for the ideological organisation of society... The point is that what is crucial in ideology is not the meaning of its assertions but the mode of understanding which it inculcates in people... It is a collection of exercises in how to comprehend... That is why Soviet people, without any initial discussion among themselves, without any hints from the leadership, react more or less uniformly to events both at home and abroad, to scientific discoveries, to natural phenomena.

If Zinoviev is right, it would be premature to hail the events of 1989 and 1990 as necessarily signalling the 'death' of Communism. What has been remarkable (and something which Zinoviev as far as I know has never predicted) is the speed with which the 'textual' aspects of Communism disappeared such as the slogans, exhortations, statues, pictures, etc. What is less certain is whether modes of thought and behaviour associated with that ideology have changed. There is good reason to doubt that it has.

JRF clearly takes the Teacher's observations on the difference between ideological theory and practice to heart, because he incorporates almost identical statements into the Scoundrel's manuscript:

> Мировоззрение (идеологическое учение) говорит человеку, что из себя представляет в общих чертах мир, общество, сам человек. Практическая идеология прививает определенные навыки поведения в принципиально важных ситуациях, – правила идеологического поведения.
>
> (ZhD I:262–3)

A world view (or ideology as doctrine) tells one in general terms how to view the world, society, man himself. Practical ideology inculcates particular forms of behaviour in particularly important situations, i.e. inculcates rules of ideological behaviour.

What that kind of behaviour is JRF explores via his remarks on 'our man' (*nash chelovek*) in Volume II.[7] Man is a complex creature, says JRF, but Soviet man is super-complex, which is only to be expected given that he is the highest form of matter:

> НЄ человек по одному и тому же вопросу способен иметь взаимоисключающие мнения, по одному и тому же поводу испытывать противоположные эмоции...Вот он каков!... Вот он поклялся вам что ваш разговор с ним останется тайной. А на другой день растрепал ваш секрет по всему городу. Пообещав помочь, тут же начинает копать вам яму. Начав бороться за разоружение, он удваивает производство оружия. Начав борьбу за осво-

бождение пролетариата, он кончает тем, что насилует не
только пролетариат, но даже ближайшего союзника –
беднейшее крестьянство.

(ZhD II:261)

Our [Soviet] man is capable of entertaining mutually
exclusive opinions about one and the same question, of
feeling opposing emotions about one and the same occurrence... Here's what he's like! ... He swears that the
conversation you've just had with him will remain con-
fidential. The next day he's blurting it out all over the
place. He promises to help you and then promptly starts
to undermine you. He begins a campaign on disarmament
and doubles the rate of arms production. He begins the
struggle to liberate the proletariat and ends up by oppressing not only it but its closest ally, the poorest peasantry.

To the objection that probably people like that exist outside
the Soviet Union, JRF responds that Soviet man is an international phenomenon. Let us not be taken in by that throw—
away remark. We recall that his social laws are universal, that
in his view civilisation is the history of attempts to harness
their force, that Western civilisation (at the time of writing
this novel, at least, although he is beginning to have doubts)
is the greatest there has ever been, that the social laws have
experienced the fewest constraints under Soviet Communism. There may well be people like that in the West but they
do not form a 'critical mass'.

Why is Soviet man like this? According to JRF, it is
because his opinions do not count for anything, and you
don't get far on emotion alone. Soviet man lives on a
particular plane of existence where opinions, emotions and
intentions are merely remnants of the past:

Преимущеста нашего человека перед всеми прочими со-
стоят, подчеркиваю, не в том, что он имеет какие-то
особые мнения, особые эмоции, особые цели и намер-
ения, особые принципы, а в том, что он ничего подобного
вообще не имеет. Наш человек силен не наличием чего-
то, а отсутствием такого наличия.

(ZhD II:266–7)

The advantages enjoyed by Soviet man over all others do not lie in the fact that he has particular opinions, particular emotions, particular aims or intentions, particular principles, but in the fact (and I emphasise this) that he doesn't have any such thing. Soviet man is powerful by not having them.

An exaggeration? No doubt, but again we have to consider recent Soviet history. Many of the people who were in power then are still in power today. Today they speak sincerely about the need for *perestroika* and the market mechanism. Ten years ago they spoke equally sincerely about the need to educate young people in the 'spirit of Communism'. Were they being insincere ten years ago? How do we know? Are they being sincere today? How do we know? Are they engaging in another piece of ritual? And it is not just people 'in power', or rather, 'in power' should be taken to mean positions of responsibility throughout Soviet society, especially those associated with the *nomenklatura*.

The Soviet individual's opinions count for nothing, because as an individual he has no status:

Советский человек есть лишь функциональная частичка некоего более сложного целого – коллектива, но такая частичка, которая отражает в себе все качества этого целого... Они, т. е. наш человек и наш коллектив, рождаются и существуют как нечто единое и не разрывное целое...

(ZhD II:284)

[Soviet man] is only a functional component of a more complex whole – the collective, but a component which reflects all the qualities of that whole... They, that is Soviet man and our collective, are born and exist as an integral, inseparable entity...

Communist ideology (as doctrine) in the Brezhnev era is despised mainly because it is no longer adequate for a highly educated population. In the Scoundrel's manuscript JRF develops the thesis that Stalin was a consummate ideologist who stripped Marxism of its verbiage and exposed its

kernel. He then presented this in a form which the uneducated masses could understand (or not dare not to
understand!). The 'social intellect' of the 1930s and the
intellectual level of the ideological doctrine 'matched'.
Once the dream of the bright future was shattered, however, the ideology was bankrupt. Attempts to 'develop'
Marxist–Leninist theory produced the word 'developed' in
front of 'socialism' – the fruits of ideological enquiry under
Brezhnev. More importantly, however, developments in
science and education have undermined the 'sacral' power
of the old ideology, and something radically different is
required for the future. JRF makes an interesting prediction in this respect: 'Ia povtoriaiu, nastaivaiu i pod-
cherkivaiu: pridet vremia, i na novom etape kto-to povtorit
delo Stalina (t.e. moe) i prevzoidet Ego' (ZhD I:263) ('I
repeat, insist and emphasise: a time will come when someone will do again what Stalin did...only better'). Were there
to be a crack-down in the Soviet Union and a return to a
more repressive regime, there would certainly be an
attempt to reconstruct an ideological 'force-field'. Will
Gorbachev or his successor outdo Stalin as an ideologist?
In the view of this writer that is a matter of considerable
doubt.

ALIENATION

Alienation is a powerful current running through *Zheltyi
dom*, not surprisingly given Zinoviev's disenchantment with
the Soviet regime and its treatment of him. The aspects
which are of most interest are those which preoccupy both
JRF and SRF. Both of them yearn for the romance of bygone
ages and bemoan its absence in contemporary Soviet reality.
Himself illustrates JRF's dilemma succinctly: 'Ty est' ditia
dvukh epokh: krovavoi, no romantichnoi, leninsko-stalin-
skoi i soplivoi, no sravnitel'no blagopoluchnoi khrush-
chevsko-brezhnevskoi.' (ZhD I:60) ('You are a child of two
epochs: the bloody but romantic Lenin-Stalin one and the
soppy but relatively prosperous Khrushchev-Brezhnev one').
His friend the Poet agrees: 'Ty est' voploshchennaia toska po
ischeznuvshei romantike' (ZhD I: 60) ('You are the embodi-

ment of yearning for a bygone romanticism'). He makes the point in verse:

Как Глас Небес приказ звучит:
Товарищи, Москва за нами!
Не опозорим наше знамя!
Труби атаку, трубачи!
Я из ножен рву клинок,
В бока коня вонзаю шторы,
И... просыпаюсь под забором,
Бесчувствен, грязен, одинок.

(ZhD I: 60)

There thunders out the brusque command:
Defend, O comrades, Moscow's walls!
Hold high our banner, duty calls!
If die you must, die sword in hand!
I pluck from scabbard trusty blade,
To noble gallop spur my roan
And... waken numb, depressed, alone,
Beneath a fence, hung o'er instead.

For the Poet, romanticism is a state of mind, not a way of life. The powers that be have robbed the population of a genuine romanticism and foisted on it one that is false (ZhD I:62).

On the other hand, when JRF discusses this question with his egos (ZhD I:101–2) in relation to the early Soviet period, they point out that there was precious little romanticism then either. Or, as Iron Felix points out, it was as genuine as today's. Look at any newspaper, he says, and you will see nothing but 'With a feeling of righteous pride... With extraordinary drive... With boundless enthusiasm', etc. JRF remains unconvinced, however, because at several points in the novel he harks back to his boyhood reading, filled with heroes like Ivanhoe, the Three Musketeers, Lohengrin. The contrast between the past and present is strikingly juxtaposed in his poem 'Complaint of the Non-Fallen':

Но так уж ведется, наверно искони:
Закроешь глаза – машут гривами,
Откроешь – увидишь не саблю и шпоры, –
Столы и бумаги постылой конторы.

И нету врага, нету гнева огня,
Нет сабли, нет шпор, нет лихого коня.
О Боже, как это дерьмо надоело!
О, где ты скрываешься, правое дело?

(ZhD I: 142)

But probably, always, the story's the same,
With eyes shut one sees horses raring to go.
When they're open you see that the name of the game
Is not sabres and spurs but office desks in a row.
And no enemy's there, in the belly no fire,
There's no sabre, no spur, no impetuous steed.
Oh, God, how this bureaucrap fails to inspire,
Where are you, Just Cause, oh, where are you, indeed?!

(TM:91)

The equation of 'romanticism' with battle is one which we encounter frequently in Zinoviev's work. He himself clearly had 'a good war', although he is keenly aware of the injustices done to his fellow service-men by the regime. We have seen examples of this in our discussion of *Ziiaiushchie vysoty* and there are echoes of it in *Svetloe budushchee*. But it is the absence of a cause worth fighting for in the contemporary Soviet Union which troubles not only JRF but also SRF. The latter discloses (ZhD II:23–6) why he enjoys going to the collective farms to help with the spring sowing and autumn harvesting. It is because the conditions are so dreadful that they remind him of his time at the front, and help to assuage his painful feelings of nostalgia. The present is grey and uneventful, the future without hope, only the past is left.

JRF regrets the disappearance of the past (especially the pre-Revolutionary past which is officially ignored or distorted for politico-ideological reasons). However, he also regrets that with that past there disappeared an appropriate sense of mystery. The present is devoid of mystery, and a reverential attitude to phenomena is not encouraged, for which JRF blames the official ideology (ZhD I:149). Himself (ZhD I: 149–50) argues that one's attitude to the past should be semi-religious, allowing one to meet death calmly in the knowledge of a lifetime richly experienced. Death is another constant theme in Zinoviev's work. It is for him the endless nothing, hence his vibrant sense of outrage at the emptiness of Soviet reality and the impossibility of leading a 'normal life' with 'normal expectations'. Life's brief spark for millions of his fellow citizens is nothing more than a life of unremitting misery for the benefit of the '*nachal'stvo*' (bosses).

A feeling of loneliness is an important aspect of alienation. It affects not only JRF, but also those who are apparently the mainstay of the regime (Petin, for example). Loneliness and yearning are explored in two related strands in *Apologiia nechistogo razuma*. Five texts are devoted to the theme of loneliness and ten poems to the theme of yearning.[8] JRF explains his own loneliness by the fact that he regards his individuality as 'sovereign'.[9] The system produces standard individual-components (reminiscent of Stalin's 'cogs'), none of which can operate individually. JRF is a non-standard component, and is recognised as such. What is non-standard about him is his rich inner world, one in which he reigns supreme. But even a super-standard component such as Academician Petin is lonely: 'Ia mog by Kanta i Gegelia prevzoiti, a ia... A glavnoe – ni odnoi zhivoi dushi krugom. Odin!' (ZhD I: 203) ('I could have surpassed Kant and Hegel, but I... But the most important thing is... there is not a single decent human being around. I'm alone! Quite alone!') Why Petin has this sense of loneliness is exposed by JRF in a short four-line verse entitled 'Toska akademika' ('Regrets of an Academician'):

> Трудами моими завалены полки,
> Но своих никому не раскрою я карт.
> Я известен и в чине. Да что в этом толку?
> Все равно я не буду Ньютон и Декарт.
>
> (ZhD I:203)

> With works of mine the shelves are lined
> But my torment I let no one see.
> I've fame and power, but here's the bind:
> A Newton I will never be.

The shelves may be lined with his 'works', but he knows that he did not write them. He cannot trust anyone. He is outwardly respected but knows that he is really a nonentity.

These ten poems are linked by the word '*toska*' which appears as part of the title of each of them. It is a difficult word to translate, but suggests at once 'longing', 'nostalgia' and 'regret'. Zinoviev cleverly uses these short poems (ostensibly composed by JRF) to give a cross-section of the 'longings' of representatives of various strata of the population. There is the yearning of the Party Secretary to become Brezhnev's replacement (ZhD I:227) and the longing of the army colonel unworthy of his rank to become a marshal unworthy of his rank (ZhD I:219). On the other hand, there are poems devoted to the longing for a real-life Juliet and the chance to die like Romeo (ZhD I:210), to a bygone Russia which will never return (ZhD I:233), and a particularly robust one on the desire for a decent domestic life and the impossibility of achieving it (ZhD I:260–1).

If JRF does not find a way out of his situation other than by bouts of drinking himself into oblivion or dragging any one of a series of women into his bed, SRF does. His solution is to seek an alternative life in sleep. Fourteen texts are devoted to this topic in *Apologiia prakticheskogo bezumiia*.[10] SRF's solution, of course, is a metaphorical one. Although he purports to have discovered the science of '*spunologiia*' (the science of *active* sleep), his in the main tedious disquisitions on this topic contain interesting points. Central is the notion of escape from the 'forcefield' of normal Soviet reality. The solution is to opt out completely and to spend as much time asleep as possible. In one's dreams, one can live a much more fulfilling life. Not everyone can succeed in this, however, but only those who live a 'righteous' (*pravednyi*) life. In two important passages (ZhD II:145–6; 154–6) SRF outlines 'rules of behaviour' which are very reminiscent of Zinoviev's rules of self-conduct which he developed in his own life. Sleep becomes a kind of haven, a reward, almost a heaven for those who lead a life apart from the life-style foisted on people by the regime in which they live. The impression is given that it is a solution on offer only to 'decent' people. Careerists and enthusiastic supporters of the regime have their own rewards, which in SRF's view are not worth having.

'INTELLIGENTSIA' vs. 'NAROD'

In an interview with Zinoviev for *Radio Liberty* in March 1980 Kanievskaia suggested that people were describing him as a russophobe (Zinoviev, 1981b:100). Zinoviev predictably denied the charge, but there can surely be no doubt that when he was writing *Zheltyi dom* his opinion of his fellow Russians was at its lowest. As usual, he treats the topic in a variety of styles and tones, but the underlying sentiment rarely changes. It is a mixture of affection and contempt, exasperation and resignation. As usual JRF is the mouth-piece, although not the only one. In his very funny 'Epistle from Stalin to Lenin' (ZhD I: 113) there is a reference to the 'narod' ('the people') and the necessity of putting large numbers of them in corrective-labour camps. There are also his views on his neighbours in his communal flat, who are 'typical Russians':

Сегодня они меня подносят последними словами, завтра как ни в чем не бывало лезут целоваться. Сегодня поднимают скандал из-за копеечных расчетов по поводу платы за свет, завтра готовы пропить с тобой же сумму в десять раз больше. И наладить какие-то устойчиыве и предсказуемые отношения с ними никак невозможно.

(ZhD I:71)

Today they will curse me under the sun, tomorrow they'll come and embrace as if nothing had happened. Today they'll raise the roof about some piddling calculation of who owes what for the electricity, tomorrow they're pre-pared to drink with you to the tune of ten times that amount. And it's impossible to have stable and predictable relations with them.

On another occasion he discusses this issue with his egos, one of whom (Beria) is much more scathing:

– Сволочной народ, ничего не скажешь. Теперь ты сам видишь, что с ним иначе нельзя, чем мы в свое время делали. Этому народу репрессии, доносы, манифестации и прочая мразь нужны как воздух... пороть этот народ

надо! Он любит, когда его порют. Он не любит, когда о
его жалком положении начинают правду говорить. Но в
жалкое положение он сам себя загоняет охотно. Подлый
народ. Холуйский. Рабский. И никто меня в этом не
переубедит.

(ZhD I: 112)

They're a rotten lot, the 'people', that's all you can say.
Now you can see for yourself that there's no other way of
treating them than the way we did in our time. These
people can't live without repressions, secret informing,
official demonstrations and stuff like that... they need to
be whipped, these people. They don't like it if anyone
starts to tell the truth about their miserable situation. But
they land themselves in that miserable situation with
alacrity. They're rotten people. Sycophantic. Slavish. No
one can tell me otherwise.

JRF's colleague Dobronravov is equally scathing:

Конечно мы можем дикарей поднять до своего полу-
дикого уровня. Но цивилизованному миру мы несем явное
занижение всех лучших продуктов цивилизации, если
не сказать большего. Мы заражаем мир серостью, халт-
урой, ленью, враньем, ненадежностью, лицемерием, ков-
арством, пошлостью, насилием, и т. д. и т. п.

(ZhD I: 123)

Of course, we can raise the savage to our semi-savage level.
But as regards the civilised world, we have a deleterious
effect, if not worse. We infect the world, denude it of
colour, pass on our totally sloppy way of doing things, our
indolence, mendacity, unreliability, hypocrisy, slyness,
banality, coercive methods, etc., etc.

This outburst prompts JRF's very funny 'Epistle to the
Russians'.[11]
  The 'narod' as described so far does not exclude the
'intelligentsia', as Dobronravov is at pains to point out on
another occasion (ZhD I:128–9), yet it is clear that members
of the intelligentsia are regarded by 'workers and peasants'

with suspicion, if not outright contempt. There is already a
hint of this in the attitude of JRF's neighbours towards him.
Much more scathing is the attitude of country dwellers like
Matrena-Dura and Mao-Tse-Dun'ka.[12] JRF sums up the position neatly thus in a passage devoted to this very topic:

> ...народ воспринимает интеллигенцию как свою собст-
> венную часть (такое же дерьмо, как и мы), стремящуюся
> жить как начальство (ишь чего захотели!) Народ уважает
> интеллигенцию, так как это – почти что начальство, но
> презирает ее, так как это – вовсе не начальство.
>
> (ZhD I: 178)

> ... the 'people' regards the intelligentsia as part of itself
> ('they're the same shit as we are') striving to live like the
> leadership ('they don't half fancy themselves!'). The
> 'people' respects the intelligentsia, for it is nearly like the
> leadership, but despises it, because it is not at all like the
> leadership, really.

JRF's isolation is thus complete. On the one hand he does
not fit into his collective (he is a 'non-standard component')
and, on the other, as a member of the intelligentsia, he is
not accepted by ordinary Russian people. This of course
does not mean that he has no relations with them, simply
that he is apart from them.

TOWN vs. COUNTRY

The countryside and the demise of the Russian village have
been major themes in Soviet literature for the past forty
years. For obvious reasons Soviet writers who were concerned about the passing of traditional cultures and values,
and critical of the transformation of collective farms into
state agribusinesses, had to be circumspect. Many of them
thus dwelt lovingly on descriptions of peasant life-styles,
moral values, attitude to the land, scenes of natural beauty,
and so on, unable as they were to confront directly the issue
of the effect of Soviet power in the countryside. Two well-
known examples of this kind of writing are Solzhenitsyn's

Matrenin dvor (*Matrena's House*) and Rasputin's *Proshchanie s Materoi* (*A Farewell to Matera*). Both of these works were written and published in the Soviet Union and in neither of them does the author directly discuss the question of what makes the Soviet countryside *Soviet*, in the sense that the issues discussed would be equally valid in a non-Communist setting. For instance, the flooding of the island in *Proshchanie s Materoi* has its clear parallel elsewhere, notably in France. Matrena's problems seem to me not to be specifically Soviet. She is old, infirm, hard-working, obliging, easily exploited, but also content. Her counterpart is no doubt to be found in villages and hamlets in Spain, in France, in Italy, in Germany. All over Europe people are leaving the land, especially the young. Modernisation, urbanisation and consumerism are international phenomena and the encroachment of the town on the countryside is by no means a uniquely Soviet phenomenon.

Zinoviev, on the other hand, with his usual economy of style paints a picture of the Soviet countryside which demonstrates beyond all doubt what makes it Soviet. The setting is a collective farm in the Moscow region. The context is the autumn 'battle for the harvest' – the annual campaign to get in the harvest with the help of 'volunteer' brigades from the town. SRF is a member of one such brigade, as is JRF.

Again Zinoviev looks at the problem from various aspects. There are texts associated with the campaign as such.[13] Another series contains the reflections of the brigade on life down on the (Soviet) farm.[14] A third contains the wisdom of a certain Matrena-Dura[15] and a fourth is devoted to Mao-Tse-Dun'ka, another representative of the 'people'.[16]

Unfortunately there is not sufficient space to deal with these various aspects in detail and we can do no more than give a brief description of each aspect and encourage the reader to find out more for him/herself. The composite picture is both hilarious and serious.

The 'battle for the harvest' strand describes how the campaign progresses, both officially and unofficially. The official account is one of brave endeavour in the face of difficulties, full of ideological claptrap, and totally untrue. The unofficial account is given by SRF and is entirely plausible: people up to their knees in mud, constant rain, lorries stuck up to their axles, farm machinery which does not work, special clothing which has not arrived and consequent widespread illness, slacking and skiving, heavy drinking, the absence of storage facilities, the preparation of holes in the muddy field to 'store' the rotting vegetables, and so on.

The conversations in the barn which SRF's brigade conduct provide an intellectual comment on the whole town/country issue. But they cover other issues as well, notably that of the individual *vis-à-vis* the collective and the problem of preserving one's individual identity. Zinoviev uses the barn as a setting where individual members of the brigade can recount some experience of their own, each one of which illumines some aspect of Soviet reality.[17] The barn in which SRF's brigade is billeted belongs to Matrena-Dura, that very same Matrena whom the 'Great Writer' observed and whose example he hoped and thought could be the salvation of Mother Russia. Here it becomes clear that Zinoviev's former respect for Solzhenitsyn has become severely adulterated. He admires him above all for his courage to speak the truth as he sees it at all times, but he disagrees vehemently with Solzhenitzyn's opinions on how to improve the Soviet Union. Matrena-Dura is a robust representative of the 'Russian people', full of folk-wisdom about things she knows nothing about and ready to spout it at the drop of a hat. She is particularly voluble about life in the West.[18] On the other hand, she survives by a mixture of cunning, common sense and bullying. She is quite ready to change her opinions, depending on whom she is sleeping with. She is not averse to receiving stolen goods and will resort to blackmail if necessary. She is as unlike Solzhenitsyn's Matrena as it is possible to be, yet no less plausible. Zinoviev's point is that it is naive in the extreme to look to the past for a solution to the problems of the Soviet countryside.

If Matrena-Dura represents the collective farmworker, Mao-Tse-Dun'ka represents the local activist who progresses from the 'village community' to the Soviet equivalent of local government. She is 'one of the people' who now sits in authority over the same people, but who never forgets that she is 'one of them'. She is in charge of the 'department of agricultural affairs' on the local town Party committee and thus oversees on its behalf the 'battle for the harvest'. She thus represents the link between the 'country' and the 'town'.

Zinoviev's portrait of her is not unaffectionate. She is coarse, domineering, can drink with the best of them, but is one hundred per cent in favour of the regime. Her attitude to the farmworkers varies according to their sex. She encouages the women by referring to them as 'men' and shames the men into action by calling them 'women'. What matters is effort and commitment, not results. She is full of encouraging clichés such as 'We'll be alright! We shall overcome! We won't give in! We've seen worse than this!' But like the leadership everywhere, she is perfectly capable of substituting the desirable for the real. Zinoviev, almost predictably, provides us with excerpts from 'the thoughts of Mao-Tse-Dun'ka'.[19] In the main, these are reminiscent of those of Matrena-Dura, but from the point of view of the 'leadership'. They are delivered with more authority and are essentially a combination of contempt for the West and a perception of the need for 'more discipline'.

Zinoviev's portrait of the Soviet countryside, of course, differs in many respects from those of other writers. For a start he does not describe it. However, detailed description of flowers, plants, trees, fields and what grows in them is not necessary for his purposes. What he does more successfully than these other writers is expose the *Sovietness* of that countryside and thereby highlight the specific problems of *Soviet* agriculture, or more generally, the life-chances of people who have to live and work in it.

STALIN

The portrait of Stalin which Zinoviev gives in *Zheltyi dom* anticipates the portrait which he offers in his later book *Nashei iunosti polet* (*Flight of our Youth*). The latter work provoked strong negative reactions on the part of some readers and he was accused of being an apologist for Stalin and Stalinism.[20] In *Zheltyi dom* Stalin appears in several guises, yet once more they are all linked with the figure of JRF. First he appears as JRF's mentor (Himself). It is not, however, clear that Himself is Stalin until very near the end of Volume II.[21] Secondly he is one of JRF's egos. Thirdly he is the subject of the long series of 'excerpts' from Scoundrel's manuscript (written, as we know, by JRF.) Finally, Stalin figures as the central character of Petin's play, as written by JRF.[22] Zinoviev thus achieves a means of depicting Stalin from four different perspectives: Stalin as the interpreter of his own past, Stalin as a parody of himself, Stalin as the personification of the post-Revolutionary, post-Lenin development of Soviet society, Stalin as bureaucrat *par excellence*.

In sum the portrait is not unsympathetic. In JRF's view he is an intellectual nonentity, but outstandingly so. He was as much a product of Stalinism as its cause, in the sense that the circumstances were such that a nonentity like Stalin could become a dictator of unrivalled power. JRF's version of Petin's drama shows Stalin as the patient bureaucrat working behind the scenes, dealing with the boring, routine, but necessary problems of organisation and administration, leaving the 'heroics' – the speechifying, the policy-making, and so on – to people like Trotsky, Lenin and Bukharin. The latter were associated with the 'froth' of history, the former with its deep-flowing, fundamental current. Moreover, compared to the present-day 'jackals' or 'rats' who run the system, he was a 'lion' or a 'wolf' (ZhD II:354).

It is probable that Zinoviev respected Stalin for his individualism, his obvious non-collectivism. But that, in a sense, is the obverse side of his contempt for the collectivist mentality, the readiness on the part of people to suppress their own individuality and their even greater willingness to participate in the oppression of those who were not so ready to toe the collectivist line. Zinoviev has also repeatedly voiced his opinion, both on his own behalf and through the mouths of his characters, that the collectivisation of agriculture was an event of outstanding historical importance, that it was seen as such, and that it was not a period of universal suffering. Many profited by it. He has also refused to condemn it.

Perhaps the most interesting facet of Zinoviev's portrait of Stalin is his role as the 'outstanding Marxist' who boiled Marxism down to its essence and turned it into an ideology which was adequate for the 'social intellect' of the time. This is surely one of the most damaging aspects of Stalinism. For decades no one was allowed to be as brilliant as Stalin, on any subject. The language of intellectual debate was reduced to a level bordering on the infantile.[23]

Finally, Stalin as a theatrical figure, participating in a spectacle of gigantic proportions, dramatically underscores Zinoviev's view that Soviet society is one based on illusion, make believe, *prestigitation.* Yet that is not quite accurate. Grandiose events like the first five-year plan the cultural revolution, collectivisation, the show trials, the Stakhanovite movement, the purges, the deportation of entire nation- alities, the gulag, were in no sense 'make believe', yet they were, literally, 'spectacular'. In the post-Stalin era, at least until recently, the 'spectacles' have been less dramatic. The latest 'spectacle', of course, is *perestroika,* and Gorbachev is a kind of pale reflection of Stalin. But he has lacked Stalin's ruthlessness. The great difference between 'Gorbachevism' and 'Stalinism' is the relative 'tawdriness' of the former. There is no grand ideological underpinning – the market mechanism is not a great rallying cry in the Soviet Union – and the impotent quasi-democratism of the Gorbachev era has something of the counterfeit about it. Today there is nostalgia, not for Brezhnev, not for Khrushchev, but for Stalin, the 'firm hand', the age-old Russian desire for strong government. Zinoviev's portrait of Stalin draws attention to Stalin's strength while underlining Stalin's outstanding non- entity as an intellectual force. The great irony underlying this portrait is Zinoviev's perception that the 'strong' in- dividual can be superior to the collective, but by default. One gets the impression that Zinoviev believes that the Russians deserved Stalin, that they were in large measure responsible for his creation, that they regret his departure and that his like will return.

THE WEST

The theme of Western incomprehension of the Soviet Union was an important theme in *Ziiaiushchie vysoty.* It is even more important in *Zheltyi dom.* In 1979 Zinoviev was experiencing

at first hand Western attitudes to the Soviet Union. Previously he had met Westerners in Moscow, including many
foreign correspondents. His portrait of the naive Western
journalist in *Ziiaiushchie vysoty* is almost certainly based on
correspondents whom he himself had known. In 1979, too,
the Soviet Union invaded Afghanistan, the SS-20 missiles
had long been installed, NATO's 'twin-track' policy in
relation to Cruise and Pershing missiles had been set in
motion and was already being vehemently opposed by a
variety of Western peace organisations. The theme of Western attitudes to the Soviet Union would henceforth become
predominant in a whole series of Zinoviev's works which
appeared between 1980 and the advent of Gorbachev.

In *Zheltyi dom*, the West is a constant subject for comment
in the conversations of the various groups of characters
associated with the different settings. JRF and his colleagues
at the Institute discuss the West, so do JRF and his egos, so
do the members of his brigade in Matrena-Dura's barn, so
does Matrena-Dura, so do the guests in the rest-home in
Part IV.[24] In sum, their views reduce to the following
propositions:

(a) The West represents the best that civilisation has to
offer; the Soviet Union is the greatest threat to it.
Civilisation equals effort, sweat, struggle, Communism
equals '*raiskoe bezdel'e*' ('heavenly indolence') (ZhD
I:82–3).

(b) Westerners are naive in the extreme and are incapable
of understanding the Soviet experience (ZhD II:
10–11).

(c) The world-wide victory of Communism is inevitable
(ZhD II:181).

(d) The Soviet Union is a parasite, living off the West, in
the hope of eventually destroying it (ZhD:345).

In 1979 Zinoviev was clearly very concerned at Western
naiveté in the face of Soviet cynicism. Yet already there is an
awareness that the West presents a constant threat to the
stability of the Soviet system. That threat, of course, is not
military – Zinoviev has little but contempt for what he sees
as West European reluctance to stand up to the Soviet bully.
The threat is ideological. The authorities can no longer

stem the flow of information from the West about the West
which enters the Soviet Union in many forms: impressions
of Soviet people who have been to the West, foreign radio
and television stations, Western youth culture in terms of
dress, music, life–style, the great increase in the number of
foreign visitors to the Soviet Union, and so on. On the other
hand, as JRF's ego nicknamed 'Zapadnik' (Westerner) puts
it: 'Dlia menia... "Vostok" i "Zapad" sut' poniatiia
sotsial'nye, a ne geograficheskie. Bor'ba Vostoka i Zapada
idet kak na Zapade, tak i u nas.' (ZhD I:82). ('"East" and
"West" for me are sociological, not geographical, concepts.
The struggle between East and West goes on in the West just
as it does here.') That is perhaps the most important point
of all. Currently the 'West' is in the ascendant, but there is
no guarantee that it will stay there.

Constraints of space prevent further analysis of this gigantic
work. As it is, we have been unable to discuss many individual texts of great interest. We should by way of conclusion,
however, make one or two observations about its strengths
and weaknesses.
    Its great strength lies in its detailed, almost panoramic
description of the Soviet system. The philosophical issues
are serious contributions to our understanding, backed up
by hilarious demonstrations of the effects of the irration-
alities which bedevil Soviet reality in its day-to-day manifestations. As usual, his characters are sketched, rather than
drawn in great detail, with the notable exception of JRF,
and to a lesser extent, SRF. The mixture of wit, intelligence
and insight is as potent as it has ever been. It is a remarkable
compendium of anecdotes, jokes, humorous poems, serious
discussion; it is illuminating, provocative, educative.
    Set against its merits, its demerits are clearly outweighed.
It is not obviously a 'novel' in the conventional sense.
Novels to do conventionally have 824 short chapters averag-
ing between one and two pages in length. It is beyond the
scope of much of conventional literary criticism. However,
there are quite serious criticisms to be made. Reference has
already been made to the most obvious one, namely the
totally anomalous status of Part III, *Apologiia prakticheskogo
bezumiia.* Its only structural connection with the rest of the

work is its title, otherwise it could be excised completely without the reader being any the wiser – Parts II and IV would join up entirely naturally.

In addition, however, several of the strands are tedious. It is doubtful whether the strand 'Sex and Revolution' contributes much to our understanding, and the idea behind it – a multi-authored book by a research team at JRF's institute – is hardly plausible. A similar comment seems justified in the case of the 'Sexual Tragedy' strand. These short dramatic scenes are not particularly funny, and the main point – that Soviet students will sleep with their professors for an appropriate degree classification or award – is somewhat laboured. There is also a strand devoted to 'flying saucers', in which JRF meets people from outer space. There is no motivation for this strand, it seems to be pure whimsy on Zinoviev's part, contributes nothing to our understanding and is, in consequence, a tedious appendix which could have been excised with profit.

The charge could also be made that Zinoviev has merely discussed the same range of issues that he discussed in *Ziiaiushchie vysoty*. It is true that certain problems discussed in that work reappear in *Zheltyi dom*. It is also true that the tenor of the discussion of those problems is similar. Similar, but not identical. One of the pleasures to be had from reading Zinoviev is to study the reformulations of similar issues. The charge of repetitiveness is not really sustainable, however, since *Zheltyi dom* takes us a stage further than *Ziiaiushchie vysoty* and *Svetloe budushchee*, as I have tried to show. *Zheltyi dom* forms a watershed in Zinoviev's artistic career. It points back to life in the Soviet Union, indeed it is predominantly concerned with it. But it also points forward. Half of it was written in the West, and the West, appropriately, receives considerable attention. From now on Zinoviev will be less intent on revealing the 'essence' of Soviet reality. He will be more preoccupied with the analysis of the 'struggle between East and West', initially as it unfolds in the West, but increasingly (after the advent of Gorbachev) from the perspective of how that struggle manifests itself in the Soviet Union.

6 *Kommunizm kak real'nost'*

Kommunizm kak real'nost' (KKR) was published in 1981. An English translation appeared in 1984 under the title *The Reality of Communism* (TRC). *Kommunizm kak real'nost'* is a collection of over one hundred shortish essays on various aspects of Soviet reality, which Zinoviev, however, presents as a theory of Communism as such, quite unperturbed by such questions as whether the Soviet Union is not better described as a system of 'state capitalism', whether the Soviet Union can truly be described as socialist, never mind Communist, etc. It is the first of four such volumes of essays to date, all of them prompted by Zinoviev's real concern at what he perceives to be Western incomprehension of Soviet reality and the threat which Communism poses to mankind. The others are *Die Diktatur der Logik* (1985) (*The Dictatorship of Logic*), *Die Macht des Unglaubens* (1986) (*The Power of Disbelief*) and *Gorbachevizm* (1988), which first appeared in French (*Le Gorbatchévisme*, 1987). It is worth emphasising that the views expressed in *Kommunizm kak real'nost'* belong to Zinoviev himself, rather than to any of the characters whom we have met before, such as Shizofrenik, Boltun, Anton Zimin or JRF. In the case of the work under discussion, Zinoviev can attribute the views expressed to no one but himself. Also this book is at once a culmination and an introduction. On the one hand it systematises and catalogues Zinoviev's views on the many aspects of Communism and Communist society which he has treated in his previous works. In that sense it is a useful summary of his thinking up until 1981. At the same time, it is a wide–ranging introduction to his philosophy of Communism for those who have not encountered his earlier work. Moreover, since it provides a detailed picture of Communism in the Brezhnev era, it serves as an excellent yardstick against which we can measure the Gorbachev reforms, a task which we shall undertake in the remaining chapters of this book.

The reception of *Kommunizm kak real'nost'* was respectful,

but not uncritical. The respect with which it was received in France, for instance, was reflected in the award to its author of the Alexis de Tocqueville prize in 1982. Simone Veil in her address on the occasion of the presentation of the prize drew attention to Zinoviev's 'point de départ révolutionnaire' and noted that his 'rigorous analysis, intelligence and courageous approach to his subject' had helped to expose aspects of the Soviet system which until then people had chosen either to ignore or even to conceal. Sidney Hook, Philip Hanson and others were less fulsome in their praise but accepted that *Kommunizm kak real'nost'* was a work worthy of serious attention. We shall consider their criticisms below, in the context of our analysis of the structure and the content of the work itself.

The 110 separate texts can be conveniently grouped under six headings: the nature of Communism as such; the nature of an adequate analytical apparatus for the scientific study of Communism; the roots and origins of communal behaviour and the psychological and moral consequences of a collectivist philosophy; the nature of power in Communist society and how it is disseminated within the social structure; the nature, role and significance of ideology in an environment in which it can flourish unopposed; the stability, vitality and adaptability of the Soviet system and its prospects for the future. Our analysis will be facilitated if we relate it to those six headings, suitably abbreviated.

THE NATURE OF COMMUNISM

If we number the texts in *Kommunizm kak real'nost'* from 1 to 110 we shall see that, of the first twenty (which interweave the topics of our first two headings), the nature of Communism as such is the subject of texts 2–9, 14 and 15. The essential points to note are the following: (a) Communism developed 'immanently' ('*immanentno*') in the Soviet Union, it was not imposed as it was in Eastern Europe (about China Zinoviev is silent) (KKR:7; TRC:12); (b) Communism is what you have in the Soviet Union, and there is no difference between Communism and socialism (KKR:11–12; TRC:-16–18); (c) Communist social relations are not confined to the Soviet Union, they exist in the West as well, but they only become *dominant* under certain circumstances (KKR:-15–16; TRC:21–22); (d) Communism arises out of what Zinoviev calls 'communal relations' (see below), and is a more deep-rooted phenomenon than capitalism (KKR:17; TRC:23); (e) Communism is the antithesis of civilisation, and the two tendencies are locked in eternal conflict, at all times, in all societies (KKR:21–3; TRC:27–30); (f) Communism requires to be studied as a unique phenomenon before it can be compared with other systems (KKR:35–37; TRC:44–6); (g) Communism is not the same as totalitarianism (KKR:38; TRC:47).

Critics, not surprisingly, have had difficulty with some of these assertions. Sidney Hook, for example, (1984:365) accuses Zinoviev of not taking into account historical contingency, arguing that, whereas America would sooner or later have been discovered if Columbus had never lived, it is not so certain that there would have been an October 1917 Revolution if Lenin had never lived. Communism in the Soviet Union was not therefore inevitable. He also disagrees with Zinoviev's 'cavalier' attitude to the relationship between socialism and totalitarianism (admitting that Zinoviev does not like the latter term), arguing that, where political democracy is present, 'there is no correlation between the degree of enforcement of socialism and the presence of coercive social controls.' Zinoviev has never shown any interest in debates about what would have happened if what actually happened had actually not happened, but in any case he has never claimed that Communism was inevitable in the Soviet Union – his main argument, after all, is that Communist tendencies exist everywhere. As regards Hook's second objection, Zinoviev would deny that political democracy as such is compatible with Communism (or socialism), a point which Hook (1984:366) himself makes: 'Granted, in the absence of political democracy there is a potential for coercive controls on every level in a complete socialist economy.'

Professor Hanson also has severe doubts about Zinoviev's claim that Communism is a universal phenomenon, arguing that the experience of Hungarians or Poles would not match that of the average Soviet citizen (Hanson, 1982:38; 1988:165–7). Hungarian or Polish Communism, in other

words, differs from Soviet Communism. He also has difficulty
with the status of the term 'Communism', regarding it as
unclear as it appears in Zinoviev's theory (Hanson, 1982:39).
My own position is the following. It seems to me that Zinoviev's definition of Communism (socialism) applies to a
society in which the socialisation of the mean of production,
distribution and exchange has occurred *in toto*, entailing
thereby the elimination of all forms of private property. The
Soviet Union is the first country in which that transformation
came about. To put the point another way, one might ask the
following question: given the goal of socialising the mean of
production, distribution and exchange *in toto*, what kind of
system would be required (a) to carry out the transformation, (b) to maintain it? If 'socialism' is the 'administration of things', in someone's famous phrase (including, as
it turns out, people), especially if it is to be 'egalitarian',
clearly an immensely complex bureaucratic and coercive
system is required. How, otherwise, can 'things' (all things,
including people) be 'administered'? I am thus less inclined
than Philip Hanson to draw comfort from the hope that,
while 'the establishment of communist regimes in Cuba,
Laos, Cambodia and China is evidence that it is not necessary
to be Russian or invaded by Russians to become communist
[it] may, however, be necessary to be either underdeveloped
or invaded by Russians' (Hanson, 1988:167).

This *total* reconstruction did not occur elsewhere (except
Albania?) and I would argue that Communism in Eastern
Europe differed mainly in terms of degree, i.e. there was
never, in any one country, quite 'as much' of it as there was
in the Soviet Union. I believe that any qualitative differences can be shown to have their basis in that quantitative
difference. There seems every reason to suppose that Zinoviev would accept as a definition of Communism 'clause 4'
socialism as it appears in the British Labour Party's Constitution. Moreover, if one accepts that definition, it is easier to
understand Zinoviev's contention that there is no difference between socialism and Communism in institutional
terms. As for the 'abundance' distinction between socialism and Communism, Zinoviev points out that the condition
of 'abundance' has been to a much greater degree achieved
under capitalism.

Philiip Hanson also draws attention to Zinoviev's distinction between Communism and totalitarianism (Hanson, 1982:39–40). Pointing out that Zinoviev's claim that Stalin's totalitarianism had a social basis, whereas Hitler's did not, Hanson asserts that Zinoviev's definition of 'social basis' seems to be circumscribed 'by the Marxist ideology he despises'. If I have understood Hanson correctly, he seems to imply that Zinoviev's view of 'social basis' derives from a Marxist theory of class structure. Zinoviev in fact rejects that theory. The 'social basis' of Stalin's totalitarianism relates to the socio-political structure of the Soviet Union, whereas the 'socialisation' *in toto* of the means of production etc. had already occurred, unlike Nazi Germany, where the socio-economic structure remained capitalist. Nazism did not grow out of the destruction of a previous social order but was superimposed upon it. Nazism could in turn be destroyed without the destruction of that social order. Communism could not be. The defeat of Communism entails destruction of its socio–economic structure. Current developments in the Soviet Union demonstrate that the 'textual' aspects of Communism can be adulterated relatively easily and that it is precisely the socio-economic structure which is proving to be the main obstacle to reform. It should be noted, incidentally, that the 'adulteration' has been accompanied by a reduction in the degree of 'socialisation', reflected in (extremely limited) private access to the means of production in the form of small enterprises and the growth of a range of services offered by the 'private sector', in addition to access to the means of 'reproduction' (of audio, visual and printed material).

THE SCIENTIFIC STUDY OF COMMUNISM

Zinoviev's view of what constitutes a 'scientific' study of Communism contains some of his most controversial statements. The texts in *Kommunizm kak real'nost'* which discuss this issue include the following: 2, 3, 10, 11, 12, 13, 16–20. The main points are these: (a) understanding a society is not the same as unmasking its defects (KKR:9; TRC:14); (b) from a scientific point of view, people can simultaneously

dislike a particular social system, accept it, prefer it to any
other and be prepared to defend it (KKR:24; TRC:31); (c)
sociology offers the possibility of a scientific description of a
society, history does not (KKR:26–32; TRC:33–41); (d) the
'dialectical method' of analysis has been neglected, but
(used properly) can lead to important insights (KKR:41;
TRC:50–1).

Not surprisingly, Zinoviev's claim to offer a 'scientific'
approach to the study of Communism has been strongly
challenged. Two main lines of attack are discernible. One
seeks (successfully, in my view) to show that his 'scientific'
stance is undermined by his moralism. The other (less
successfully) challenges his claim on purely scientific criter-
ia.

Anne-Marie Roviello (1982:86) points out that Zinoviev's
desire to present a 'scientific' description of Soviet society
encounters a major terminological difficulty in that the
terms which he uses to describe Communist society cannot
be divorced from the ethical judgements which underlie
them. His basic premiss, that the 'social laws' governing
human behaviour can be reduced to the formula 'dog eat
dog', contains an ethical judgement, irrespective of his
claim that the behaviour described by that formula is neither
good nor evil. His view that Communism and civilisation are
mutually exclusive terms is another instance. Hanson
(1982:47) points out that 'for all his strenuous (or at any
rate ingenious) attempts to disguise the fact, Zinoviev is an
impassioned moralist.' On the other hand, unlike Roviello,
he regards the moralising and analysis in *Kommunizm kak
real'nost'* as being clearly distinguished. Geoffrey Hosking
(1988:176) directly asks whether it would not be better to
conclude that Zinoviev, despite his claims to be a scientist,
should be regarded rather as a 'remarkable artist and
moralist' and goes on to state: 'His status as a moralist is
apparent even in *The Reality of Communism,* where he is most
scrupulously trying to restrain moralism in the interests of
science.'[1]

Critics have tended to be harsher in their attacks on
Zinoviev's 'scientific' approach from the point of view of
science as such. Hosking (1988) and Hanson (1982, 1988)
have exposed perhaps more clearly than others specific

departures in *Kommunizm kak real'nost'* from accepted scientific method. Both writers quite properly draw attention to Zinoviev's annoying habit of ignoring all known scholarship on anything to do with the Soviet Union and his equally annoying habit of making it clear that he ignores it because he thinks it is no good, or, more accurately, that it embodies the 'philistine' approach to cognition which he criticises in an early chapter in the book (KKR:24–5; TRC:31–3). They also uncover Zinoviev's habit of putting forward one thesis in one text and its antithesis in another, without tackling the inherent contradiction. Both writers also agree on what they think is the weakest link in Zinoviev's argument, namely his neglect of the upper reaches of power in the hierarchy (Hosking, 1988:176; Hanson, 1982:42–3). We shall look at this point in more detail in the appropriate section below. I have expounded my own view of the status of Zinoviev's claim to be a (social) scientist elsewhere (Kirkwood, 1990a). Here I shall confine myself to the following observations. I think that there is a distinction to be made between scientific method *per se* and accepted scientific procedures. Sometimes the latter can constrain, rather than promote, scientific enquiry. Scientific paradigms associated with particular fields constrain the range of problems which can be tackled within those paradigms. Moreover, many problems which can be (and are) treated within them are trivial. In his professional field Zinoviev found the constraints of two-value logic restricting for those reasons and developed many-valued logic as a way of extending the range of problems which could be treated with the same formal rigour. I suggest that he has done something similar in respect of his studies of Communism. Soviet (Communist) society he regards as a phenomenon susceptible to insightful description beyond the paradigms of the social sciences as they are currently constructed. In this respect he is a 'deconstructionist'. However, his underlying approach is scientific in spirit, in the sense that he is intent on describing a complex phenomenon in a way which takes account of its complexity. To borrow a metaphor from linguistics, if the surface structure of his approach is arguably unscientific, the deep structure is scientific.

COMMUNAL BEHAVIOUR AND THE COLLECTIVE

Under this rubric can be grouped texts numbered 21–55 inclusive. They contain important elements of Zinoviev's theory which we reproduce here in summarised (and therefore markedly simplified) form.

The individual is biologically programmed to seek to defend or improve his position in society. (Even those who seem to lead a life of complete altruism may also be acting selfishly.) (KKR:54–5; TRC:62–4). Individuals live in communities, and when these communities exceed a certain size, the laws of communalism come into operation. These laws are the 'social laws' first adumbrated by Shizofrenik in *Ziiaiushchie vysoty*, although, of course, not invented by him. Communism is a direct product of communalism, given certain circumstances (KKR:50–1; TRC:58–60). Communist society can best be understood via the study of its fundamental or primary component, its 'primary cell' (KKR:50–1; TRC:58–60). This primary cell is an example of a 'complex social (or communal) individual' defined thus: 'Two or more people form an integral *communal individual* if, and only if, the following conditions are fulfilled: (1) this group of people relates to the environment as a unit; (2) there takes place within it the same distribution of "body" and "brain" functions as [can be] observed in the case of the individual person, the former being governed by the latter; (3) there is a division of functions among the individuals who are governed' (KKR:58; TRC:64). Complex individuals vary in size and complexity, but behave as individuals, i.e. they observe the laws of communalism. In this respect the Soviet government can be seen as a complex communal-individual which behaves like 'the average Soviet citizen'.[2]

Communal behaviour is by nature hypocritical. The individual improves his social position by appearing not to wish to improve his social position. Mediocrity must be presented as talent, flattery as sincerity, cowardly acts of secret denunciation as evidence of courage and principle, and so on (KKR:59; TRC:69). Relations within the cell, or 'commune', operate according to the following basic principle: 'be like everyone else'. Since everyone by definition wants to improve his position, the individual seeks to act against that

principle while everyone else is interested in his conforming
to it. Oppression of the individual in its daily, regular
manifestation, therefore, is not exercised by the 'authorities' or the KGB, but by the primary cell. Moreover, since
the cell structure embraces the overwhelming majority of
the population, oppression is a constant, ubiquitous phenomenon.

As noted above, this summary is a highly simplified
account of Zinoviev's theory of communal behaviour and its
relationship to Communism. We have, however, encountered enough examples of Zinoviev's 'communal laws' in
operation in previous chapters for the general picture to be
clear, and we have already noted (in Chapter 3) the views of
other critics on the issue of the validity of these communal-
laws with reference to *Ziiaiushchie vysoty.*

THE NATURE OF POWER UNDER COMMUNISM

The texts which deal mainly with the above topic are the
following: 56–72, 74–92. Clearly we cannot discuss each of
them, so we shall concentrate on those which are of primary
importance. Zinoviev's discussion of this issue has met with
least approval on the part of his critics, mainly on the
grounds that his account of how the commune fits into the
system as a whole is less than totally convincing.

There are various aspects of the problem which need to
be separated. Zinoviev's first point relates to the sheer
numbers of people involved in the administration of power
(KKR:122; TRC:140) in Communist society. Given the extent
of the network of communes which permeates the whole of
society, the number of bosses together with their families
adds up to a state within a state, except that they themselves
in turn are subordinate to other bosses. Given the structure
of Communist society, the number of bosses required will
not fall below a certain (extremely high) number. Moreover,
and this is important in the context of perestroika, power in
a Communist society is negative. That is, it is incapable of
carrying through the smallest reform but capable of suffocat-
ing any initiative. Why this is so seems to be first because (a)
so many people have positions carrying *some* power for

whom reforms constitute a threat to their interests, (b) even if they wish to implement a reform, they themselves are enmeshed in a local power network which significantly constrains their freedom to act. Secondly, for most people power is experienced at the level of the commune. For instance, the commune cannot give permission for one of its members to travel abroad, but it can prevent that member obtaining permission from the appropriate quarter (KKR:125; TRC:144). Thirdly, power at the level of the primary collective is not experienced as coercion. Bosses, while in the same collective as their subordinates, are 'one of us', their relationship to their colleagues is *not* that of employer to employee. Power at this level is democratic, but gives rise to highly undemocratic power at the level of the district, region, ministry, etc. (KKR:125; TRC:144). He does not explain, however, precisely how this happens.

This is a pity, for the proposition that power operates from below forms a cornerstone of his theory of the structure of power in Communist society. What is true, however, is that an inordinately large number of people have a little bit of power, ranging from, say, the head of a small department down to the lift attendant, doorman, or the famous '*dezhurnye*' ladies, 'guardians of the room-keys', in Soviet hotels, not to mention petty bureaucrats, shop assistants, dentists, craftsmen, and so on. In a country notoriously deficient in basic goods and services, such power becomes tangible and it is at that level that most people, most of the time, feel the exercise of power upon themselves. If we then imagine that this situation is mirrored all the way up the hierarchy to the very top (ministries vying with each other for resources, regional party organisations protecting their positions, and so on), we begin to see how the influence of power from below counteracts the flow of power from above. In simple terms, decision-making power tends to be negated by a wide range of obstacles, many of which derive from the power to obstruct, delay, modify, etc., invested in myriad organisations located at different points in the overall power network.

Decision-making power, in other words, is limited by the sheer size of the administrative system and the cell structure of Communist society. In this respect the power of the Party is likewise subverted. Zinoviev's account of the Party as an instrument of state power mirrors to a large extent conventional Western accounts. For instance, he distinguishes between the Party *apparat* and the primary Party organisations operating at the micro-level of the primary collectives. Less conventionally, he insists that an understanding of the Party and its functions can only be achieved via a study of the Party at that micro-level.

He rejects the idea of the Party as a 'partocracy' in the sense of a Party elite relying on the army and the KGB to exercise oppression on the rest of the population. At the level of the primary collective, the Party organisation is a blessing, since it is the only force capable of restraining what would otherwise be rampant communalism. It protects people from themselves and provides the stimulus for whatever slight progress can be recorded. Two points are of crucial importance: (a) people join the Party voluntarily, whether directly or for reasons connected with their (chosen) profession. This voluntary commitment, according to Zinoviev, grows into the most unfettered oppressive power. Coercion is the resultant force of the free-will of individuals, not the evil design of tyrants (KKR:130; TRC:150); (b) Party members are *selected*. In other words, people *want* to participate in the exercise of power, and will be selected if they are deemed to be suitable.

At the level of the primary collective, according to Zinoviev, Party leaders are more dependent on the leadership of the collective than on the district Party committee (they depend on the latter for their selection, but on the former for material benefits). Although the director is a Party member and is subordinate to the Party Secretary, the latter rarely abuses his position: the director is still the most powerful individual in the institution, but not just because of his managerial position. He represents Party power, is its protégé, and is assisted by the Party bureau and the Party organisation. They supervise him to a certain extent, but to a greater extent obscure the fact that in reality power is essentially a non–Party phenomenon.

The role of the Party organisation is twofold: (a) it represents the interests of the whole collective; (b) it represents the organs of power of society as a whole in that sector of society, and thus acts as a link and regulator of the relationship between the power of the people and the power of the state. The cell structure of Communist society is such that there is no place for political parties (or even one political party), since there is no one for them to represent. People are represented at primary collective level in the system of power (KKR:133; TRC:153). Finally, Zinoviev argues that the situation at the lowest levels of Party life affects the formation of the Party line taken higher up. Stalinism was not only imposed from above, it also grew from below – as did the Khrushchev/Brezhnev brand of 'liberalism'.

Zinoviev, as we noted, conventionally separates the *apparat* from the Party cell and concentrates on the latter. There is no doubt that his account of life in the individual primary collective (communalism restrained by the Party organisation) is much more detailed than his account of the relationship between the individual commune and the hierarchy of communes within which it is embedded. As Philip Hanson has written, Zinoviev has displayed communal life and its role in the Communist order 'in a brilliant and pitiless light', whereas the workings of the upper reaches of power are 'more fitfully illuminated' (Hanson, 1982:48).

Bearing in mind that the account Zinoviev gives relates to the situation as it was in 1981, let us now consider some of the criticisms which have been levelled against it. Hanson (1988:162) argues that the primary collective under Communism cannot be accounted for simply by reference to basic human drives and the inner logic of the workplace collective but that it derives its special power from the overall hierarchy within which it is embedded. Elsewhere (1982:43) he maintains that, in the terms of Zinoviev's own argument that hierarchy must exist in any large human organisation, the sort of hierarchy that could be avoided is precisely the unified national hierarchy of a Communist state. I confess that I fail to follow Professor Hanson's reasoning as regards the latter point. However, in general, one might respond thus. Given that there are 'workplace collectives' in non-Communist societies which are in some ways different from those in Communist countries, the differences must be accounted for in terms of the different

hierarchies in which they are embedded. But if one argues
along those lines, my response would be that if the state
controls everything, the nature of its administrative apparatus will be uniform (and unified). Complex, of course,
indeed much more complex than the administrative apparatus of capitalism, but uniform nonetheless. In other words,
the unified national hierarchy of a Communist state is
precisely not avoidable.

Geoffrey Hosking argues that Zinoviev ducks the key issue
of establishing the ultimate locus of power. With particular
reference to the issue of power in the primary collective,
Hosking (1988:175–6) writes as follows:

> [Zinoviev] maintains that in any given institution the
> primary party organisation is dependent more on the
> collective within the institution than it is on superior party
> organs, and that the director of the institution, not the
> party bureau, is the principal power within the collective.
> But as he then proceeds immediately to point out: 'The
> director of the institution is a representative above all of
> party authority. He is an appointee of the party apparatus,
> and he is selected for that purpose by the party appar-
> atus.' Two lines later he again changes horses in mid-
> stream by talking of the 'non-party essence of political
> power'.

Hosking then goes on to express surprise that Zinoviev does
not pay more attention to the *nomenklatura* appointment
mechanism, which, as he says, most observers would see as
the link between the power structure and the collectives.

In point of fact, Zinoviev does not talk about the non-
party essence of *political* power. The word 'political' has
been supplied by Professor Hosking.[3] Indeed, as noted
above, Zinoviev makes a point of denying both the existence
of political power as such in Communist societies (KKR:124;
TRC:143) and the idea of any opposition between Party
power and managerial/governmental power, power in Communist societies being one and the same (KKR:128;
TRC:147).

Whole books, of course, have been written about this
issue and we cannot discuss it here in any detail. One might

make the following observations, however. First, if Zinoviev believes that there is no opposition between Party and managerial power, how does he account for the impotence of the Party under Stalin and its weakened position in the Soviet Union today, when in both contexts managerial power remained relatively undiminished? Secondly, Zinoviev's contention that power is diffused throughout Communist society (KKR:122; TRC:141) is in my view correct and accounts for the apparent inconsistency to which Hosking draws attention. It is, I think, possible for a director to be a Party appointee, to be its protégé, and yet to administer his power in his capacity as *director*, in a context in which for the most part management decisions will relate to matters which have nothing to do with the Party. On the other hand, since his powers to manage are so circumscribed by other factors such as the Plan, instructions from various ministries (and Party organisations, too), his room for manoeuvre is obviously greatly restricted. What that means, however, is that much of his energy goes in to 'putting on a good show', 'keeping the authorities off his back', 'maintaining a healthy atmosphere in the collective' and so on. Thirdly, the power to govern is circumscribed by the administrative apparatus for the execution of decisions. The aspiration to govern everything (administer everything) leads to the sort of impotence which confronts the Soviet leadership when they wish to introduce change, a paradox well described by Zinoviev himself.

IDEOLOGY

Zinoviev devotes ten texts (93–102) to the discussion of ideology, in which he sets out an explicit, multi-faceted account of the role, nature and importance of ideology in a Communist society. Some of what he sets out in *Kommunizm kak real'nost'* he has described in earlier works through the mouths (and pens) of various characters. We shall not refer to that material here but concentrate on two aspects which he sets out in more detail in the work under discussion than elsewhere.[4] The first aspect concerns the functions of ideology in Communist society. We have noted on several occasions that Zinoviev attributes so much importance to ideology that he regards it as *the* main distinguishing feature of a Communist society. It is thus difficult to understand Besançon's remark (Besançon, 1982:155–6) that Zinoviev fails to give sufficient weight to the role of ideology in Soviet life. For Zinoviev, ideology is not only doctrine, it is daily, routine activity. He regards ideology (including the ideological *apparat*) as having four main functions (KKR:195–6; TRC: 220–1).

Its first function is to acquaint citizens with the officially recognised ideological doctrine, to force them (by means of compulsory tests, examinations, seminar contributions) to master at least the elementary basics of that doctrine and to accept it. This acceptance is not a one-off event – acceptance must be regularly and publicly exhibited. The second function of ideology is to monitor everything which goes on in the cultural sphere (literature, the arts, science, the press, etc.), prohibiting everything not in conformity with the doctrine and encouraging everything that is. Its third function is to interpret everything that happens in the world, including major political events, scientific discoveries and the like, in the light of the fundamental principles of the ideology. Finally, perhaps its most important function is to coerce citizens into being not mere passive recipients of ideology who acquire an indoctrinated way of looking at the world, but active, creative participants in all sorts of ideological spectacles at all levels of society, from the very top to the smallest social groups. We note again that *belief* in the ideology is not required.

This creative, participatory aspect of ideology is perhaps Zinoviev's most original contribution to a theory of ideology. His demonstration that ideology seen as doctrine can be at once nonsensical, powerful and publicly endorsed is an impressive indictment of a regime which attributes so much importance to it. We in the West have not only tended to underestimate the role of ideology in the Soviet Union, we have in the main failed to take sufficient account of it, or have even discounted it in our descriptions of the workings of Soviet society.

The second aspect, to which Zinoviev in the work under discussion devotes more space than to any other, is the relationship between ideology and morality (KKR:208–11; TRC:234–8). Communist society aspires to a morality shaped by its ideology, which Zinoviev equates with pseudo-morality, and which seeks to destroy any germination of a personal morality, or morality in the proper sense of that term.

At the root of truly moral behaviour, argues Zinoviev, is the principle of a voluntary decision on the part of an individual to restrain the force of the social (communal) laws in his behaviour towards others. A moral act is one performed voluntarily, not in response to juridically determined norms, rules or laws. Zinoviev argues that morality in that sense comes into conflict with Communist 'morality' and constitutes a real threat to it:

> Ideological 'morality' has undeniable advantages over morality. It releases people from internal self–restraint. It justifies every crime committed by the country's government *vis-à-vis* the population and against other peoples... The lower levels of the population in turn are compelled by truths and untruths (especially untruths) to adapt themselves to the conditions of life, repaying the torrent of lies and violence streaming down on them from above with lies, idleness, theft, drunkenness, hack-work, and other phenomena of this kind. Corruption, deceit and coercion penetrate the whole of society from top to bottom.
>
> (TRC:237)

The consequence, notes Zinoviev, is that people in the Soviet Union do not believe in the moral qualities of their neighbours and place no reliance on them, which is the deepest source of immorality in society (KKR:210; TRC:238). The picture Zinoviev paints of the moral quagmire of Soviet (Communist) society is recognisable. It confronts us, however, with the question of the nature of the morality of the Soviet citizen. Hanson (1982:48) regards Zinoviev as passing moral judgement on the whole of the Soviet population, an action which he rejects on the grounds that Zinoviev cannot know the moral attitude of every Soviet citizen. This is obviously true. But it does not logically follow that we must therefore discard the possibility of making a moral judgement about the nature of Communist society, a society based on a morality which specifically rejects a personal morality.

There are three other points which should be made in this connection. First, leaving morality aside, it is legitimate to wonder whether Soviet people think that non-Soviet people think like they do, or not. Can the Soviet mentality conceive of a non-Soviet mentality? If not, we must expect Soviet people to think of us as they think of each other, that is to assume that our moral qualities are not to be relied upon. At government level this is a serious matter. Secondly, the combination of Soviet education and Soviet history has presented so many people with so many moral dilemmas that it is not surprising that the question of reassessing the past is so difficult and so painful. Nor is it surprising, perhaps, that Party members of fifty years or more standing and who were in charge of rounding up peasant families for deportation can still live in the same village community as the relatives of their victims without apparently attracting any opprobrium.[5] Thirdly, there is the matter of adaptability. Zinoviev points out on numerous occasions that *homo sovieticus* is remarkably adaptable, that he can, with equal sincerity, propound one set of views in conformity with one particular Party line and the opposite set of views with equal sincerity when the Party line is reversed. There have been countless examples of this behaviour since Gorbachev came to power.

STABILITY AND VIABILITY

The last eight texts (103–10) deal with individual aspects of Communism which, nonetheless, can be grouped under the above rubric. Zinoviev clearly saw their function as summarising the cardinal features of the system and leaving the reader with a clear impression of what the inevitable consequence is when the ideals of Communism are realised in practice. We shall highlight these features in the paragraphs that follow.

Texts 102 and 104 consider the problem of large societies as examples of complex systems. Zinoviev's purpose is to demonstrate the systemic problems which flow automatically from the existence of such systems. His main point seems to be that the number, range and combinatorial possibilities of events produced by the system is so vast that describing the system in terms of cause and effect relations is impossible. There is a so-called 'systemic coefficient' which reduces the extent to which the wishes of leadership can be realised (KKR:215; TRC:243).

The Soviet system under Brezhnev was considered to be stagnant and inert. In fact, as not only Zinoviev has shown, the inertia and stagnation are to a significant extent the result of the complexity of the decision-making and decision–implementing process. Changes introduced in some parts of the system are cancelled out by those in other parts. Stagnation and inertia are non-dynamic terms, whereas Zinoviev continually emphasises that the system is dynamic. Stagnation is maintained by dynamic processes, as it were. Dynamic stagnation, however, is perhaps not so different from stability.

The question of stability, indeed vitality, of the Communist system is the subject of text 105 (KKR:219–21; TRC:246–9). Zinoviev regards Communist society as highly stable thanks to the following characteristics: (a) homogeneity of the structure of all its parts, organs, fabric, strata and groups, (b) standardisation of the conditions of life, (c) centralised government of all aspects of social life, (d) a mighty, unified system of power, (e) a single ideology and powerful conditioning of the population, (f) ability of a huge number of people to occupy any government post, (g) absence of a serious opposition movement and the presence of a powerful network of organs to repress manifestations of discontent, (h) ability to preserve cohesion of society in the face of great losses, (i) ability to impose a low standard of living for a long time without there being serious protests.

Zinoviev then goes on to make a strong claim:

Communist society is stable to such a degree that forces serious enough to destroy it simply do not materialise within it. It is, therefore, senseless to hope that the internal requirements of Communist countries will give rise to radical changes in this society in the direction of Western countries.   (KKR:219; TRC:247)

The extent to which Zinoviev's claim in the context of the Gorbachev era and post-1989 Eastern Europe has been invalidated is a question which will be examined in later chapters of this book. Here, however, we may note that the claim seems to be less valid in the case of Eastern Europe than in the Soviet Union. However, we might observe that none of the East European countries (with the exception of Albania) possessed the full range of features enumerated above. The term 'post-Communist' has gained rapid currency, but it is perhaps too early to be sure of the long-term validity of the concept.

Zinoviev also claims that the tendency to expansion and hegemony is inherent in a Communist society. Philip Hanson has challenged this claim (1982:46), arguing that Soviet expansionism (as exemplified by Cuba, Vietnam, Angola) almost certainly entailed a net loss of Soviet resources and an increase in the base for comparisons unfavourable to Communism. The economic argument in a Soviet context, however, is somehow less than compelling, given that the Soviet political elite is less constrained by economic considerations than their Western counterparts. The halt to Communist expansionism has arguably more to do with Western resolve to counter irresponsible Soviet military blackmail, as reflected in the Nato 'twin-track' strategy to counteract the installation of the SS-20 missiles in central Europe. One might add that the tendency to hegemony and expansionism is not exclusive to Communist societies. It seems, on balance, reasonable to assume that Communism *does* have that inherent tendency and that therefore it should be resisted.

Two other aspects which Zinoviev discusses are the related issues of the way of life (KKR:224–5; TRC:252–4) and discontent (KKR:226–8; TRC:254–7). As regards the way of life, Zinoviev makes the following points. First, the ordinary life of the average Soviet citizen is not as dramatically bad as it is depicted by dissidents and critics, nor as good as it is depicted by apologists. Millions of individuals lead ordinary lives like anywhere else. By contrast, however, and this is his second point, the relevant characteristic of Communist life is its despondency, greyness and boredom:

Everything is grey: the feast-days, the week-days, the speeches, the books, the films, the successes, the defeats, the crimes, the joys, love and hatred. Even the lying, which is meant to brighten life up, is grey.

(KKR:224; TRC:252)

This is a description which anyone familiar with the Brezhnev era would instantly recognise. The extent to which things have changed in the area of the public press, the media and the arts are precisely *departures* from the Communist way of doing things. Whether these changes are irreversible is a matter of considerable doubt. Thirdly, everything under Communism is made difficult: eating, living, recreation, entertainment, getting ahead, and so on. These difficulties are not temporary but endemic. The prevalent tendency is downward. People's expectations are that things will get worse.

What, then, of discontent? The first point that Zinoviev makes with some force is that there is a very high level of acceptance of the system accompanied by very widespread discontent (KKR:226; TRC:254). This discontent takes various forms. There is first the general mood of the people. The pressures of life make them short-tempered, tense, suspicious, rude, unhelpful, spiteful. Beyond that, however, Zinoviev distinguishes three types of activist: those who want to improve things within the existing system, those who want to reform the system but preserve the regime, and those who oppose the system as it stands and want to change it.

Activists of the first category are regarded by Zinoviev as a bulwark of the regime. They want slight improvements in the system and large improvements for themselves. Reformers want more radical changes while preserving the regime, but encounter opposition from many quarters, including many in the first category. Reformers talk about introducing a tenure-system in agriculture, for example, or industrial self-management.

Zinoviev devotes most space, however, to the oppositionists. He maintains first that their composition is always heterogeneous and inconstant. Their recommendations can be radical enough to include recipes for the replacement of

Communism with something else. Many oppositionists belong to various sects and religious groups whose solutions to
socio–political problems hark back to a pre-Revolutionary
past. Their recommendations do not add up to a programme for action, they are not supported by the population
at large and they do not represent any important con-
stituency. The reason is connected with the structure of
Communist society and a person's position in society. His
conclusion (in 1981) is bleak:

> It is practically impossible to originate a serious pro-
> gramme of reform such as would hold the attention of
> broad strata of the population deeply or for a sufficiently
> long period. People are condemned to fight for their own
> individual livelihoods by their own methods, or through
> their primary collectives... [But] for the time being one
> has no grounds for hoping that the opposition will play a
> discernible role in the country's social structure. For the
> time being the position is that the population of a Com-
> munist country is on balance inclined to fight for its
> unfreedom against those who wish to free it.
>
> (KKR:227; TRC:257)

This is another prediction which has turned out to be at
odds with the course of events since 1989, although there
are indications at the time of writing tht it has not been
totally wrong. That, however, is a matter for a later chapter.

As we noted above, *Kommunizm kak real'nost'* is at once a
culmination and an introduction. It is his most theoretical
exposition of classical Communism as he understands it, a
system which he has explored in great detail in a wide
variety of modes in earlier works, most of which we have
discussed. It provides a most useful bench-mark from which
to measure change in the Gorbachev era, not only in the
Soviet Union but also in Eastern Europe. As Wenzel Daneil
(1988:153) has written:

> In the Soviet Union an experiment is taking place the
> outcome of which will decide whether Zinoviev has given
> us a lasting analysis of Soviet reality or merely a fleeting

impression of a particular epoch in Soviet history, of the period of stagnation under the Brezhnev leadership.

I would argue that it is still too soon to be certain, although I am inclined to believe that some aspects of Zinoviev's theory have turned out to have had remarkable predictive power, whereas others have not. His predictions about the self-perpetuation of the ideological machine have turned out to be wrong. One of the most surprising developments has been the speed of the demise of the 'textual' component of Communism, due entirely to the advent of *glasnost'*. It is unlikely that Communism will be resurrected as a doctrine in the near future. That is not to say, however, that the ideological mind-set of the Soviet population has changed. I believe, in fact, that the non-textual aspects of the ideology will prove to be much more difficult to eradicate. Soviet political discourse has not radically changed, in the sense that the ideological damage wrought on the language of public discourse has not been undone, nor will it be for perhaps many years to come.

Another manifestation which Zinoviev's theory has not predicted, or even incorporated, is national unrest. He devotes less than one half of one page to the 'national question' in *Kommunizm kak real'nost'*, in which he says: 'I will only remark that the Communist regime deals successfully with national problems' (KKR:163; TRC:186). Ethnic strife has turned out to be one of Gorbachev's most intractable problems. In this respect the predictions of Western scholars, notably Carrère–d'Encausse and Bennigsen to name but two, that sooner or later the national issue would explode, have turned out to be all too well-founded.

On the other hand, the advent of *glasnost'* was a non–Communist manifestation and has acted as an accelerator to the speed of developments within the Soviet Union and, by extension, within Eastern Europe, developments which were anti–Communist in spirit. The question is whether developments in the political and economic arena have become irreversible, or whether a return to totalitarian methods is still possible. I do not yet believe that a return to a Brezhnev-style system is impossible, although I do believe that there would be a new ideological doctrine. Some of the main

features of classical Communism as Zinoviev describes it
have been relaxed, or even removed. But important features
remain in place. One is the nature of the totalitarian economic and administrative structure (the loss of Party influence may be of less importance for the stability of the
regime than one might have supposed). Another is the
degree of support for the old system and the hatred of
perestroika (and of Gorbachev). A third is the KGB.

Another matter of considerable importance is the extent
to which *perestroika* has been sabotaged. On the one hand
there is the 'systemic effect', to which reference has been
made in this chapter. On the other there is the matter of
genuine communication. Soviet public discourse allows people to present sincerely points of view which adapt effortlessly to changes in the political breeze. Communist traits,
as Zinoviev describes them, such as eye-wash, procrastina-
tion, hack-work, muddle, are not likely to disappear overnight. The ability of the regime to introduce meaningful,
lasting reform is rated by Zinoviev as close to zero. So far,
especially in the economic domain, Zinoviev has been shown
to be right. He has also been a keen student of developments under Gorbachev, of course, and has been assiduous
as ever in writing about them. It is accordingly to a consideration of Zinoviev's views on the Gorbachev era that we now
turn.

Part Three
The Gorbachev Era

7 *Gorbachevizm*

At the time of writing (February 1991), it begins to look as though the era of *perestroika* is going into decline. Individual republics, particularly in the Baltic region, wish to go their own way. This centrifugal tendency has provoked a reaction from the centre, and there are signs that the military and the KGB are exerting an increasing influence on Gorbachev's policies. National unrest, economic chaos, the rise in crime, the breakdown in law and order, to say nothing of widespread dissatisfaction with *perestroika* among the majority of ordinary Soviet citizens, and strong, almost universal, dislike of Gorbachev himself, have combined to render meaningless programmes based on a premise of Union-wide cooperation and effort and directed towards a collectivist solution of the Soviet Union's profound social, economic and environmental problems. From the perspective of anyone who agrees with Zinoviev's analysis of Soviet society, this development was entirely predictable. In this chapter we shall consider what Zinoviev had to say about the Gorbachev era in the first book he wrote about it, and juxtapose his views with those of leading Western experts writing about the same time. Since he completed the manuscript in 1987, it is clear that Zinoviev is commenting only on the period which Geoffrey Hosking has characterised as 'Perestroika Mark 1' (Hosking, 1990a:459).

The following anecdote is perhaps symbolic of the gulf which exists between Zinoviev and Western experts. In 1987 the well–known French Sovietologist Michel Tatu published a book entitled *Gorbatchev. L'U.R.S.S. va-t-elle changer?* I came across it in a Lausanne bookshop while it was being promoted. In the same shop, tucked away on a back shelf, I found another book which had just been published – Zinoviev's *Le Gorbatchévisme ou les pouvoirs d'une illusion* (Zinoviev, 1987a). It is somehow typical that, while Tatu's book should receive the publicity, it is Zinoviev's book that is the more revealing of the two. The temptation to devote this chapter to a comparative analysis of these two books has been hard to resist.

I decided not to attempt such an analysis mainly for textological reasons. Although the above-mentioned books were published within months of each other, Zinoviev published *Gorbachevizm,* a revised and extended version of *Le Gorbatchévisme,* in Russian the following year (Zinoviev, 1988b). In that same year there appeared *Katastroika. Gorbatchows Potemkinsche Doerfer* (Zinoviev, 1988a), a book which shares no less than 32 chapters (out of 35) with *Gorbachevizm,* but which includes several additional chapters. A Hungarian translation of *Katastroika* appeared in 1990, as did an Estonian translation of *Gorbachevizm,* which reputedly sold out in an hour and a half. An English translation also appeared. Our discussion is based on the Russian version of *Gorbachevizm* (G). Although I decided not to compare *Le Gorbatchévisme* and Tatu's *Gorbatchev,* reference is made to the latter work where appropriate.

In structure, *Gorbachevizm* is similar to *Kommunizm kak real'nost'.* It consists of 33 short chapters (with titles) together with a preface and a conclusion. The structure is thus typical of a Zinoviev work and facilitates his preferred *pointilliste* approach to his subject matter. On the other hand, many of these chapters can be grouped under general headings relating to various aspects of the Gorbachev phenomenon. The most important of these seem to me to be the following: Gorbachev himself, *glasnost,* the Soviet Union and the West, the economy, the government, the opposition.

GORBACHEV

The first point that Zinoviev makes about Gorbachev (G:2) is that he and his contemporaries are the careerists he described in *Ziiaiushchie vysoty.* Typically he refuses to interpret current events in the Soviet Union in terms of Gorbachev's personal qualities, arguing that the circumstances of the time required a reformist approach and that therefore a reformer emerged. Zinoviev's line is that historical processes are 'objective' and that 'outstanding' individuals emerge as a consequence (G:7). Gorbachev and his contemporaries were the ones who gambled on 'liberalism' as a career-option under Khrushchev, compromised under Brezhnev, and emerged under Andropov.

One might object that Zinoviev's account of how Gorbachev came to power ignores the mechanisms by which precisely Gorbachev and no one else was elected to the post of General Secretary. He might reply that there already exist numerous such accounts and that he is merely seeking to redress an imbalance by focusing on the extent to which the historical context in which an individual comes to prominence is also important. Moreover, he is keen to show that Gorbachev merely inherited a 'Party line' inaugurated by Andropov.

It is important for an account of Zinoviev's interpretation of the Gorbachev phenomenon to emphasise this connection. According to Zinoviev, the prestige of the KGB grew during the Brezhnev era, and Andropov himself was probably the person best informed about the true state of Soviet affairs, both at home and abroad. The complexities of how Andropov came to be General Secretary need not detain us here, but no doubt two of the contributary factors were, first, the growing awareness among the leadership that something had to be done to arrest the decline of the Soviet system before it threatened their own position, and, secondly, that Andropov was too old and infirm to last longer than necessary to administer a short, sharp campaign against corruption and the erosion of labour discipline.

Andropov's approach to relations with the West was radically different from what had gone before. Under Stalin and Khrushchev, ideological warfare with the West had emphasised Soviet man's 'superior' moral qualities and, more generally, the <i>differences</i> between East and West, predicting the eventual demise of 'rotten' capitalism and the world-wide triumph of Communism. The defects of capitalism were highlighted, those of Communism concealed or denied. Andropov discovered, during his chairmanship of the KGB, that more was to be gained from stressing not the differences but the <i>similarities</i> between 'Soviet man' and his Western counterpart. A new sophistication in Soviet diplomacy, right down to the way Soviet diplomats dressed, replaced the old, truculent 'worker-and-peasant' approach of the Khrushchev period. Andropov discovered that the

West was not permanently shocked by revelations of Soviet atrocities committed during the Stalin era, that open acknowledgement of Soviet economic problems brought greater benefits than attempts to conceal their existence, that many people in the West wanted to be encouraged in their wishful thinking about the extent to which the Soviet military 'threat' was an invention of NATO. From here it is but a short step to Gorbachev's talk of 'our common European home', an extension, be it noted, of the decades-old cliché of the Soviet 'common Soviet home' in which all the 'appartments' were occupied by fraternal Soviet nationalities. The hollowness of the latter concept has been repeatedly and mercilessly revealed in the last few years.

As for Andropov's campaigns against corruption, Zinoviev is equally scathing. Campaigns have been a feature of Soviet life since its inception. They are regular phenomena which are always doomed to failure but which serve an ideological purpose at the time. The campaign against corruption led easily to a campaign against the abuse of alcohol, and talk of 'democratisation', '*glasnost*' and 'acceleration' (*uskorenie*) led quickly to talk of *perestroika*. We shall have more to say about these phenomena below. Here we seek to demonstrate the links between policies associated exclusively with Gorbachev and those of his predecessor.

Zinoviev's approach to the *persona* of Gorbachev necessarily differs from those writers who emphasise the importance of Gorbachev's personality as a catalyst for change in the Soviet Union. It provides a useful counterpoint to the detailed accounts of Gorbachev's rise to power by acknowledged experts like Archie Brown and Michel Tatu, neither of whom is unaware of the parlous state of the Soviet system at the end of the Brezhnev era. What differentiates Tatu's approach to the future from Zinoviev's is the former's goodwill towards Gorbachev and his cautious optimism. Tatu is aware of Gorbachev's qualities, which include a well-developed ability to dissimulate. On the other hand, part of what Gorbachev had hidden during his climb to power was a measure of idealism (Tatu, 1987:11), and Tatu is prepared to give 'democratisation' the benefit of the doubt:

...ce serait déjà un bon résultat si la 'démocratisation',

elle, progressait régulièrement pendant les vingt proch-
aines années, si l'économie soviétique retrouvait un second souffle et si l'architecte de tout cela restait en place
tout ce temps. Bonne chance tout de même, Mikhail
Sergueevitch!

(1987:17)

Zinoviev's sentiment is the opposite. Gorbachev is a
careerist looking after his own interests above everything
else. The Soviet Union is a complex, almost model, Communist society and is therefore unreformable. Consequently, *perestroika* will fail.

GLASNOST'[1]

Zinoviev's approach to the development of *glasnost'* in the
Soviet Union is to emphasise the extent to which it is an
alien phenomenon in Communist society. Not only is Communist society deeply inimical to the idea of *glasnost'* as it is
understood in the West, it is a society pervaded by secrecy
(G:91). This secrecy, to use Elster's distinction, is not the
passive negation of *glasnost'*, but its active negation. Secrecy
is a dynamic phenomenon in Communist society, manifested in many ways: secret institutions, closed meetings, secret
instructions, permits, passes, signed undertakings to preserve confidentiality, secret departments, special sections,
etc. (G:91).

Glasnost' for Gorbachev, therefore, according to Zinoviev,
is scarcely anything more than a propaganda campaign
designed to influence Western opinion in the required
direction (G:92). A clear example of the absence of genuine
glasnost' was the attempted cover-up after Chernobyl. *Glasnost'* from above is not a genuine democratic phenomenon
but a cynical means of disinformation and manipulation of
public opinion (witness the persecution of the editors of the
unofficial journal *Glasnost'*, Grigoriants, Timofeev and Shil-
kov).

Official attitudes to *glasnost'* have been affected by the
information revolution. The Soviet government is no longer
able to restrict its citizens to Stalinist norms of information,

nor to conceal from the West things that it would rather not reveal. Zinoviev then argues that 'official *glasnost"* is a subtle campaign against genuine *glasnost'* (G:95). What looks like increased freedom of information is essentially more up–to-date methods designed to improve control over the flood of information from the West which, for a time under Brezhnev, escaped such control. Zinoviev's argument is somewhat opaque and leaves room for considerable doubt. To this observer at least, it seems that the flow of information from the West has increased immeasurably under Gorbachev. On the other hand, it seems at least possible to see 'official *glasnost'* as another manifestation of Soviet *'imitatsiia'* of the West, in the sense that in the Soviet Union *glasnost'* is 'top-down', whereas in the West it is 'bottom-up'. Some support for this view is offered by Remington, who (referring to the period up until 1987) argues that 'a good deal had been done to generate the *semblance* of openness without the substance of debate' (Remington, 1989:61–2).

Where it seems that Zinoviev may have got it right is in the area of speculation about the likely future of *glasnost'*. His view (G:96) is that 'official *glasnost'* is too subtle a weapon for a Communist society and that in time it will be accompanied by increasingly harsh methods of control. At the time of writing (February 1991) the phrase 'the death of *glasnost'* is already quite commonly encountered and there have been several examples of these 'increasingly harsh methods' being applied. Remington made a more specific prediction (Remington, 1989:74), suggesting that when negative publicity passed from criticism of the Brezhnev era to criticism of the *perestroika* era, in particular criticism of the performance of officials appointed under Gorbachev, enthusiasm for *glasnost'* would wane.

So far we have been examining Zinoviev's view of *glasnost'* in its general manifestation. However, there are two particular aspects which he singles out for special treatment, namely the widespread revelations about the Soviet past (and present) (*samorazoblachenie* or 'self-revelation') and the so-called (in the West) 'cultural renaissance'.

Zinoviev's attitude to the flood of 'self-criticism' pouring incessantly from the Soviet media is best indicated by the proverb he quotes: '*Zastav' duraka Bogu molit'sia, on i lob*

rasshibet' (loosely translated: 'Force a fool to pray [by pros-
trating himself] and he'll bruise his forehead'). The abrupt
change from 'self-praise' to 'self-criticism' has been quite
remarkable. Something of the effect was brought home to
the present writer during a recent trip to Moscow. A few
years ago he had been contemplating the ravaged landscape
of suburban Moscow from the window of his hotel, watching
citizens tramp through the mud from one soulless building
to the next while listening to a wash of Soviet hyperbolic
rhetoric on the radio about how good life was. At the time
he thought that such propaganda was ineffective, since the
gap between the picture offered by the media and stark
reality could scarcely have been greater. On his recent trip,
however, he found the constant flood of reporting about
how life was *exactly* as it looked from his hotel window
infinitely more depressing. One might wonder, therefore,
about the effect of such '*glasnost'*' on people's determination
to 'fight for *perestroika*'.

Zinoviev's point about self-criticism is a different one.
While he is aware of the fact that the undifferentiated
criticism of the sytem pouring from the media is no more
representative of a genuine, democratic form of control of
information than the previous undifferentiated praise, he
nevertheless emphasises that a subtle form of censorship
still exists. That is to say, he draws attention to the relative
unimportance of such things as the abuse of alcohol. *Glasnost'* with respect to alcohol, argues Zinoviev, is a form of
concealment of the true reasons underlying particular
phenomena (G:20). The Soviet press, in short, can permit
itself any revelation it likes about Soviet society, so long as it
does not attack the foundations of that society:

> In this regard there has always been, still is, and always will
> be one particular taboo, and that is any recognition of the
> fact that the Communist social order gives rise to defects
> which are common to Communism and capitalism, may
> even intensify them and in addition spawn new ones.
>
> (G:20)

This prediction has turned out to be false, if for no other
reason than the fact that press freedom has currently es-

caped total government control. The abolition of censorship is another example, as are the facts that *Gorbachevizm* has already appeared in Estonia and that *Ziiaiushchie vysoty* has been serialised in a Soviet journal.[2]

Zinoviev is also scathing about cultural developments under Gorbachev. He regards the so-called cultural 'renaissance' as a farce compared to the real damage that the Soviet authorities inflicted on the flowering of a genuine Russian literature in the environment of '*samizdat*' and '*tamizdat*'.[3] This view is part of his larger view that Gorbachev and his colleagues were instrumental in crushing the dissident movement, purloining their ideas and presenting them later as official Soviet policy. He has nothing but scorn for the 'aitmatovs' (*aitmatovy*) who publish 'daring' works with permission of the authorities and offer 'personal' invitations to Western personalities to discuss cultural matters at a chic resort on Lake Issyk-Kul' (G:101). The reality, he maintains, is that Soviet society is destined to perpetuate mediocrity and that there will be no development in 'permitted' Soviet literature. This may be true, but in fact since Zinoviev advanced that view there has been a tremendous flood of publication in the Soviet 'thick journals' of foreign and previously unpublished Soviet and émigré literature which reflects a degree of editorial freedom not seen since the 1920s.[4]

Writing about the same time, Tatu argued that Gorbachevism amounted to little more than a new information and cultural policy (Tatu, 1987:139), making the important point that progress in these areas should be measured in relation to the Soviet past and in no sense to the situation in a Western democracy. To that extent he and Zinoviev are in agreement. It is a measure of how far *glasnost'* has developed since 1987 that both Zinoviev and Tatu were then emphasising the extent to which important subject areas were taboo. Thus while Tatu could point to new topics and institutions which were open for discussion, there were still large '*zones opaques*': the military, foreign policy and politburo/secretariat discussions, not to mention the provincial press, which was still to a much larger extent under Party control than the metropolitan press. He could also say that *glasnost'* had not been accompanied by any institutional change worthy of the name and that it could be annulled from one day to the next (Tatu, 1987:148–9).

In short, although both writers raised questions about the long-term future of *glasnost'*, Zinoviev was bolder in his prediction that *glasnost'* would sooner or later be suppressed. His confidence (not shared by Tatu) derives from his theoretical position: *glasnost'* is incompatible with Communist society, Communism is here to stay, therefore *glasnost'* will be be suppressed.

Glasnost' is viewed from a different (and more frequently encountered) angle by James Scanlan (Scanlan, 1988) who links it to a discussion of the prospects for the development of a civil society under the 'new thinking'. He shows how Gorbachev initially argued for *glasnost'* primarily as a means of permitting freer discussion of social, political and economic issues in order to combat inefficiency and corruption. What Gorbachev did not seem to envisage was that people would express opinions which did not necessarily contribute to the common good. Scanlan then goes on to look at the general question of individual rights in a Marxist-–Leninist context, demonstrating that the official Soviet view continues to be that individual rights are indissolubly linked to duties and are socially based. His conclusion is that the prospects for the development of a civil society in the Soviet Union are not particularly good and that therefore *glasnost'* will not develop far enough to contribute to a fundamental alteration in the existing relationship between society and the state. Scanlan is thus closer to Zinoviev than to Tatu, since, like Zinoviev, he believes that there will be no fundamental change in the system. Tatu is more circumspect, preferring to leave open the question of the prospects for radical change, while being under no allusion whatsoever about the massive obstacles which stand in the way of genuine, lasting reform.

Geoffrey Hosking is perhaps slightly more optimistic. He too agrees that *glasnost'* in its initial phase was little more than an encouragement of the media to probe inefficiency and corruption (Hosking, 1990a:459). However, in its later stages, having been accompanied by an impressive replacement of cadres in many areas of the media and the ideological apparatus, it provided an atmosphere in which thousands of unofficial, 'informal' organisations could flourish, testifying to a vigorous, and varied, 'alternative culture'. Moreover, the increasingly open, wide-ranging and critical review of Soviet history unfolding in the Soviet media leads Hosking to suggest that it has almost reached the point 'at which *glasnost'* becomes freedom of speech'. (Hosking, 1990b:157).

While subscribing to Zinoviev's general view that *glasnost'* will in the end be suppressed because of the nature of Communist society, the present writer would suggest that the ultimate threat to *glasnost'* is economic. Without the ownership of the means of production and reproduction and the guarantee of financially independent distribution systems, a free, non–State-controlled press is not possible. Remington's interesting study of the changes in cadres accompanying Gorbachev's policy of *glasnost'* (Remington, 1989:62–70) leads one to conclude (noting in particular the large percentage of editors and media bosses who were 'parachuted' into their posts from the Party, not promoted from within the media (Remington, op.cit.:67)), that a decision to clamp down on *glasnost'* would be reflected in a cadres policy which would be the reverse of Gorbachev's. I see no reason to suppose that the editorial policy of a publication like *Ogonek* could not be changed overnight by replacing Korotich with his ideological opposite. The absence of a financially independent press guarantees the absence of genuine press freedom.[5] The formation of a financially independent press, however, entails a level of *economic perestroika* of which the Soviet Union will not be capable.

THE SOVIET UNION AND THE WEST[6]

As usual Zinoviev takes a swipe at Western attitudes towards the Soviet Union. Formerly, people in the West thought of the Soviet Union as a gigantic labour camp; now they trust the Soviet leadership more than those who have suffered the Soviet experience at first hand. There is certainly some justification for that view, given the extremely enthusiastic reception of Gorbachev in the West, characterised in some of the tabloids as 'Gorbiemania'. On the other hand, not everyone in the West shared that attitude, notes of warning being sounded by many people of international renown, including Zbigniew Brzezinski, Richard Nixon, Henry Kissinger, Jeane Kirkpatrick and Margaret Thatcher.[7]

What needs to be understood, argues Zinoviev, is that the Soviet Union is a new *social* order, not just a political system, and that that new order is unreformable. Currently we have the unique situation in which the Soviet leadership is expressing lack of confidence in Communist ideals and in specifically Communist methods of organising society, and trying to cure specifically *Communist* problems by quasi–Western, *non*-Communist means (G:35).

Zinoviev points out that, as far as closing the economic gap between the Soviet Union and the West is concerned, that gap was narrower under Stalin than it is now. Moreover, the structure of Soviet society prevents restructuring along Western lines, permitting only the *imitation* of Western institutions. Imitation cannot touch the foundations of society. The introduction of cheque-books, for instance, he regards as a frankly ludicrous innovation in a country where most people are so poorly paid that they are more or less broke by pay-day, where the shops are empty and where money is a mere 'imitation' of its Western counterpart. Only the *'privilegentsiia'* would find any use for a cheque-book, but they managed perfectly well without them!

More serious, however, is the attempt to emulate the West in terms of cost-efficiency at the level of the factory or enterprise. One of the great benefits of Communism is the guaranteed right to work and the elimination of unemployment. The price is high: low labour productivity, poor quality goods, low wages, forced labour. In Soviet circumstances, attempts to imitate the West in terms of increased efficiency will lead to unemployment without Western-style social security systems. Soviet 'solutions' like lowering the age of retirement, merely reduce the standard of living of large numbers of people. If, therefore, people are asked to choose between striving to 'catch up with the West' or 'achieve the highest world level' and their own (Communist) system, they will choose the latter. And, Zinoviev maintains (in 1987), they have already done so. Gorbachev's

perestroika is already destined to become just another piece of
theatre (G:53). Any benefits will be the result of Western
help or Soviet exploitation of the West, but they will be short-
lived and the old problems will re-emerge and be dealt with
by old-fashioned Communist methods. That is his firm prediction (G:54).[8]

In an important chapter on mutual misunderstanding
Zinoviev argues that it is in principle impossible for East and
West to achieve a genuine understanding of each other.
Why should this be so, given that many factors exist which
promote mutual understanding? Millions of people are well-
educated. There are books, newspapers, journals, radio,
television, the cinema, cultural exchanges, countless tourists, diplomats, journalists, thousands of spies. Zinoviev
argues that the will to achieve genuine, objective, non-
ideological understanding is not there, on either side. On
both sides, professional investigation and interpretation is
biased by the need or desire to create a more refined, but
still ideologised, version of the 'truth' about each other.
Thus whole teams of -ologists spend decades not understanding each other. Political leaders 'understand each
other' only in so far as it helps them to solve their own
problems. The Soviet Union is destined to build up its war
preparations and to continue its exploitation of the West,
without which it cannot maintain a decent economic and
technological level. The desire of the Soviet Union to be
integrated into the world economy is a desire to be an even
greater parasite than it has been hitherto (G:146).

One difficulty about such a vision is the fact that opinions
both in the East and West vary. Both sides have 'hawks' and
'doves' and species in between. Also, Zinoviev's argument is
self-serving to the extent that it implies that his version of
Communism is the only valid one since it alone is 'scientific'.
On the other hand, one might argue that a more fundamental
reason for mutual misunderstanding derives from opposing
systems based respectively on the view that the individual is
paramount and that the individual is not paramount. The
fundamental basis for misunderstanding, in other words, is
the gulf between individualism and collectivism. But at that
point national boundaries disappear and we are confronted
with the familiar situation where hawks of whatever national-

ity tend to despise any species of dove. Individualists and collectivists are to be found in every society. On the other hand, people in the West have not had to live for decades in an atmosphere where they are used to saying one thing in public and the opposite in private. This is a major experiential difference which likewise cannot be bridged. People in the Soviet Union are having a break, currently, from that experience but are having difficulty in replenishing the husk of Sovspeak with new conceptual content.

Zinoviev's scathing dismissal of Gorbachev's 'new thinking' as a new way of hoodwinking the West is in tune with the opinions of Western observers who are not inclined to take what Gorbachev asserts at face value. Gerhard Wettig (Wettig, 1988) offers a convincing analysis of Gorbachev's 'new thinking' in the sphere of defence policy which reinforces Zinoviev's theory that foreign policy is following a line laid down originally by Andropov. That is, ideological confrontation based on class struggle has been downplayed, since it was getting nowhere, and has been replaced by the idea of the 'all-human' goal of saving mankind from nuclear destruction, a danger which is entirely due to the Western doctrine of nuclear deterrence. The Soviet goal is the removal of nuclear deterrence, allowing superior Soviet conventional forces to intimidate Western Europe, and ultimately to extend Soviet influence to *all* of Europe. (This was written, of course, before the momentous events of 1989 which have led to a situation in which, currently, about 300,000 Soviet troops are stationed on German (i.e. West European) territory.) It aims to involve *all* likely Western groups: CND, environmentalists, pacifists, proponents of aid to the Third World, etc., as well as 'reasonable' forces within the political establishment of Western countries. This arguably realistic view is supported by Krauthammer (Krauthammer, 1989:121–30) who doubts whether Gorbachev's foreign policy initiatives amount to more than a second period of détente, allowing the Soviet Union a respite from the arms race and another opportunity to extract Western credits and technology. Less adamant, but nonetheless cautious, interpretations of Gorbachev's foreign policy initiatives are offered by Mendras (Mendras, 1989:127–62) and Light (Light, 1989:169–88).

Mendras explores the idea that it is easier for the leadership in the Soviet Union to make progress in foreign policy
than in domestic policy. Her position is close to Zinoviev's,
arguing that the West is perceived both as a threat to the
stability of the Soviet state and as an arena for expansion
and source of material and technological support. If things
go wrong in international affairs, the government can evade
responsibility. In the area of domestic policy the evasion of
responsibility is much more difficult, as Gorbachev is finding
to his cost. Mendras suggests, however, and again she is
close to Zinoviev, that Gorbachev has tried to persuade
Western leaders that Soviet rulers reason like them and
accord priority to internal development and social progress
(1989:134). She too has observed that Soviet rhetoric has
changed and that the former confrontational approach
associated with Khrushchev and Brezhnev has been replaced
by the concept of interdependence, a point noted also by
Light (1990:178).

But whereas these writers have reacted with various degrees of caution to this new Soviet policy of 'interdependence', most searchingly examined by Wettig, the reaction
of George Kennan has been to take it at face value. In an
extraordinary essay (Kennan, 1989:63–72), Kennan argues
that those who doubt the sincerity of Gorbachev's talk of
'mutual dependence' and the necessity of 'a new dialectic of
the common human and class interests and principles in
our modern age' reveal a lack of understanding of Gorbachev's position 'that borders on the bizarre' (1989:67).
Similarly, Jerry Hough (Hough, 1989:111–13) argues that
the United States should encourage Gorbachev's 'embrace'
of Europe, seeing nothing to be worried about in the idea
that the Soviet Union 'needs' Europe. Whether Europe
'needs' the Soviet Union is a question he does not address.
Moreover, he suggests that Gorbachev needs to convince his
countrymen that 'Russia is integrating into the higher
civilisation of Europe, while avoiding the bourgeois crass-
ness of America' (1989:112). Such views by Western experts
on the Soviet Union make Zinoviev despair.

THE ECONOMY [9]

The Soviet system, observes Zinoviev, was built by 'pre-Soviet' people ('*dosovetskie liudi*'). Real Soviet people have had their fill of ideas about 'progress'. Communist society is organised in such a way that dynamism does not pay. Dynamic people fall foul of the conservative majority, which will do all in its power to obstruct Gorbachev's reforms. Personal initiatives are neutered by the complexity of the social system in which predominate *not* competition and free enterprise but mutual connections and obstructionism. [10] As one American management consultant put it, Communist society is risk-free. But economic relations in Communist society, according to Zinoviev, are in any case not primary, as we have noted before. The primary relations in Communist society are communal. The West's greater economic effectiveness is at the expense of unemployment and the intensification of labour processes. In the Soviet Union there are no resources to re-employ sacked workers or to provide social security for them or to pay high wages for intensified labour. A major problem for Gorbachev is the fact that even the idea of unemployment undermines one of Communism's most attractive features. Since all 100 per cent of Soviet firms are unprofitable, any that will be shut down will merely be scapegoats and will probably be in unimportant sectors of the economy (i.e. *not* heavy industry, not the military sphere, not agriculture, etc.). The main task of government is to keep what has to be governed within the bounds of governability. There are thus built-in limits to economic or any other processes. [11]

Zinoviev's views on decentralisation and privatisation have also been prophetic. The centralised administration of people, he argues, is adequate for Communist society and will be present for as long as Communism exists. On the other hand, within the centralised system, individuals find some scope for action which very often takes the form of deception, corruption, illegal or criminal activity. The most that can be hoped for from decentralisation under Gorbachev is the legalisation of what is already going on, an outcome which will improve the environment for even more criminal activity (G:75–6). Private enterprise in Communist society quickly becomes criminal and arouses the ire of the masses, since it creates a relatively privileged stratum among the underprivileged. On the specific matter of 'privatisation' or 'destatisation', incidentally, Philip Hanson notes the huge disparity in the scale of British and Soviet programmes and observes that 'even the comparatively tiny British programme, conducted within an existing framework of market institutions, has been problematic and is not yet complete' (Hanson, 1990:100). One can begin to imagine the size of the task facing those elements of the Soviet leadership who are in favour of the sale of state-owned assets.

The question of 'unrealistic prices' (for instance, the heavily subsidised price of bread) is linked by Zinoviev to a discussion of the relevance of Western economic theory in the Soviet context. It is time, he says, to ask why it is that, after seventy years in a huge territory with everyone working, the country cannot feed itself. Surely it is time to stop blaming economic difficulties on extraneous factors? Surely the weather has not been bad for seventy years? Surely shortages cannot be blamed on historical circumstances? After all, since the end of the Second World War both Japan and Germany have reached an economic level which the Soviet Union will not reach in a hundred years. Is it not time to consider that the difficulties might result from the very structure of the Communist system itself? The science of economics, he seems to be suggesting, has no relevance for Communist society.

It is not that the Soviet Union is short of economists. There are tens of thousands of them. But, he argues, they employ terms and concepts borrowed from Western economic thought, terms and concepts which are alien to the Soviet system (G:127–8). He asserts that there is still no respectable economic theory in the Soviet Union. On the other hand, the Soviet Union needs to survive in the world as it is, where economic forces and laws operate 'objectively'. Gorbachev's increasingly desperate attempt to integrate the Soviet economy into the global economy is a strategy with the aim of preying on the West to an even greater extent than it does at the moment (G:146).

What are we to make of all this? On the one hand he appears to be arguing that a 'Communist economics' is theoretically possible. Yet elsewhere he has argued (at length) that scientific laws are 'objective' or 'universal'. But a 'Communist economics' in Zinoviev's understanding would probably not resemble economics so much as sociology, and it certainly would not resemble Marxist economic theory. If one were to project the Soviet system to encompass the world, what force then would economic laws have? The present writer is not an economist and is not prepared, therefore, to attempt to discuss that matter, but it seems *a priori* reasonable to suppose that they would operate, if at all, with considerably less force. On the level of common sense, however, Zinoviev's views are persuasive. Much of what he predicted in 1987 has turned out to be the case in 1991. The rise in economic crime (and in crime generally), public resentment of cooperatives, sullen opposition to talk of 'realistic' prices, 'streamlining', 'profitability' and so on, provide evidence for Zinoviev's view that the system is unreformable, and for the reasons which he adduces.

Gorbachev, however, did not launch his programme of *perestroika* whimsically. Most observers agreed that the Soviet Union was facing economic catastrophe and that something would have to be done to reverse the decline. It is generally agreed, however, that the economy is now in much worse shape than it was before *perestroika*. That economic situation is now accompanied by a great measure of social breakdown and the erosion of centralised power. Again Zinoviev was right. He predicted that attempts to reform the system would make the system worse.

GOVERNMENT[12]

He also predicted that any relaxation of firm, centralised control would lead to anarchy and a breakdown of law and order. He blames the catastrophic economic situation on a lack of understanding on the part of the leadership of the mechanisms of Communist society. This lack of understanding is also largely responsible for the breakdown in the centralised system of administration and control.

We discussed Zinoviev's view of the power structure in the

Soviet Union in the previous chapter. We need now to consider Zinoviev's view of Gorbachev's problems in the context of that discussion. The first problem raised by Zinoviev is connected with the sheer size and complexity of the Soviet administrative and governmental apparatus. In *Kommunizm kak real'nost'* Zinoviev wrote of a 'coefficient of effectiveness'. In *Gorbachevizm* he employs the metaphor of a 'ceiling of effectiveness' which cannot be raised (G:39). The limits to reform are prescribed by the size of the apparatus. We might note in 1991 that if this was true of the system under Brezhnev, it is at least as true of the system under Gorbachev. Zinoviev's argument has always been that power flowing from the top is neutralised by power exercised in a variety of ways down below. Now power from the top is much weaker. As Gorbachev has assumed more and more personal power, his decrees and pronouncements fail more and more to be implemented. The power of the Communist Party had already been greatly weakened by factionalism along national lines as well as in relation to policy even before its 'leading role' was legislated out of existence. New institutions of representative government have weakened it still further. The current situation is best summed up by the word *mnogovlastie* (something like 'multiple authority' in the absence of clearly-defined spheres of authority), a word which is increasingly encountered in the Soviet press.

Zinoviev makes another point about the bureaucracy. The October Revolution was a bureaucratic revolution. By this he means that the destruction of the old order was replaced by a totalitarian system in which the bureaucracy of the state reached an unprecedented size. The chief results of that revolution have been that (a) the Communist economy is incapable of competing with the capitalist economy, and (b) the Communist system reveals a strong tendency to stagnation. Thus Gorbachev's battle against bureaucracy is a battle against the very foundations of the Communist social system. His prediction is that Gorbachev will fail in one respect and succeed in another. On the one hand he will not manage to implement his reforms. On the other, the Soviet Union, with Western help, will regain confidence and reintroduce Communist ways of solving Communist problems.

The greatest crisis facing Communism, argues Zinoviev, is not economic, it is ideological. (This is perfectly consistent with his view that Communist society is above all an ideological society.) On the one hand, almost no one in the Soviet Union any longer believes in the paradise on earth promised by Marxism-Leninism. Exhortations to do so in the current climate of *glasnost'* are pointless. On the other hand, many people are inimically disposed to capitalism, and value the practical achievements of the Communist system. The aim of Communist enterprises is not in the first instance to achieve profitability but to guarantee work for their workforces and to afford them the necessities of life, free from the defects of capitalism. Thus when Gorbachev and his supporters argue for the reintroduction of 'Western' reforms in the Soviet context such as private property, self-financing, real money, etc., they are perceived by a growing percentage of the Soviet population as counter-revolutionaries. Gorbachev's chief enemy is the mass of the Soviet population. This prediction in 1987 is paralleled in February 1991 by the findings of an opinion poll carried out in the Soviet Union which reflected an approval rate for Gorbachev of just 13 per cent.[13]

Zinoviev is also at pains to point out that the distinction between 'supporters of *perestroika*' (*perestroishchiki*) and 'conservatives' (*konservatory*) within the leadership and administrative apparatus is a false one which does not exist in reality. It was the invention of those who tended to view Soviet society in terms of *a priori* categories. In reality there is no such division: people can be both. For instance, in the Khrushchev years, former Stalinists participated in the de-stalinisation campaign. Now, the nimble conservatives of the Brezhnev period have taken over *perestroika*. The kernel of Gorbachev's leadership, who were cynical careerists and Brezhnev toadies, have become 'supporters of *perestroika*' for career reasons. They excel, he alleges, in cynicism and resourcefulness, qualities evident to everyone in the Soviet Union but ignored in the West. The implication is that even those supposedly in favour of *perestroika* will oppose it as soon as it suits them.

Again one is struck by Zinoviev's mix of insight, simplicity and cynicism. As political science it is no doubt defective,

yet genuine political science is stymied to a large extent by a
lack of data about the workings of Soviet government at the
upper levels. Furthermore, many expert analyses of Soviet
government based on models of one sort or another seem to
attempt to fit the Soviet system into categories which have
been developed for non-Soviet systems.[14] On the other hand,
it may well be, as Archie Brown suggests (Brown, 1990:153),
that the Soviet Union has changed from being a highly
authoritarian system to a mixed political system with plural-
ist elements. Whether the process of dismantling the pillars
of the Communist system has gone beyond the point of no
return, however, is perhaps still open to question. Ultimately
it may turn out that the difficulties inherent in 'destatisation' are too great and that the socialist economic base will
force the return of an authoritarian superstructure.

THE OPPOSITION[15]

A survey of the main themes of *Gorbachevizm* would be
incomplete without a reference to Zinoviev's account of
what he regards as the Gorbachev leadership's theft of ideas
for reform first proposed by an opposition movement which
Gorbachev and his peers allegedly did much to crush when
they were making their way up the careeer ladder under
Brezhnev. His argument is simple:

> Before they obtained the highest positions of power,
> Gorbachev and his acolytes obtained positions of power
> on lower levels and participated in the power structure in
> every way and at every level. Moreover, they tried harder
> than others, in order to achieve still greater personal
> success. They assiduously served their superiors. If they
> had not done so, they would not even have obtained the
> lowest positions of power.
> The destruction of the dissident movement is what has
> distinguished their 'service' above all. It was one of the
> biggest feathers in their cap. They proved to their masters
> that they were capable of dealing with opposition and at
> the same time making use of it in the leadership's interest.
> (G:80)

Here we detect Zinoviev's continuing contempt for the 'liberals' whom he has satirised in his works of fiction from the beginning.

As usual Zinoviev is sensitive to paradox. He points out, for example, that the overwhelming majority of the government/administrative apparat is *against perestroika*. The main opposition, therefore, is perhaps located within the ranks of those who allegedly support it. Secondly, he wonders whether it is possible to have a constructive opposition with a programme of reforms which would be an alternative to Gorbachev's reforms, and decides that it probably is not possible. Thirdly, is a constructive dissident opposition with a serious programme directed not at the government but at society beyond government, possible? Again he thinks not, for two reasons: first, in the Soviet Union there is no society which functions independently of the system of administration and government; secondly, there is no possible alternative programme of reform, for in current circumstances *any* programme of reform which retains the Communist social order and its administrative-governmental system will not substantially change the way of life of that society (G:88). We should note here that he does not mention the CPSU.

His remedy is a form of social opposition, the contours of which he first outlined in a series of articles in *Kontinent* (Zinoviev, 1987c, 1987d, 1989d). Essentially he advocates a form of social opposition which should be based on criticism of each and every action of the authorities. Its main task should be a thorough, ongoing critique of the whole social system, power structure and ideology. What is required, he suggests, is 'the formation of different groups, including illegal ones, for the purpose of studying and disseminating ideas for opposition' (G:89). In this respect at least, the formation of upwards of 60,000 'informal' groups must give him some encouragement. Some, but perhaps not much. Although the 'administrative-governmental system' is being radically restructured, there is little sign of the emergence of a system which would make room for a genuine opposition along the lines of Parliamentary democracy. '*Edinovlastie*' (unified power) is giving way to '*mnogovlastie*' (fragmented power), but what any system of power has to adminis-

ter in the Soviet Union continues to be a huge conglomerate
of state-owned assets and a socialist economy which is still
incapable of responding to 'market forces', together with an
unruly population, the majority of which have no interest in
giving up the 'achievements of socialism'.

CONCLUSION

With the benefit of hindsight we can see that Zinoviev's first
book on the Gorbachev period can in many respects hold its
own with the writings of other commentators which appeared about the same time and provides a perspective
missing from virtually all of the Western analyses.

His main purpose was to underline for the Western
reader the most significant features of the Gorbachev phenomenon as he understands it. First, Gorbachev was for many
years a Party careerist who served under Brezhnev and who
was a protégé of Andropov. His charismatic image in the
West is not duplicated in the Soviet Union. Secondly, his
call for '*glasnost*' was initially to impress the West and to
attempt to control the impact of Western influence. The
emphasis here is surely wrong. Gorbachev quite clearly
seems to have called for '*glasnost*' as a way of combating
inefficiency and corruption, while (naively) expecting
people to use *glasnost* exclusively in the interests of the state.
Neither Zinoviev nor Gorbachev foresaw the extent to
which freedom of expression would flourish under the
guidance of radical and courageous editors, authors, film–
makers, television programmers and other representatives
of the intelligentsia. Thirdly, the Soviet Union is living
through a *Communist* crisis, which is primarily an *ideological*
crisis. Here again, Zinoviev probably did not foresee the
rapidity with which the extraneous ideological trappings
would be dismantled. Fourthly, although there are problems which are classed by Western observers (and Soviet
observers as well) as *economic*, they are in fact *social*. Communist 'economic' problems cannot be solved by 'Western'
economic means. He predicts the end of *glasnost'* and a
resumption of *Communist* methods for the solution of *Communist* problems (authoritarianism, coercion, absence of

glasnost', etc.). At that point ideology will re-emerge as the most immediate concern. Fifthly, the system is unreformable. The inordinate complexity of a totalitarian system[16] is self-regulating. Reforms in one area produce counter-measures in another. Counter-evidence in the shape of the new governmental structures, the elimination of the central role of the CPSU, etc., which he, of course, did not foresee in 1987, he will regard as evidence of a progress of disintegration, not reform. Whether the Communist system is *indestructible*, however, is a question for a future chapter. In 1987 he is confident that the crisis is surmountable, that Communism has a long future ahead of it, and that the current period is merely the *first* genuinely Communist crisis and probably not the last. After all, capitalism too has its crises, and yet it still survives.

No doubt many observers would disagree with much of the foregoing, but it is also true that many would not. In terms of Remington's 'pessimistic' and 'optimistic' schools of thought about the chances of 'regime transition' (Remington, 1990:160), Zinoviev belongs to the former. However, he offers a perspective which is by definition absent in Western accounts. The perspective is that of *homo sovieticus*. In *Gorbachevizm* his accounts of Soviet bureaucrats and their careerist aspirations would probably be discounted by observers as 'unscientific', possibly even 'unfair'. It is nonetheless an important perspective. How important, we shall discuss in the next chapter.

8 *Katastroika*

Katastroika: A Tale of Perestroika in Partgrad was completed by Zinoviev towards the end of 1989 and published in 1990. An excerpt had already appeared in issue 57 of the journal *Kontinent* (Zinoviev, 1988c). The work to some extent owes a debt to Saltykov-Shchedrin's *Istoriia odnogo goroda* (*History of A Town*), although characteristically Zinoviev goes out of his way to deny that *Katastroika* is a satire (K:29). A satire, however, it nonetheless is, and once again Zinoviev offers an insight into the workings of Soviet society via a description of the absurd practices which are endemic to it. If the humour is occasionally strained, there are more than enough brilliantly funny passages to compensate for the infrequent lapses. Read in conjunction with *Gorbachevizm*, it provides a useful counterbalance to expert Western analyses.

The structure of the work consists of 103 short texts with titles, arranged in loose sequences which can be grouped together to form four separate sections, framed by a prologue and epilogue. As usual, texts are related to each other by means of a range of devices, including juxtaposition, title and theme. Via the reappearance of characters and places from earlier books such as *Svetloe budushchee* and *Zhelty dom*, Zinoviev incorporates what is essentially a critique of *perestroika*, and by extension, of Gorbachev, into his (still) unfolding mega-text. Upstarts and toadies encountered at an earlier stage of their careers in, say, *Svetloe budushchee*, are now Gorbachev's advisers, colleagues and friends, people like Mitrofan Lukich Portiankin, Petr Stepanovich Suslikov, Korytov and others. There are also links with works not discussed in this volume: *V preddverii raia* (*On the Threshhold of Paradise*), *Idi na Golgofu*, (*Go to Golgotha!*) and *Zhivi!* (*Live!*). Mao-Tse-Dun'ka returns from *Zhelty dom*, from which Zinoviev also borrows the 'True tale of the good collective-farm chairman' (K:169–70), albeit in truncated, slightly adapted form. This is counterbalanced by the 'Parable of the factory director' (K:169–70), which provides the collective-farm chairman's industrial counterpart. By enmeshing

196

Gorbachev in his own interminable description of Soviet society as he sees it, Zinoviev neatly underlines the extent to which he believes Gorbachev is bound to fail.

The structure of *Katastroika* is rather neat. The prologue tells us of the intention of the central authorities to turn Partgrad, a provincial Russian 'closed' city, into a 'beacon' of *perestroika*, an attraction for Western tourists. The epilogue tells us that the plan was successfully accomplished. In between we have four reasonably distinct sections dealing with what one might call respectively 'the project', 'the history of Partgrad', '*perestroika* in Partgrad' and 'realisation of the project'. These different sections provide Zinoviev with a wide range of perspectives, both synchronic and diachronic. A discussion of the genesis of the project allows him to dissect the Gorbachev leadership's motives with his usual cynical clarity. His unusual foray into pre-Revolutionary history allows him to satirise Soviet historiography to hilarious effect. His account of *perestroika* in Partgrad is a review of Gorbachev's reforms from their beginnings, and his account of how the project is realised allows him to examine in detail his important, even central, distinction between reality and the appearance of reality, action and the appearance of action, truth and the appearance of truth.

THE PROJECT[1]

The book opens with Mikhail Sergeevich ruminating in the limousine which is taking him from the Kremlin to his dacha outside Moscow. Not everything is going well. The workers are not taking to his mineral-water-as-a-substitute-for-vodka campaign. Moreover, it is proving more difficult to supply them with mineral water than it was to supply them with vodka. Then there is *glasnost'*, which is also not going according to plan. People are not exercising sufficient self-restraint. His wife wants to go on another shopping trip to Paris, since the years are passing, and if she doesn't keep up appearances in a few years' time she will again be upstaged in the beauty stakes by Nancy Reagan. He wouldn't mind a trip to Paris himself, but he cannot afford the time. Every day is taken up with promoting some new reform or other, sometimes even two or three. Also, he needs to keep an eye on his comrades. At the first opportunity they will accuse him of all sorts of deviation and get rid of him and he'll end up in Novodeviche beside Khrushchev instead of in the Kremlin wall. Just wait till he gets full power, however...

He decides to talk things over with his nextdoor neighbour and friend Petr Stepanovich Suslikov over a cup of tea. Suslikov is in charge of all the departments which monitor the West, educate it in a pro-Soviet direction, and exploit it in the interests of the Soviet people. Suslikov, of course, fawns and flatters Gorbachev, who is perplexed by the fact that *glasnost'* has led to a situation where only the failures of Communism are exposed and none of the achievements. They hit on the idea of exploiting favourable Western public opinion by turning a closed provincial town into a tourist attraction. Suslikov suggests Partgrad, since that is where he progressed from a rank-and-file spermatozoid to First Secretary of the Oblast Party Committee. If things work out, he reasons, it might even be renamed after himself – Suslikovgrad!

The main purpose of the project is to hoodwink the West. Zinoviev's contempt for Western public opinion can scarcely be exaggerated. In the Prologue he argues that the advent of Gorbachev heralds a new period in Soviet history. The first period – the era of concealment of defects – has come to an end. Henceforth defects will be acknowledged and laid bare. Laid bare for the benefit of the West, of course, since there is no need to reveal them to the Soviet population. This coincides with a change in the West, where people are no longer interested in the fact that life in the Soviet Union is bad, but in the fact that the Soviet Union officially acknowedges that things are bad. They have forgiven the Soviet Union for all the evil things which have happened there and (because of it) elsewhere, simply because it has admitted to a tiny part of that evil. Since this is now the way the West looks at things, why not invite as many Western tourists as possible to come and see for themselves how *perestroika* is working in practice, how people are confronting their huge problems, wrestling with these problems, bravely, courageously, openly, etc.?

The implementation of the plan is entrusted to Suslikov and he decides to call a meeting of his subordinates at which he can demonstrate the new approach to problem-solving in the *perestroika* era. Again what is most striking is the cynicism with which Suslikov exemplifies the 'new thinking':

... наша задача состоит в том, чтобы на конкретных примерах показатаь западным людям сущность и ход нашей перестройки...мы, товарищи, начали жить по-новому. Нам ничего скрывать не надо. Недостатки замазывать не следует, но и успехи таить не надо. Пусть иностранцы посмотрят учреждение, где процветает бюрократизм и коррупция, и учреждение, где эти пережитки прошлого уже преодолены. Пусть на живого взяточника поглядят. Можно и суд над ним показать. Западные люди любят такие зрелища...

(К:17)

...Our task is to show Western people on the basis of concrete examples what precisely our *perestroika* is and how it's developing... We have begun, Comrades, to live in a new way. We don't have to hide anything. We shouldn't try to cover up our defects, but nor should we conceal our successes. Let foreigners see an institution where bureaucracy and corruption are flourishing, and an institution where these defects from the past have already been overcome. Let them look at a real bribe-taker. You might also let them see his court case. Westerners love that kind of thing...

The whole purpose is to keep relations with the West in good order:

На данном этапе нашего развития... нам чрезвычайно важны дружеские отношения с западом. С его помощью мы быстрее и лучше преодолеем временно возникшие трудности.

(К:17–18)

At the current stage in our development... friendly relations with the West are extremely important for us. With its help we'll be able to resolve our temporary difficulties more quickly and successfully.

It is deemed necessary to send a commission from Moscow to oversee the implementation of the project *in situ* and Suslikov chooses his closest subordinate Korytov as Chairman. Since Korytov would be the first to oust Suslikov, given half a chance, Suslikov has to be careful how he briefs him on his mission. Korytov, however, has no difficulty in getting Suslikov's drift:

Перед тем, как пойти на радикальный поворот в нашей политической стратегии, мы должны были дать ясный ответ по крайней мере на такие вопросы: 1) сможем ли мы своими силами, без помощи преодолеть наши трудности или нет, 2) способны мы защитить себя с имеющимся у нас оружием или нет, 3) наступит в ближайшие годы экономический спад на западе или нет? По всем трем вопросам мы пришли к отрицательным выводам. Поэтому мы пошли на перестройку.

(K: 19)

Before introducing a radical change of course in our political strategy we had to have a clear answer to the following questions at least: 1) can we solve our own problems with our own resources, without the help of the West or not, 2) can we defend ourselves with the weaponry we've got at the moment or not, 3) is there going to be an economic decline in the West in the near future or not? We decided in all three cases that the answer was negative. Therefore we engaged in *perestroika*.

But:

Мы зашли слишком далеко. Перестройка породила непредвиденные последствия, угрожающие основам нашего социального строя. Ее минусы уже теперь очевидны, тогда как обещанные плюсы сомнительны. Если дело и дальше так пойдет, партия потеряет кредит доверия в массах населения...А главное - преодолеть кризисное состояние без использования наших собственных методов мы не можем, какой бы ни была помощь запада.

(К:20)

We went too far. *Perestroika* gave rise to unforeseen consequences which threaten the foundations of our social order. Its minuses are now clearly visible, while the pluses are doubtful. If things go on the way they are, the Party will lose the confidence of the mass of the population... But the most important thing is – we can't get on top of this crisis without using our own methods, no matter what help we get from the West.

The conclusion is clear: 'Prodolzhat' prezhnii kurs-znachit katit'sia k katastrofe. Nado gotovit'sia k povorotu' (K:20) ('Continuing on our present course means heading for disaster. We must be prepared for a radical reversal of policy').

One can imagine the dilemma facing many a Suslikov and Korytov in 1988. For careerists who had opted for the *perestroika* option, things were already looking less than rosy. Suslikov's reasoning is sound, if cynical. At what point, however, does the careerist actually change sides? Suslikov does not trust Korytov enough to feel that he can speak frankly. Korytov, on the other hand, is even less fortunate. It is all very well for his boss to tell him what the current thinking is (albeit in veiled fashion). No doubt he represents powerful forces in the apparatus of power, but which ones? Or is he secretly plotting? Korytov is clear about how he is going to act: 'Kak predannyi idealam kommunizma chlen partii, kak staryi apparatchik, kak russkii patriot on, Korytov, budet postupat' tak, kak podskazyvaet ego sovest'' (K:20) ('As a Party member dedicated to the ideals of Communism, as an old "apparatchik", as a Russian patriot, he, Korytov, would act as his conscience dictated'. In other words, he will look out for number one.

We already have a clear picture of the difficulties facing Mikhail Sergeevich. His closest associate and friend is a fawning careerist who apparently agrees with everything Gorbachev says, helps to plan a project in the spirit of the times, but then starts to undermine it, partly to safeguard his own position. Suslikov, in turn, cannot trust Korytov, who has even less reason to trust Suslikov and who will, therefore, look out for himself. The mixture of cynicism, unwillingness to take risks and duplicity is one with which we are by now familiar. The extent to which it is responsible for the increasing chaos in the Soviet Union we can only guess at, but we may suppose it to be anything but negligible.

THE HISTORY OF PARTGRAD [2]

Zinoviev has always been ambivalent about the value of history as a means of interpreting the present. On the one hand he has tended to regard sociology as more important in that respect. On the other, he has frequently used Soviet history as a means of explicating the Soviet present. He has always been careful, however, to distinguish between what he calls the 'froth' (what we would regard as history proper, i.e. the events which are deemed sufficiently worthy of note to be recorded, evaluated and commented upon) and the 'deep current' of the historical process (by which he means the unseen actions of millions of people whose activity constructs and maintains a particular social order). On the whole he has been inimical to theories of continuity, regarding the Soviet state as the embodiment of Communism, which was a social order built on the ruins of what had gone before and owing little, if anything, to the past. In his short 'history' of Partgrad Zinoviev has two digs at historical theory. He reverses the continuity argument by projecting Soviet attitudes back into the past and at the same time makes fun of Soviet historiography by satirising the 'Marxist-Leninist' perspective on Russian history.

The name Partgrad is perhaps not particularly amusing. It is not in the same league as the very funny list of place names associated with Vozhd' (Leader) which appears at the beginning of *V preddverii raia*. On the other hand it is the logical name for a town which has always named itself after the most important contemporary ruler. This becomes clear after reading the text devoted to the history of the toponym (K:23–5). In Kievan times the 'legendary Prince Oleg' (Kniaz' Oleg), on his way to do battle with the Khasars, stopped in 'some town or other', which then named itself Kniazev in his honour. When Ivan the Terrible took the title Tsar, Kniazev renamed itself Tsarev. After the 1917 Revolution it was re-christened Trotsky, then in succession Tukhachevsky, Ezhov, Dzhugashviligrad, Khrushchev, and Brezhnevsk. It was Andropov who ordered the town to be called Partgrad, assuming that this would be an appropriate way of continuing an old Russian tradition. How long the name will last, notes the chronicler, is a matter of some doubt. Applications to call it Gorbachevsk have been turned down since that name is reserved for his birthplace Stavropol'. The most likely candidate is Suslikovgrad.

The chronicles of Partgrad (K:26–9) underline its total isolation and insignincance. Information about it is contained in the earliest manuscripts, then nothing more is heard of the town until Partgrad scholars unearthed some material in connection with the celebrations of the 1,000 years of Christianity in Russia in 1988. Apparently the legendary Prince Igor, grandson of the legendary Prince Oleg, was baptised as a Christian two weeks ahead of the Kievan Prince Vladimir, who was dithering between adopting Christianity or Islam. Igor was apparently a reformer, too, in the Gorbachev mould. Thanks to his reforms, Partgrad was as advanced as anywhere else in the world of that time. Since the acme of progress was feudalism, there were slogans on the palace and church like 'Long live feudalism – the bright future of all mankind!', 'Forward to the victory of serfdom!' And of course, Prince Igor thought of opening a window to the West long before Peter the Great. The only problem was that he got the direction wrong and opened a window to Asia, as a result of which Partgrad was engulfed by a dark age, during which a 'period of stagnation' set in which lasted until Gorbachev himself. After the Mongol invasion there was another slogan which undertook to 'pay five years' tribute in four years'.[3]

In this harmless, amusing account of Partgrad history there is a hint of Zinoviev's scathing attitude towards his own people, which was very strongly expressed in earlier works, notably in *Zhelty dom*. It also, of course, makes fun of the Marxist theory of historical stages of development. In a 'commentary' (K:29), the narrator denies any similarity between the chronicle and Saltykov-Shchedrin's satire in the same vein, going on to point out that it is necessarily a simplified account of a long historical period. He then goes on to talk about a local Partgrad historian who had written a multi-volume history of the region, full of mind-numbing tedium and endless statistics about unbelievable trivia.

The 'history', of course, continues right up to the advent of *perestroika,* much of it written in the same vein as indicated above. But beneath the humour there is Zinoviev's continuing concern with what constitutes the 'Stoff' of history. This point is made seriously in the text entitled '*glubinnaia istoriia*' (roughly: 'the hidden depths of history'). Again he draws the distinction between 'froth' and 'current'. Writing about the historical events of the Soviet period, he says the following:

Но все то, о чем говорилось выше о советском периоде, составляло лишь ничтожную часть подлинной истории Партграда, причем – часть десятистепенной важности. Это была лишь пена партградской истории, а не ее глубинный поток. Последний заключался в том, что можно было назвать социальной жизнью масс населения, а именно – в различного рода социальных процедурах, ритуалах и мероприятиях, которые стали привычным элементом повседневной жизни людей: принятие в октябрята, в пионеры, в комосомол; октябрятские и пионерские сборы; комсомольские собрания; принятие в партию; партийные собрания; общественная работа; общие и профсоюзные собрания; митинги, демонстрации; пропагандистские кружки и семинары; комосомольские и партийные школы; университеты марксизма-ленинизма; заседания органов власти и управления на всех уровнях, начиная первичными коллективами и кончая высшими органами власти области; руководящие совещания, указания, контроль.

(K:51)

But everything that has been said above about the Soviet period relates to only a tiny part of the real history of

Partgrad, moreover a part of tenth-rate importance. That was merely the froth of Partgrad history, not its deep current. The latter consists in what might be called the day-to-day life of the mass of the population, namely the different procedures, rituals and undertakings which have become a familiar element of people's everyday lives: becoming an October Child, then a Pioneer, then a member of the Komsomol; October Children and Pioneer meetings, Komsomol meetings; joining the Party; Party meetings; community service; general meetings and meetings of the trade union; public meetings and demonstrations; propaganda circles and seminars; Komsomol and Party schools; universities of Marxism-Leninism; meetings of the organs of power and administration at all levels, beginning with the primary collectives and finishing with the highest organs of power in the region; management meetings, instructions, monitoring exercises.

That, for Zinoviev, is what Soviet history *is*, an endless round of ritual. It consists of the unimportant, the humdrum, the routine. Everything else is merely the means and the material needed to support that form of social life. Factories and enterprises are there primarily to provide a means of organising people into Communist collectives and only secondarily to engage in some kind of production. The amount of time and resources spent on Communist ritual far exceeds that spent on the mining of coal or the smelting of ore. If you add up the number of meetings at the various levels enumerated above, multiplied by the number of localities in the Soviet Union, multiplied by the number of years during which the Soviet Union has existed, says Zinoviev, you will get a sense of the type of progress achieved in Partgrad during the years of Soviet power. He has made this point before, but not quite with such eloquence. We might note that the advent of *perestroika* will, of course, have increased the number of meetings. The advent of *glasnost'* has increased (enormously) the range of permitted opinion, which in turn has led to a vastly more complicated situation than the one Gorbachev originally set out to improve. Before we consider, however, how Partgrad responded to the challenge of *perestroika*, we should note

Zinoviev's estimation of the nature of the crisis facing the Soviet Union.

As we noted in the previous chapter, he regards it as the first specifically *Communist* crisis in history.[4] His reasoning is as follows. World War Three did not happen. He had expected that it would. He had warned the West ever since his arrival there that the Soviet Union was preparing for that war and that it would probably win it, or at least not lose it, or at the very least survive it better than the West. Without an obviously much more prosperous West, the Communist authorities would be able to present Communist achievements as the pinnacle of human endeavour. But the war did not happen and the West became the yardstick for the measurement of progress. Moreover the pressure exerted by the West on Communist regimes, particularly in the area of human rights, became irresistible. There are many obvious signs of crisis: shortages, inflation, corruption, crime, ideological cynicism, and much else besides. But the specifically *Communist* feature of the crisis is the breakdown of the system of power.

In the absence of Western-type features like private enterprise, a property-owning class, a free market, political pluralism, etc., the administrative/power system takes on a particular role. It permeates every level and branch of society and becomes in effect the foundation of that society. The breakdown of that system beyond a certain point can lead to its destruction. What has happened is that the top leadership has lost control of the administrative system, and the administrative system no longer administers the administered. Why this has happened is to a large extent a consequence of the growing complexity of the system, a point made by many Western observers, who in the main, however, have not emphasised the extent to which the administrative system and the system of political power form an indivisible whole, nor the extent to which it permeates society.

His verdict on Gorbachev's reformist zeal is uncompromising:

Именно реформаторская активность Горбачева способствовала развязыванию кризиса. С нее потенциальный кризис превратился в актуальный, стал реальностью. Процесс вышел из-под контроля советского руководства и вынул его на такое поведение, о котором оно и не помышляло. Перестройка явилась попыткой предотвратить кризис, проявлением и следствием кризиса, а когда кризис стал фактом – попыткой выйти из него на пути поверхностной, иллюзорной и принудительной западнизации советского общества.

(К:62)

It was precisely Gorbachev's reformist zeal which provoked the crisis. Because of it, a potential crisis has become a real one. The whole process has escaped the control of the Soviet leadership and forced it to behave in a way it had never dreamed of. *Perestroika* was an attempt to avert a crisis, then a manifestation of a crisis, then the result of a crisis, and when the crisis became a fact, *perestroika* became an attempt to resolve it by means of a superficial, illusory and enforced Westernisation of Soviet society.

For Zinoviev, however, the crisis is temporary. He is not ready to concede that the Communist era is over. As he observes of the citizens of Partgrad through his narrator:

Им было безразлично, как называется то свинство, в котором они жили испокон веков и обречены жить до скончания века, – крепостничеством, военным коммунизмом, развитым социализмом или посткоммунизмом.

(К: 165)

It was all the same to them what you called the swinish conditions in which they had lived since time immemorial and in which they were destined to live eternally – serfdom, War, Communism, developed socialism or post-Communism.

PERESTROIKA IN PARTGRAD

Given Zinoviev's interminable 'text', he is paradoxically delightfully succinct. His text entitled '*Katastroika*' (K:69–70) encapsulates the difficulties Gorbachev's reforms have en-

countered from the start, exemplified by their reception in
Partgrad. The main difficulty is their interpretation by
ordinary Soviet citizens who have been well used over the
decades to various hare-brained schemes devised by 'Them
Up There'. Pensioners and old Party members regard the
reforms as counter-revolutionary and a betrayal of Lenin.
The *glasnost'* campaign leads to the besmirching of all the
ideals of Communism. The 'informal' groups which mush-
roomed out of nowhere, and which were previously vilified
as a manifestation of the corrupting influence of the West,
offend ordinary citizens. When people begin to lose their
jobs and certain enterprises are shut down as ecomonically
unviable, something akin to panic sets in.

Krutov, Gorbachev's placement as Oblast Party Committee Chairman, cannot afford to report this state of affairs
to Moscow in case he is branded as a conservative and
opponent of *perestroika*. He appeals instead for calm, basing
his plea on the cynical argument that things will 'blow over'.
Alcohol will be forthcoming, even if they have to mine it out
of the ground. The bureaucrats who have lost their jobs will
be found new ones. Factories which have shut down will re-
open with new names. The local youth will discover that
rock music and chewing gum are not enough. They will
have to acquire an education, a training, a job, a career, in
short they will have to learn to live according to the real laws
of life (i.e. communal laws) and not according to short-lived
slogans (K:70).

One may suppose that Krutov represents a large number
of Soviet Party functionaries. Again we are confronted with
the problem of Soviet discourse. The Krutovs can instantly
pay lip-service to the ideals of *perestroika* and go out of their
way to undermine it. We may easily imagine the countless
meetings at which Soviet colleagues parade their support of
perestroika in front of each other, while everyone remembers
the occasions at which the same colleagues paraded their
support of 'trust in cadres' or the invasion of Czechoslovakia
or Afghanistan.

Until 'things blow over', however, Partgrad has to be seen
to be implementing the programme of *perestroika* dictated
by Moscow. Zinoviev's account is both highly amusing and
highly plausible. At first the authorities assume that it is just

another campaign ordered by Moscow and adopt their usual attitude. There are meetings at every level of the regional administrative apparatus to discuss 'implementation'. Every enterprise and factory initiates a programme of *perestroika* which is, of course, merely a simulacrum of such a programme; everyone is aware that it will be quite impossible to change things in reality. Thus certain leadership posts are suppressed and others set up. People are forced to retire who were already on their last legs anyway. People are accused of corruption who are already facing such charges or have been sent to prison or labour camps, and so on. This time, however, things turn out to be different. Moscow seems to be in earnest about its programme, and this causes a certain amount of alarm, again because it is clear that nothing fundamental can be done to change the way Partgrad life is conducted. People begin to worry seriously about their own position. Everyone becomes volubly in favour of *perestroika*. Everyone begins to berate 'conservatives' and 'reactionary elements' and to call for 'a new way of thinking and acting'. The result is entirely predictable. The wiliest, most cynical careerists come out on top. There is an increase in inefficiency, confusion, empty chatter, eye-wash and corruption. In order not to have to lay the blame at the feet of the entire Communist system, scapegoats are found and scores are settled. Amusing as Zinoviev's account undoubtely is, Partgrad life as he describes it is entirely within the bounds of plausibility, and indeed even the most cursory reading of current Soviet publications (which need not even include notoriously outspoken ones such as *Ogonek* or *Argumenty i fakty*) will provide convincing corroboration of this claim. As Zinoviev has predicted from the beginning, any relaxation of central authority in a Communist system simply allows the laws of communalism to operate with even greater force.

Having given a general picture of Partgrad's attitude towards *perestroika* as a whole, Zinoviev then devotes a series of texts to an analysis of individual parts of Gorbachev's programme, dealing in turn with the anti-alcohol campaign (K:70–2), the fight against bureaucratism (K:73), *glasnost'* (K:75–6) and economic reform (K:77–9).

Lack of space unfortunately makes it impossible to present an analysis of each of these texts. Like the majority of texts in this work they make serious points in a highly amusing manner. The outcome of the anti-alcohol campaign is an increase in the amount and intensity of alcoholism, in the manufacture of truly dangerous beverages from toothpaste and old gramophone records, as well as a rise in alcohol-related crime. The fight against bureaucracy is hopeless from the start, since bureaucracy is endemic to Communism and cannot be seriously reduced. The apparent struggle *against* bureaucracy is in reality a fight *among* bureaucrats. The campaign for *glasnost'*, having got off to a sticky start because of local bewilderment at the idea of actually reporting disasters and the like, leads to a 'hurricane' of disclosures of drug-taking, prostitution and homosexuality, ending in a sharp rise in prostitution after a local newspaper interviews two old prostitutes and records that their earnings from prostitution exceed the salaries of professors, engineers, stewardesses and even pilots (K:76). As for the economic reform, attempts to make use of imported, electronically operated factory equipment founder under Soviet conditions, since the quality-control robot rejects every Soviet-produced component offered for inspection. The Soviet solution, however, is to lock the robot-arm permanently in a position from which it can no longer actually reach the components (K:78)!

In a text devoted to the dilemma of the provincial careerist-bureaucrat (K:74–5), Zinoviev makes a point about *perestroika* which is worth describing in some detail. Krutov, Gorbachev's man-in-charge in Partgrad, takes his orders from Suslikov and is desperate to do Moscow's bidding. Moscow, however, does not seem to be of one mind. The guidelines given to him by Suslikov seem ambiguous. On the one hand he is supposed to promote *perestroika* more vigorously, but on the other he is advised not to be too zealous about it, to conserve experienced cadres and not to neglect the political education of the population in the required direction. Krutov's solution is to interfere less and less in the day-to-day administration of his fiefdom. At all levels of the administrative appartus, in factories and enterprises, the process of 'doing things for show' (*pokazukha*) becomes so refined, on such a scale, that some people even begin to be taken in by the gigantic imitation of *perestroika* and to regard it as the real thing. And at some point the switch occurs. The limits of the possible are breached and the imitation of the positive intentions of *perestroika* become in fact a genuine regional crisis. People no longer believe that as a result of the reforms life will improve, but, on the contrary, and thanks to the stupidity of the Gorbachev leadership, that life has become much worse. The crisis has been induced from above, it has not developed spontaneously in the region. Partgrad has slowly and steadily been enmeshed in a crisis which germinated in what first seemed to be the usual empty talk, originating in the highest reaches of power, about the need for reforms.

Thus far we have been considering Zinoviev's scathing account of how Partgrad reacted to the earlier part of Gorbachev's campaign of reform, i.e. to his battles with alcoholism and bureaucracy. We now turn to his account of Partgrad's implementation of the full programme of *perestroika*. One string of texts is devoted to a description of attempts on the part of the authorities to reform various institutions such as those connected with the administration of justice, the church, the crematorium 'complex', the old people's home, and so on.[6] Another describes the antics and aspirations of various 'informal groups' which spring up in the new conditions of freedom of speech and freedom of assembly.[7] With these two strings Zinoviev neatly captures Gorbachev's central dilemma. On the one hand the authorities are incapable of implementing his reforms and/or unwilling to do so. On the other, the fantastic growth of 'informal groups' beyond central (Party) control creates enormous counter-pressure, leading rapidly to the chaos which now engulfs the Soviet Union.

Again constraints of space impose the need to be selective in our treatment of these two strings. Not all of the texts are equally funny. His descriptions of *perestroika* in the church and the crematorium complex are exaggerated and in questionable taste. On the other hand, his description of the administration of justice and reform of the psychiatric hospital is highly amusing. Once more his contempt for Soviet liberals comes to the fore. His account of liberal ideas for *perestroika* in the area of penal reform is highly sarcastic.

Defendants when arrested consult their lawyers, then go off
to a rest-home while preparations for the trial are made.
They have the right to choose the judge as well as the jury.
Any judge who has been rejected three times is disqualified.
Prisoners will regulate their own activities in prisons, which
will be free of barred windows and other features which
offend their dignity as prisoners. They will be allowed
freedom of movement and activity for twelve hours per day,
and so on.

In the psychiatric hospital the inmates are not told about
perestroika, but more and more patients arrive who imagine
themselves to be Gorbachev, Yeltsin, Sakharov, Solzhenitsyn, Trotsky, Bukharin, Nicholas II, Anastasia, Stolypin
and others who, formerly denounced as reactionaries, enemies of the people and traitors, are now the innocent victims
of the Stalinist terror, ideological opponents of Stalinism,
and geniuses singing the praises of Gorbachev's *perestroika*.
They are not easy to distinguish from ordinary supporters of
perestroika, and the population takes the ravings of the
mental patients to be the further development of Gorbachev's ideas. Moreover, the new patients demand control
of their own affairs, the non-interference of the medical
staff in the 'healing process', the transfer of the hospital to
a regime of 'self-healing' by analogy with 'self-financing' in
industry, and the freedom to go mad as an inalienable
human right. All the other patients regard this as counter-
revolution and demand the introduction of martial law. As a
consequence they are released and the streets of Partgrad
begin to be filled with Napoleons, Lenins, Robespierres,
Khomeinis, Mao Tse-tungs, Hitlers, Mussolinis and other
representatives of a bygone age. They create such chaos that
ordinary citizens begin to ask to be committed to the
psychiatric hospital, since according to rumour there is now
full democracy there.

If Zinoviev's descriptions of Partgrad institutions under
perestroika are hilarious, his account of the antics of the
various democratic movements are even funnier. Occasionally, however, in the midst of laughter, we suddenly
realise that Zinoviev's descriptions are in fact uncomfortably
close to the truth. When he describes the local nationalities
question (K:117–8) and the local national minority's de-

mands for autonomy, the right to use their own language, to have their own constitution and currency (convertible, moreover!), the reader is reminded of the real demands of some of the real national minorities.

The Partgrad equivalent of 'Pamiat'', like its Moscow namesake, begins by restoring historical monuments. Since there are very few of those, however, it rapidly proceeds to the anti-Semitic phase of its programme. However, there are very few Jews in Partgrad, and even they have forgotten that they are Jewish. This is proof of Jewish cunning! Partgrad is too good for Jews! Partgrad's swinish conditions are only good enough for long-suffering Russians! The Jews have all dug themselves in in Moscow, nearer to the West!

The local democrats fare no better at Zinoviev's hands. After they publish their democratic programme which, among other things, calls for the end of the one-party system, privatisation of state-owned property and the re-moval of the command function from the local organs of power, Partgrad citizens become swamped in discussion of such questions as: What does one do if the workers refuse to join another party? What means of production are going to be handed over to teachers, doctors, policemen, book-keepers, actors? Who is going to be in charge of industrial production? What happens to the railway and the airline services? Who gets the prisons and the labour camps?

It is noteworthy that, whereas Zinoviev makes fun of 'nationalists', 'democrats' and 'liberals' in *Katastroika*, he tends to be sympathetic to what one might call the 'Nina Andreeva' viewpoint, expressed by the 'neo-Communists' and the 'neo-Stalinists', young people under the age of twenty, who are shocked by the behaviour of their elders (K:93, 123).[8] This no doubt reflects Zinoviev's growing sense of outrage at the extent to which under Gorbachev everything Soviet is denigrated. No one has subjected the Soviet system to more merciless analysis than Zinoviev, yet he cannot stomach the way in which those who formerly sang its praises can effortlessly switch to showering abuse upon it. There is real feeling in the following passage which forms part of the 'neo-Stalinists'' call-to-arms:

Неужели все прожитое нашей страной есть лишь черный провал в истории?! Неужели наши прадеды напрасно шли на виселицы, в тюрьмы, на каторгу?! Неужели был ошибкой выстрел Авроры ?! Неужели наши деды ни за что погибли на фронтах Гражданской войны, мерзли, голодали, жертвовали самым дорогим в жизни и самими жизнями?! Неужели были впустую пятилетки и великие стройки, массовый героизм и энтузиазм?! Неужели зазря погибли миллионы наших отцов, матерей, братьев и сестер на фронтах Отечественной войны?! Зря горели в самолетах, бросались со связками гранат под вражеские танки?! Разгром фашизма – зто тоже не в счет?! А покорение космоса?! А тот факт, что на нас боятся напасть?! Мы пережили страшную, но великую историю. Любой другой народ гордился бы такой историей. А мы? Что делаем мы? Мы сами черним и оплевываем нашу великую и многострадальную историю. И инициатива этого осквернения исходит сверху, от циничных и тщеславных карьеристов и авантюристов, готовых за ничтожную похвалу на Западе предать все то, за что жертвовали жизнью наши прадеды, деды, отцы. Позор этим изменникам! Мы, внуки и правнуки их, протестуем против этого. Защитим дело Леина и Сталина от предателей!

(К:123)

Has everything that our country has suffered merely been a dreadful historical failure?! Did our forefathers go to the gallows, to prison, to exile and hard labour in vain?! Was the shot fired by the *Aurora* really a mistake?! Did our grandfathers die fighting in the Civil War for nothing?! Did they freeze, go hungry, sacrifice what was dearest to them in this life and life itself for nothing?! Were the five-year plans, the 'great constructions', the heroism and enthusiasm of the masses merely a waste of time?! Was it for nothing that millions of our fathers, mothers, brothers and sisters died in the Great Fatherland War?! Did they burn in aeroplanes, throw themselves with a grenade under enemy tanks for nothing?! Does the destruction of fascism also count for nothing?! What about the conquest of space?! And the fact that people were afraid to attack us?! We have

lived through a terrible history, but a great one. Any other
nation would have been proud of such a history. But are
we? What do we do? We ourselves blacken our great, long-
suffering history and spit all over it. And the initiative has
come from above, from cynical and vain careerists and
adventurers who are ready to betray everything for which
our forefathers, grandfathers and fathers sacrificed their
lives in exchange for worthless praise from the West.
Shame on these traitors! We, their grandchildren and
great grandchildren protest. We will defend the cause of
Lenin and Stalin from those who would betray it!

As someone who was proud to defend his country and share
in a large part of Soviet history, there is little doubt that
Zinoviev has a great deal of understanding for such sentiments. There can be little doubt, also, that millions of Soviet
citizens share those sentiments.

The state of affairs in Partgrad degenerates to the point
where only the priests can save the town from religious
obscurantism, only the neo-Stalinists can save it from the
excesses of democracy, and only the mafia can protect it
from the efforts of private entrepreneurs. Krutov gives up
any attempt to control events and spends the day fishing or
drinking vodka in his office. It is at this point that Suslikov
telephones him to warn him that a commission is coming
from Moscow.

THE MOSCOW COMMISSION IN PARTGRAD [9]

The final part of *Katastroika* relates the attempt on the part of
the authorities, with the help of the Moscow commission, to
turn Partgrad into a 'Potemkin village' for Western visitors.[10]
Zinoviev uses the clever device of different tourist itineraries
to provide the framework for systematic comment on Partgrad's attempt to hoodwink the foreigners. The itineraries
are as follows: (a) the Partgrad sights; (b) Partgrad industry;
(c) Partgrad living conditions; (d) Partgrad culture; (e)
Partgrad's care of the elderly and its provision for the spiritual needs of its citizenry; (f) the Partgrad labour-camp; (g)
Partgrad farming; (h) privatisation in Partgrad. As we see,

Zinoviev gives himself ample scope for satire.

The whole Partgrad project is based, of course, on deception. But the deception is multi-layered. There is the level at
which, say, the workers deceive the management by pretending to work. The management reciprocates by pretending to
pay, as the old joke has it. Within the power apparatus
subordinates deceive their superiors and vice-versa. When
the commission comes from Moscow, Partgrad functionaries
are fully aware of the need to deceive them too. But the
members of the commission have got where they are by
climbing a bit higher up the same career ladder and are
aware of all the tricks. Now forces have to be joined in order
to deceive the foreigners. The business of deception, of
imitation, however, is one in which they are far in advance
of the West and neither Korytov (head of the commission)
nor Krutov are in any doubt that they will succeed.

There are, of course, certain logistical problems. One is
the empty shops. Another is the completely run-down nature
of Partgrad industry. A third is the dreadful housing. A
fourth is the fact that the era of *perestroika* has arrived.
Previously deceptions mounted for visiting dignitaries had
a strict time-limit. Selected shops were stocked just before a
visit and destocked just after. But *perestroika* shows no sign of
ending, so there will be a problem keeping the shops which
foreigners visit permanently stocked. Fortunately there is a
local shady operator who will be able to solve the problem,
given police and KGB protection. Other problems are less
easily solved, such as run-down factories and the dreadful
housing. The solution is to put up hoarding where possible
and to blame things on the 'period of stagnation' in cases
where concealment is not possible. Zinoviev's point is that
perestroika and the 'new thinking' have changed nothing.
The time-honoured, tried and tested procedures of cover-
up and prevarication continue to be applied.

The Moscow commission's tour of all the projected itineraries provides ample scope for mockery of the West and
mockery of the excesses of *perestroika*. We have already
touched on examples. Again not all the itineraries are
equally funny, but taken together they provide an im-
pressively sarcastic critique. Particular mention should perhaps be made of the cultural programme. Zinoviev, for all

the examples of scatology in his own works, has no time for
gratuitous vulgarity. He shows little but contempt for avant-
garde Soviet theatre and cinema, much of which he regards
as poor imitation of Western mediocrity. Two blisteringly
scathing texts deal with Soviet theatre and cinema respectively (K:154–7, 157–8). The first describes a contemporary play entitled '*Krovavoe koleso*' (*The Wheel of Blood*),
and the second a contemporary film with the title of '*Poshel
ty v zhopu!*' (*Up Your Arse!*)

The play purports to criticise the falsifiers of Soviet
history by enacting it in a provocatively forthright way,
which is supposed to 'put the record straight'. It contains
Soviet versions of audience participation. Actors wear offensively smelly clothes and mingle with the audience, challen-
ging individuals to answer the question 'What did *you* do
during the period of stagnation?' Members of the audience
who are overcome by the smell are led off to the sound of
actors chanting 'How do you think your victims felt?' Old
people suspected of being Stalinists or Brezhnevites are
hauled onto the stage and roundly mocked. The whole
spectacle radiates crudity, falsity and mediocrity. Korytov
thinks that it will go down well with Western audiences and
that it will enable the Partgrad authorities to kill three birds
with one stone. First, they will earn some hard currency;
secondly, they will appear to demonstrate a critical attitude
to their own past; thirdly, they will appear to permit a
hitherto unimaginable degree of artistic freedom.

The film is even more vulgar and we are not even told
what it purports to be about. All we learn is that it consists
largely of swear-words and naked love scenes. Korytov thinks
that it should be the Soviet entry to the Cannes Film Festival,
as an example of how the Soviet Union is becoming like the
West. His reasoning is as follows:

На Западе смотрят на нас, как на дикарей. Если мы
начинаем делать что-то похожее на них, они начинают
похлопывать нас по плечу и награждать премиями наше
запоздалое дерьмо. А если уже делать дерьмо, то в этом
отношении мы можем перегнать запад в два счета. Одним
словом, додермим и передермим запад в культуре, – вот
наша установка на данном этапе.   (К: 158)

The West thinks of us as savages. If we begin to copy them, they clap us on the shoulder and award us prizes for our somewhat belated crap. And if it comes to producing crap, we can overtake the West in two ticks. In a word, our current line is to out-crap the West in the cultural field.

One of the Partgrad retinue recalls with a sigh a time when the Soviet cinema produced films which amazed the whole world. Korytov's ironic rejoinder is that it was during the 'cult of personality', when people still had ideals, when they did not hanker after the West, when... He leaves the end of his thought unspoken, but everyone understands anyway.

Here we may draw our analysis of *Katastroika* to a close. On the whole it is a very successful work of satire. As we observed at the beginning of this chapter, the structure is admirably simple, yet allows Zinoviev tremendous scope. His verdict on *perestroika* as it developed up until the time of the 19th Party Conference is unmistakable. It has been a catastrophic miscalculation on the part of the Gorbachev leadership. Gorbachev has tried to solve Communist problems by looking for non-Communist solutions – and has demonstrably failed.

On the other hand, Zinoviev has not yet conceded that Communism as a social order is finished. On the contrary, at the time of writing *Katastroika*, he believes that it will survive the current crisis – but only via a return to Communist methods, by which he means an end to *glasnost'*, the reimposition of central control and the re-establishment of an adequate ideology. There are many in the Soviet Union who would agree with him. There are also signs that the Communist Party, at least in the Russian Federation, is beginning to regain confidence. There is a general consensus that freedom of expression is being curtailed. There has been the re-imposition of centralised television programmes, denuded of serious current affairs programmes. There has been the mysterious shooting of the popular presenter of the Leningrad television programme '600 Seconds'. There has been concern expressed about the threatened closure of printing presses.[11] There is Gorbachev's clear alignment with forces on the political right. There have been the attempts to muzzle Boris Yeltsin, the very one-

sided media run-up to Gorbachev's March 1991 referen-
dum, to give but a few examples. There is the growing
disaffection of the Soviet population, the widespread detes-
tation of Gorbachev himself and his policies. The ideals of
socialism and Communism are still espoused by many.
Above all there is the economic base, still largely totalitarian. The prospects for capitalist solutions like free mar-
kets, private ownership, competition, and so on, are bleak
indeed. Zinoviev's belief in the validity of his model continues to be justified.

One should note, however, a distinct change in tone.
Zinoviev is nothing if not a loner. For much of his life he has
spoken out at a time when it was least safe to do so. He
pilloried the Brezhnev era when Brezhnev was still in power,
simultaneously pillorying the Stalin and Khrushchev eras
when it was forbidden to do so. He has very little time for
the 'jackals' who attack the lion once it is dead. Indeed,
when the 'jackals' attack, Zinoviev characteristically defends
the object of their attack. As we noted earlier, he was anti-
Stalinist when it was unfashionable, but defended Stalin
against those who attacked him when it was safe to do so. He
mercilessly dissected Communism when it was forbidden to
do so. Now when it is under constant attack, again when it is
'safe', Zinoviev is prepared to launch a counter-attack. He is
not pro-Communist, but he is against those who seek to
besmirch Communism in the pursuit of purely private,
selfish goals. Rightly or wrongly, he sees Gorbachev as first
and foremost a Party careerist who took a cynical gamble –
and who is likely to lose. The price, however, has had to be
paid by the Soviet population, which he now regards as
much worse off than under Brezhnev. None of what has
happened since 1985 has surprised him. The general outcome of attempts to reform a Communist system has been
predicted by him since *Ziiaiushchie vysoty*. His apparent
sympathy for the neo-Stalinists and neo-Communists is based
on his respect for people who stick by their beliefs. He does
not share those beliefs, but he is prepared to speak up in the
defence of those who do.

How realistic is the picture offered by *Katastroika*, shorn
of its humour? Is Zinoviev's caricature of *perestroika* not as
one-sided as the current Soviet picture of the Soviet past?

Surely *perestroika* has not been all bad? The quite amazing freedoms which have emerged from the expansion of *glasnost* and democratisation are surely worth a great deal? No doubt the answers to the last three questions , from a Western viewpoint. are respectively 'yes', 'no' and 'yes'. Yet, from the viewpoint of the average Soviet citizen, the answers are perhaps not so clear-cut. Moreover, Zinoviev has quite rightly been concerned to criticise what he regards as the negative sides of *perestroika*. If his picture is one-sided, it is because he concentrates on how *perestroika* affects the Communist social order as an organism, not on how it affects individuals living on the margins of Communist society. His 'social laws' continue to operate under *perestroika*. We can safely assume that they will continue to operate in the era of 'post-Communism'.

This term is now widely current in the West. It is referred to scathingly by Zinoviev at least twice in *Katastroika*. Zbigniew Bzrezinski has written a book entitled *The Grand Failure: The Birth and Death of Communism in the Twentieth Century* (Brzezinski, 1989). Zinoviev has riposted with *Il superpotere in URSS: il communismo è veramente tramontato?* (Zinoviev, 1990f). In the final chapter of this volume we shall discuss these books in an attempt to evaluate the extent to which Zinoviev's model of Communism can be said to have lasting validity.

9 *Konets kommunizma?*

In this chapter the debate is about the future of Communism. Zbignew Brzezinski, Director of the National Security Council in the Carter administration and currently a member of President Bush's Foreign Intelligence Advisory Board, has made a strong case for the failure of Communism in his book *The Grand Failure* (TGF), completed in August 1988 and published in 1989. Zinoviev has responded with a book entitled *Konets kommunizma?* (*The End of Communism?*), published in 1990 in Italian under the title *Il superpotere in URSS: il communismo è veramente tramontato?* (*Superpower in the USSR: Has the Sun Really Set over Communism?*) (henceforth IS). The question mark in the title of Zinoviev's book is rhetorical rather than interrogatory.[1] Brzezinski, for his part, is in no doubt about the demise of Communism:

> Humanity's catastrophic encounter with communism during the twentieth century has thus provided a painful but critically important lesson: Utopian social engineering is fundamentally in conflict with the complexity of the human condition, and social creativity blossoms best when political power is restrained. That basic lesson makes it all the more likely that democracy – and not communism – will dominate the twenty-first century.
>
> (TGF:258)

Brzezinski develops his argument under six headings: the political and socio-economic failure of the Soviet system; current Soviet attempts to reform and revitalise that system; the social and political consequences of the imposition of Communism on Eastern Europe; the Chinese experience; the ideological and political decline of international Communist appeal; Communism's final agony. Within that particular framework he focuses on ten interlocking debates in the Soviet Union which have produced what he calls the Ten Dynamics of Disunion. These are: economic reform; social priorities; political democratisation; role of the Party;

221

ideology, religion and culture; history (or Stalinism); internal national problems; domestic concerns over the war in Afghanistan; foreign and defence policy; the Soviet bloc and the world Communist movement (TGF:65–6).

The scope of Brzezinski's book is wider than Zinoviev's. The latter writer in *Il superpotere in URSS* focuses almost exclusively on the situation in the Soviet Union. Clearly, however, there is a great deal of overlap, most obviously related to the ten areas of debate alluded to above. But there is also a difference of focus. Brzezinski's approach inclines more to the historical, Zinoviev's more to the sociological. Nevertheless, for all that these two writers come to different conclusions, there are important areas of agreement, or at least proximity of views. Since much of this chapter considers how these two authors differ in their opinions, it will be useful to establish at the outset the areas where they do not.

For a start, Brzezinski seems to agree with two fundamental positions of Zinoviev's, namely that the nationwide consolidation of the Communist system was more important than the social and cultural innovation that dominated life in Moscow, Leningrad and a few other large cities (TGF:19), and that the 1930s, despite the atrocities associated with that decade, are still perceived by millions of Soviet citizens as a time of real accomplishment of which they can justifiably be proud (TGF:27–8). There is also broad agreement on other important issues. For instance, Zinoviev would have no objection to the following observation: 'The political obstacles to a real *perestroika* are... not only formidable but probably insurmountable' (TGF:48). He would also broadly agree with the following: 'Contrary to widespread Western speculation that the Soviet Politburo was split between "reformers" in favor of change and "reactionaries" wedded to the status quo, most top Soviet leaders accepted by the mid 1980s the need for renewal – for *perestroika* of the Soviet system – as a necessity' (TGF:54). Zinoviev says much the same thing (Zinoviev, 1990a:474): 'In Western eyes the Soviets are divided into those who are "for" *perestroika*, the reformers, and those who are "against", the conservatives. In reality, apart from a few extreme cases, this division does not exist... All Soviet leaders have the same objectives.' Two other areas in which there is substantial agreement include their recognition of the alleged 'moral rot' which is the product of Communist ideology, and the discovery by the Soviet population of the advantages of egalitarianism and the consequent reluctance to go down the capitalist road.[2]

Before we turn our attention to *Il superpotere in URSS* and consider the areas of *dis*agreement, it will be useful to summarise Brzezinski's argument in support of his thesis that Communism has failed and that the future for democracy is bright.

His case rests on two propositions: first, that there has been a growing discrepancy between Communist theory and Communist practice; secondly, that Communist regimes have been discredited by their abysmal human rights record. The early success of Communism is attributable to the fact that Communist theory seemed to work. As Brzezinski points out, the outcome of the Second World War enhanced enormously the prestige of the Soviet Union and the next four decades saw everywhere an increase in the inclination to rely on state action to cope with economic or social ills (TGF:9). The tendency to embrace one form or another of state socialism also proved irresistible in the case of the scores of newly created post-colonial states, many of whom looked to the Soviet experience for inspiration and adopted it uncritically. At the same time, much Western intellectual opinion looked upon the Soviet Union with an approval which dated back to the 1920s and 1930s, and political leftism enjoyed particular popularity on the campuses in the 1960s and 1970s. By the 1980s, however, it was no longer possible to disguise the extent of the Communist crisis.

The crisis grew out of the discrepancy between theory and practice, but the reason for the growth of that discrepancy Brzezinski sees as largely the inability of the Soviet socio-political system, as conceived by Lenin and developed by Stalin, to adapt to the accelerating pace of technological advance and the complexity of modern urban society, quite apart from the moral issues of human rights, respect for the individual, etc.

In the course of his book Brzezinski documents the extent to which Communist leaders have abandoned the

dogmas of Communist ideology.[3] Much of his case for the
demise of the Communist movement rests on the extent to
which the ideological doctrine has turned out to be unrealis-
able in practice. Communism as an ideology is thus dead
and can no longer serve as a model for the world. The other
main reason why Communism is unlikely to attract in the
future is its historical record as regards the imposition of
social change. Brzezinski presents an impressive list of
headings (summary executions, executions of political opponents, extermination of all people belonging to various
social categories deemed to be potentially hostile) under
which the cost in terms of human suffering becomes starkly
clear (TGF:239–40).

Such, in skeletal form, is Brzezinski's argument. Obviously this account does it much less than justice, and it
should be emphasised that he makes a strong case for his
point of view. His position, however, is open to challenge
and we shall review that position in the light of our discussion of *Il superpotere in URSS*, to which we now turn.

The book consists of some 86 texts, each with its own title,
the texts themselves taking the form of short essays. We thus
have a book in the mould of *Kommunizm kak real'nost'* and
Gorbachevizm. As the author says himself, the book consists
of two parts, the first of which sets out a description of 'real'
Communism in a fashion which best illustrates the 'crisis' in
Communism. The second part of the book provides an
anatomy of that crisis.

It should be stated at the outset that *Il superpotere in URSS*
is fascinating for two reasons. First, it contains much evidence of what can only be termed Zinoviev's 'revisionism'.
Secondly, it contains an unmistakable note of *sympathy* for
the state in which Communism currently finds itself, intima-
tions of which we discovered in our analysis of *Katastroika*.
The change of tone, however, is occasionally quite staggering, being at times indistinguishable from that of the worst
kind of anti-Western Soviet propaganda associated with the
era of the Cold War. His sympathies are quite clearly with
people like Nina Andreeva and Egor Ligachev (to whom he
refers with approval (IS:148)). Clearly Zinoviev is affronted
at the rate at which the Gorbachev leadership has unleashed
forces it can no longer control, and is appalled by the great

damage it has done to the Communist social order in the Soviet Union, not to mention the current demise of Communism in Eastern Europe.

The author's attempt to account for what he steadfastly defines as a 'crisis', rather than a 'failure', brings him face to face with positions which he has defended in the past and which are now clearly untenable. He is quite prepared to abandon them where necessary. However, we cannot help but observe the development of a tendency on the part of Zinoviev to dress up mere description in the guise of 'objective laws'. These 'laws', as displayed by Zinoviev in the work under discussion, occasionally reek of 'ad hocery'. On the other hand, the book also contains many convincing passages on the origin and nature of the Communist crisis, and successfully (on the whole) argues that that crisis is more a result of the growing pains of Communism, rather than a manifestation of its death agonies. His conclusion, thus, is diametrically opposed to Brzezinski's. Our analysis will be conducted along two lines. We shall chart the nature and extent of Zinoviev's revisionism and the consequent changes which need to be introduced into his model of Communism. Secondly, we shall compare and contrast Zinoviev's main arguments with those of Zbigniew Brzezinski as contained in *The Grand Failure*. These two lines of analysis will not necessarily be kept separate.

We have already alluded to Brzezinski's 'Ten Dynamics of Disunion'. Most of the 86 texts in *Il superpotere in URSS* can be grouped around the following themes: the Party, the State, power, the economy, ideology, origins of the crisis, society, ways out of the crisis. We shall consider those themes below, but first we should note Zinoviev's remarks on what he calls the 'roots' of Communism, since they form the basic premise on which his argument rests, a premise very different from Brzezinski's.

Zinoviev says nothing about the 'roots of Communism' which he has not said many times before. We recall that, for Zinoviev, a Communist society is one in which his famous 'social laws' or 'laws of communalism' predominate. These laws, however, are universal, and thus operate at all times and in all places, given sufficiently large numbers of people living in a community. Zinoviev is thus not surprised that

Communism made its first appearance, not in the capitalist West (as erroneously foretold by Marx), but in backward Russia, with a long history of communalist tendencies: a powerful, centralised state apparatus, an army of officials which could be regarded as a separate social class, a population accustomed to submitting to authority, a peasant commune. Nor is he surprised that Communism was a temptation for countries in which capitalism was only weakly developed, if at all (IS:19). Brzezinski, on the other hand, argues that Communism was generically related to Fascism and Nazism, historically linked and 'politically quite similar' (TGF:6). 'They were all responses to traumas of the industrial age, to the appearance of millions of rootless, first-generation industrial workers, to the iniquities of early capitalism, and to the newly acute sense of class-hatred bred by these conditions.' Moreover, the totalitarian regimes in Russia and Germany developed directly from the application by Lenin, and later Hitler, of the combination of a militarised vanguard party and the construction of a state based on terror. For Zinoviev, the Communist state is a natural product of the unfettered 'laws of communalism', for Brzezinski the product of the policies of a particular individual, Lenin.

THE PARTY [4]

Zinoviev's basic view of the Party remains unchanged: a distinction needs to be made between the primary Party organisations and the Party apparatus. The former constitute an element in the social organisation of the population, the latter is a part of the government apparatus, and indeed its core. As long as the social basis of Communism is preserved, something similar will always exist, whether it be called the Communist Party or not, namely a means of separating out the activists in the collectives and of forming a core element within the power structure (IS:42). Such is Zinoviev's view of the Communist Party under conditions of what he would call 'real Communism'. It is essentially non-elective, centralised and monolithic.

Under Gorbachev, of course, the Party has become democratised, decentralised and pluralistic. Zinoviev clearly sees this development as particularly dangerous for the future of Communism as he understands it: 'The crisis has affected to the strongest degree the very core of [the power system] – the Party apparat. It has lost its former control of the power system and has been cut off from... society' (IS:145). Later on he observes that by introducing an elective element into an essentially non-elective power-system, Gorbachev has brought it to the edge of catastrophe (IS:145). He notes (with approval) that Ligachev made essentially the same point in his speech to the March 1989 Plenum of the CPSU.

But it is not only at the level of the Party apparat that radical change has come about. A process of mass exodus is currently taking place from the ranks of the Party itself. Zinoviev seems to be quite shocked by that development. His explanation is that, ever since the time of Khrushchev, the Party had not been representative of the 'workers', but had become a party of bureaucrats. Increasingly, people joined the Party for purely careerist reasons, and were quite openly cynical about that fact. The current crisis is associated in people's minds with the failure of the leadership, which draws its members from the ranks of the Party. People have thus begun to blame 'the Communists' for the difficulties engendered by the crisis, and Communists are now leaving the Party ostentatiously, an act which formerly would have signalled the end of that person's career, if nothing worse (IS:147–8). He does not actually suggest why they are leaving, implying perhaps that, having joined for careerist reasons, they are now resigning for careerist reasons.

THE STATE [5]

The Communist state for Zinoviev differs from non-Communist ones primarily by the function it fulfils of guaranteeing the means of existence for the whole of its population. In this respect it takes on functions which, in Western countries, are carried out by private enterprise, banks and other non-state organisations. The key to the performance of this function is planning and the monitoring of plan fulfilment. Whatever the defects of planning, a decrease in the degree of planning is matched by an increase in social chaos.

A crisis in government, argues Zinoviev, points up a major distinction between Communism and capitalism. Capitalist countries can take governmental crises in their stride, Communist ones cannot. The crisis in government in the Soviet Union is most clearly discernible in the failure to maintain the power-system as an organic whole. '*Edinovlastie*' (monolithic power) has been replaced by '*mnogovlastie*'. Zinoviev lists additional problems: the organs responsible for the maintenance of public order have ceased to carry out their functions to an adequate degree. The police have been unable to contain the rise in crime. The organs of state security have been unable to cope with the rise of anti-government and anti-Communist sentiments and acts. The leaders themselves have deepened this aspect of the crisis by rehabilitating former dissidents and by carrying out the dissident function of drawing attention to defects. The Gorbachev leadership's 'flirtation' with the West has engendered a whole series of liberal gestures, thereby encouraging the growth of rebellious, anti-state, anti-Party and anti-Communist forces in the country (IS:144). Neither Nina Andreeva nor Egor Ligachev could have put it better!

At this point we should discuss Zinoviev's view as expressed in *Il superpotere in URSS* on the stability of the Communist state, for he introduces a radically revised version of his previous position. Let us recall what he said about stability in *Kommunizm kak real'nost'*: 'Communist society is stable to such a degree that forces serious enough to destroy it simply do not materialise within it' (KKR:219; TRC:247). In *Il superpotere in URSS* he says this:

> Communist society possesses a high degree of stability in the sense of its ability to preserve its more or less normal state... On the other hand, if a Communist society is shaken out of its normal state, it is very difficult for it to return to that state. From this viewpoint its degree of stability is relatively low.
>
> (IS:93–4)

It seems to me that Zinoviev has revised his position to the following: Communist society is highly stable, except when it is not. What he seems to be trying to do is to obscure the fact that his theory, as adumbrated in *Kommunizm kak real'nost'*, and exemplified in all his other works up to and including *Katastroika*, predicted the opposite of what has happened since Gorbachev came to power, as regards the stability of the regime. The Communist system has not yet been destroyed, but it can no longer be maintained that forces strong enough to destroy it 'simply do not materialise within it'. The forces which are in the process of doing their utmost to destroy Communism were unleashed precisely within it, albeit with encouragement from the West. The introduction of *glasnost'* and the fragmentation of the monolithic power system have turned out to be highly potent forces for destruction of the Communist order.

Zinoviev does not deny that, but he puts the blame for the unleashing of these forces squarely on Gorbachev. Note the word 'blame', as opposed to 'credit'. He accurately identifies the genesis of the crisis with the step-by-step introduction of Gorbachev's reforms, but *blames* Gorbachev for not understanding the laws of his own society. If Communism is weakened beyond a certain point, he thinks, the Soviet Union will be broken up and colonised by the West, Japan and China (IS:97). This will be Gorbachev's fault. We thus have the situation in which one of the most incisive critics of the Communist social order switches from what he has always called his 'scientific impartiality' to the position of apologist. Ironically, it may well be that Gorbachev *has* understood the laws of his own society – and has decided to destroy it because it is rotten. But whether Gorbachev has sown the whirlwind by design or accident, there is no doubt that Zinoviev despises him for it.

POWER [6]

In the context of the current political situation in the Soviet Union the most important points that Zinoviev makes are the following. First, there are only two possible types of government for a Communist state: a voluntaristic, Stalinist type, or an adaptive, *re*-active, Brezhnevist type. Any government contains elements of both tendencies, the type being determined by which tendency predominates. The Gorbachev government, of course, is Stalinist. Secondly, the importance of the '*ustanovka*' (general aim, guideline) for Communist government can scarcely be exaggerated. If this element disappears, the system of power, and society in general, is thrown into a state of confusion. Thirdly, the chief danger for the Communist leviathan is the appearance of groups outside its control. Fourthly, the sheer extent of government in Communist society incorporates a large part of the working population. The administration and organisation of Communist society involves so many people and has reached such a level of complexity that (a) it is no longer equal to the task, and (b) it is not amenable to organic reform.

Zinoviev's explanation of the crisis in government is very similar to Western accounts, although as usual he pays more attention than Western scholars to the *homo sovieticus* factor. That is to say, he attributes part of the cause to the increased complexity of Communist society itself, as a result of technological change, urban growth, changing patterns of production, etc. On the other hand, more than most Western observers, he emphasises that the main objective of people serving in the administrative apparatus is to look after their own interests first, interests which need not coincide with the 'managerial interest'. But, more importantly, the system of administration grew beyond an optimal size and gradually became divorced from what it was supposed to be administering. Society as a consequence began to function increasingly independently of the administrative system and to ignore its instructions and plans, indeed to act against them.

THE ECONOMY [7]

Zinoviev's central contention about the importance of economic relations in Communist societies is that they are secondary to social relations. The current desire on the part of the Soviet leadership to raise economic performance is primarily to seek to combat the immense pressure from the West, which is extremely demoralising for the population, given the inability of Communism to compete economically with capitalism.

We may note, in passing, how this formulation differs from Brzezinski's neat formulation of the Communist dilemma as he sees it: '[The Soviet Union's] economic success can only be purchased at the cost of political stability, while its political stability can only be sustained at the cost of economic failure' (TGF:102). What Brzezinski sees as a dilemma, Zinoviev regards as a situation which is entirely normal in a Communist society. The dilemma facing the Soviet Union, for Zinoviev, is how to combat the effects of Western economic superiority as they impinge on Soviet society. For instance, if it were possible to return to a policy of keeping the entire population in ignorance of Western economic superiority, that would be the preferred, Communist, solution.

Another interesting observation of Zinoviev's is that it turns out that Communism is most easily achieved on a basis of poverty, *not* of abundance:

Experience has shown that it is not abundance but extreme poverty which is the most adequate realisation of the Marxist ideal. An approximation to the ideal of a society without money is reflected in a ration-card system, a normative system of distribution of consumer goods, secret shops, the army, prisons, labour camps, barter.

(IS:72)

Given the size of the population and the complexity of society, however, it is not possible to dispense with money entirely. But money has a different function in a Communist economy. It is there, not primarily as a means of representing value, but as a means of facilitating the distribution of goods. Prices are fixed for basic items in such a way that a person on average income will be able to afford them. This is not an economic policy, but a social policy. In reality, of course, the system is far from perfect, owing to factors such as problems with distribution, corruption, greed, the presence of a black market, the shadow economy, and so on.

Zinoviev notes that the Soviet Union has more or less admitted that Communism cannot compete economically with capitalism. He regards the revised Soviet aim of developing the Soviet economy to 'world levels' (in place of the former aim of 'overtaking and surpassing the West') as a clear indication of that. Moreover, he sees it as a sign of unnecessary panic. According to Zinoviev, the Soviet leadership should have acknowledged the senselessness of competing with capitalism in a sphere disadvantageous to Communism.

What it has done, however, is to seek to solve Communist economic problems by capitalist economic means, with disastrous results. Zinoviev argues with force and conviction that all the attempts to dismantle specifically Communist means of regulating the Communist economy have accentuated that crisis, and indeed have *produced* a crisis by disrupting the Communist principles of distribution, and demoralising a large percentage of the population by introducing alien capitalist economic principles, against which they have been struggling for the whole of Soviet history.

IDEOLOGY [8]

We noted in Chapter 6 what Zinoviev had to say about the role and importance of ideology in Communist society. Much of what he wrote about ideology in *Kommunizm kak real'nost'* he stands by, yet there are occasional important differences of emphasis, not to say outright contradictions. In the work under discussion he enumerates what he still considers to be the main pillars of a Communist society: (a) a standardised organisation of the population into primary collectives; (b) a system of power and administration which permeates society from top to bottom; (c) a single stage ideology and the systematic ideological indoctrination of the population (IS:82–3). This is the standard Zinovievan view. We also recall from Chapter 6 that, according to Zinoviev, (a) belief in the ideology is *not* required; (b) not passive acceptance, but active participation *is* required; (c) collectivist, Communist 'morality' is highly inimical to morality as such. More generally, we recall Zinoviev's oft-repeated

belief that the West was the embodiment of civilisation, that
the history of civilisation has been the history of attempts by
society to protect itself against the unrestrained operation
of the 'social laws' or 'laws of communalism', and that
Communism is a society based on the laws of communalism.
Whereas he still maintains (a) and (b), his views on (c)
seem to have changed. In *The Reality of Communism* he wrote:
'Ideological "morality" has undeniable advantages over
morality. It releases people from internal self-restraint. It
justifies every crime committed by the country's government *vis-à-vis* the population and against other peoples...'
(TRC:237). In *Il superpotere in URSS* we read the following:

> We should not think that ideology strives to inculcate
> negative qualities in people – egotism, careerism, two-
> facedness, venality, unreliability. Ideology strives to in-
> culcate the best possible qualities. And this is not hypoc-
> risy. If ideology did not strive to do so, or *were unsuccessful
> in actually doing so* [my italics – MK], life in society would
> become an absolute nightmare and in practice impossible
> for the mass of the population.
>
> (IS:85)

There seems to be an obvious contradiction here. On the
one hand he seems to suggest that Communist ideology
produces a counterfeit morality, on the other that it does
not. Yet perhaps the contradiction is more apparent than
real. In both books he is talking about an ideology which
seeks to train a collectivist mentality, downplaying the importance of the individual in his own right, emphasising
that the individual has validity only as a *part* of something
greater, namely the collective. The point he does not address
is whether morally desirable qualities cannot be inculcated
outside the framework of the official ideology – and public
life generally – via such mechanisms as parental upbringing,
relations among close friends, religion, art, and so on.
   Given the enormous role that ideology plays in Communist society, the consequences of its being in crisis are
very grave. Zinoviev's account of the lapse into crisis is in
fact quite conventional, and similar to, say, Brzezinski's
account.[9] What is striking, however, is the unmistakable

note of *regret* at the demise of an ideology he has spent so many years deriding.

He notes, first, that Communist ideology had two very important icons: the idea of constructing a bright future under Communism according to the blueprint of Marxism-Leninism, and the presence of a powerful external enemy, i.e. the West. Like Brzezinski, (and many others) he notes the growing gulf between Marxist-Leninist theory and Soviet practice. Unlike Brzezinski, however, he berates the Gorbachev leadership for *abandoning* Marxist-Leninist theory. Some of his pronouncements are quite breath-taking, given the whole thrust of his previous work. The following is an example. Having noted that a lack of faith in Marxist ideals has been demonstrated for the first time in Soviet history by the leadership itself, he goes on to observe:

> Moreover, Marxism-Leninism was not revised or refuted on any scientific basis, but simply cast aside as something unsuitable either for propaganda or as a basis for decision-making. *And this, despite the fact that the tenets of Marxism-Leninism could as never before serve as a guiding star in the contemporary confused state of the world. Communists have betrayed Marxism-Leninism just at the point where they should have insisted upon it with particular force* [my italics – MK].
>
> (IS:151)

It is difficult to believe that the person who wrote these words is Alexander Zinoviev. It is true that he has always maintained that Marxism is a great ideology, but he, more than most, has demonstrated that ideology is not a science, its tenets are not scientific, they can be neither proved nor disproved, they are logically nonsensical, and so on. The merciless analysis he makes of the Marxist categories in, say, *V preddverii raia* is absolutely incompatible with what he writes above.[10] Once more it is impossible to avoid the conclusion that Zinoviev is on the side of those in the Soviet Union who wish to retain the 'gains' of the October Revolution, return to the 'true path' of Marxism-Leninism and the 'Communist' way of building Communism.

Zinoviev's obvious regret is neatly balanced by Brzezinski's equally obvious satisfaction at the demise of Marxism-Leninism. As regards the role of the West, their analyses are not as far apart as their attitude to these analyses. Both writers are satisfied that, economically, the West has always been superior. However, whereas Brzezinsky sees the economic sphere as only *one* in which the West has been superior, Zinoviev currently tends to regard it as the *only* one in which it is superior. Moreover, whereas Brzezinski (quite understandably, in the view of the present writer) has seen the Soviet Union as the aggressive partner in East–West relations, Zinoviev presents a standard, pre-Gorbachev Soviet view of the *West* as the aggressor.

This attitude is new. Previously (or at any rate, until very recently) Zinoviev in his books had depicted the West as, certainly, the ideological enemy of Communism, but as Communism's future victim. The West did not understand the Soviet system. The West was not ready to defend itself. The West was intimated by the Soviet Union. Western indulgence of Soviet foreign policy and its indifferent attitude to Western left-wing ideologists and Western Communist parties were helping the KGB and carrying out the Kremlin's wishes. To be fair, he also always ackowledged the West's potential as an ideological adversary and the temptation which its obvious material prosperity presented to the Soviet population.

Now (at the time of writing), Zinoviev sees the West as the potential conqueror. But conqueror of what? Of Russia? Of the Soviet Union? Of the Communist way of life? The answer seems to be: (a) of Russia; (b) the Communist way of life. He profoundly regrets both (a) *and* (b), judging by the tone in which he writes in the book under discussion. Whereas in books like *Zheltyi dom* and *Kommunizm kak real'nost'*, Communism was seen as an excrescence on the surface of the globe, threatening to spread over its entire surface, leading to the end of civilisation, Zinoviev in *Il superpotere in URSS* regards the Soviet Union as having valiantly withstood unending pressure from the West since its inception.

He is particularly strident on the subject of the Second World War. Already in *Confessions d'un homme en trop* he expresses the view that Hitler's attack on the USSR was somehow a conspiracy on the part of the West as a whole:

236   *The Gorbachev Era*

'La guerre de l'Allemagne hitlérienne contre l'Union soviétique n'était qu'une tentative des pays occidentaux pour écraser la société communiste en Union soviétique' (Zinoviev, 1990a:193). In *Il superpotere in URSS* he is even more forthright (and wrong!): 'It is a fact that the West went to enormous lengths to set Hitlerite Germany against the Communist Soviet Union' (IS:110). The difference between his attitude and Brzezinski's could hardly be greater, since Brzezinski, as we noted earlier, sees Communism, Fascism and Nazism as having common roots.

That Zinoviev appears to regard *Russia* as being under threat, rather than the Soviet Union, reveals another ideological shift, this time with respect to the 'nationalities question'. We noted in Chapter 6 that Zinoviev devoted less than half a page to this issue in *Kommunizm kak real'nost'*. In *Il superpotere in URSS* he devotes no less than four! His view had always been that nationality issues were a particular manifestation of *social* relations, an explanation of which could only be derived from a theory of Communist society. In so far as he has expressed an opinion about nationalities as such, it had always been his view that the central government discriminated against *Russians* in favour of virtually every other nationality in the Soviet Union. In the book under discussion he advances the totally (for him) new idea that Communism did not take root equally everywhere in the Soviet Union:

> Many nationalities on the planet seemed to become Communist in many respects. But experience shows that the Communist organisation of society was not carried out fundamentally and did not become the natural basis of their [way of] life. That is precisely the situation in the Soviet republics of Central Asia, Azerbaidzhan, Moldavia and the Baltic Republics. They are able, therefore, to 'reject' Communism relatively easily and to return to their pre-Communist state – capitalist, feudal, tribal.
>
> (IS:21)

This is a major departure, as regards the Soviet republics. (He has never spoken much about other countries.) Moreover, in terms of his own theory, it is difficult to see how he comes to that conclusion. Once more, one has the uncomfortable suspicion that Zinoviev is quite ready to 'palm off' on the reader 'laws of society' which just happen to fit current situations. His theory predicted a long, unchanging period of Communism, once it was established. The prerequisites we have listed before, but we recall that they include the destruction of a previous social order, the socialisation *in toto* of the means of production, distribution and exchange, and the establishment of the three pillars of Communism to which reference is made at the beginning of this chapter. Acceptance of, or belief in, the state ideology was never part of his theory, although *participation* in ideological spectacles was. Zinoviev does not say *why* in the republics he lists Communism was never fully developed. Nationalism is clearly a factor. However, another problem for Zinoviev's position is that, whereas the Baltic Republics would apparently be very happy to leave the Soviet Union, the republics in Central Asia would not. Moreover, we have yet to establish how far in fact Communism became the basis of people's way of life in Eastern Europe. So far, the omens for a shift to democracy are at best mixed. Zinoviev may well turn out to have been too hasty in assuming that Communism was less firmly rooted in the periphery of the Soviet Union than in that part of the Soviet Union which is to all intents and purposes Russia itself. He now appears ready to abandon the periphery to capitalism and to defend Communism exclusively in the land of Mother Russia.

Marxism-Leninism is currently on the ideological retreat, and Zinoviev thinks that it will be a long time, if ever, before it regains its place as the state ideology. However, he is sure that something will take its place, for a Communist society without an ideology is unthinkable. As we have already seen, some observers already detect a shift in Soviet ideology away from confrontation and towards consensus, albeit around a Soviet-inspired slogan of 'the interests of humanity' in our 'global village', in which the West continues to play the role of chief threat to the future of mankind. Within the Soviet Union there have been some interesting 'hybrid' ideological manifestations, such as '*subbotniki*'[11] in aid of various Soviet charity organisations.

In short, Zinoviev's ideological 'revisionism' notwithstan-

ding, his general theory continues to merit serious attention. The doctrinal side of Communism has suffered an
ignominious defeat. But those aspects of behaviour which
have been the product of the Soviet ideological 'magnetic
field' are arguably deeply ingrained and will take much time
and effort to eradicate. Soviet discourse is still deeply
affected by Soviet ideology. The chameleon-like behaviour
of the Soviet population is still a phenomenon to be rec-
koned with. For these reasons it is still too early to write off
Soviet ideology as a spent force. It will revive under some
other guise.

ORIGINS OF THE CRISIS

In terms of Zinoviev's theory of Communism, particularly as
regards the stability of Communist regimes, failure of the
system is not likely. We have noted, however, that he is
prepared to concede that not all Communist countries (nor
all Soviet republics) developed Communism to the point
where it became 'natural'. In these countries (and republics), the failure of Communism is apparently possible.
Where it has become 'natural', however, it will undergo
crises from time to time, these crises being an accumulation
of departures from the norms of Communist behaviour
itself (IS:118). There is, here, more than a trace of '*kus-
tarnichestvo*' ('amateurishness'), a particularly grave charge
to level at a writer who has insisted on his scientific approach to the analysis of Communism. For all that Zinoviev
has fulminated against Western inability to 'understand' the
Soviet Union, or to elaborate a 'science of Communism', he
himself previously discounted signs of impending crisis
which had already been detected in the West. Two important predictions were made by Western scholars: one emphasised that the nationalities issue was anything but 'solved', as the Soviets claimed tirelessly for at least two decades;
the other concerned the problems being stored up for the
Brezhnev leadership as a simple consequence of their advancing age. There was bound to be a crisis, as large
numbers of leaders were increasingly likely to die about the
same time as each other, give or take a few years. Zinoviev

had always discounted the 'nationalities question' and ridiculed Western 'Kremlin watchers'. His own list of contributing factors, however, merits attention. These include: the 'cancellation' of World War Three; the radical (Andropov-inspired) change in Soviet political strategy in its relations with the West; the powerful attack by the West in the field of democracy and human rights; the complete ideological switch from anti-West to pro-West propaganda, accompanied by a parallel switch from pro-Communist propaganda to anti-Communist propaganda within the Soviet Union itself; the change of leadership.

Up until the publication of *Confessions d'un homme en trop*, Zinoviev had predicted that there would be a nuclear world war, which the Soviets would win, or at least not lose. In the aftermath, Communism as a social order would prove to be more '*lebensfähig*' than capitalism. He now believes that this war has been 'cancelled', and that the consequences of an unnaturally long period of peace have put a strain on the workings of Communism, thereby leading to the crisis. Andropov's policy towards the West turned out to be a double-edged sword. The obverse side of *rapprochement* with the West was increased Western influence in the Soviet Union, both economically and ideologically. This was accompanied by a 'ferocious' Western attack on Communism's record on democracy and human rights, leading to a departure from Communist ways of handling Communist problems. The complete ideological volte-face from anti-West pro-Soviet to pro-West anti-Soviet amounted to 'betrayal' on the part of the leadership, a leadership which is neo-Stalinist in its approach if not in political outlook.

These factors contributed to the crisis, but did not spark it off. Zinoviev's argument is that Gorbachev himself 'pushed the button' (IS:129) and the bomb, i.e. the crisis, exploded. *Perestroika*, initially an attempt to combat the crisis, itself *became* the crisis:

> Gorbachev's *perestroika* itself is the real crisis. Only in a secondary sense is it an attempt to forestall a crisis and then to overcome a crisis. It may have begun as an attempt to prevent a crisis. But as such, it merely, as the saying goes, added fuel to the flames. It then turned into an

attempt to find a way out of the crisis. But as such it merely intensified the crisis and then turned into a disguised form of counter-*perestroika*.

(*IS*:129–30)

The last sentence contains the key to Zinoviev's prediction as to how the crisis will end, to a discussion of which we now turn.

THE WAY OUT OF THE CRISIS

It will be useful at the outset to compare Brzezinski's prediction with Zinoviev's. Brzezinski offers five options. *Perestroika* will lead to one of the following: (a) success; (b) protracted but inconclusive turmoil; (c) renewed stagnation, as *perestroika* runs out of steam; (d) a regressive and repressive political coup, in reaction to (b) or (c); (e) fragmentation of the Soviet Union as a consequence of some combination of (b) to (d) (TGF:100). Brzezinski's prediction is that option (b) is the most likely, with the possibility of a slide into (c). Zinoviev offers a list of three: (a) the end of Communism; (b) a hybridisation of Communism and capitalism; (c) a restoration of 'normal' Communism (IS:179). Zinoviev is inclined to bet on (c). What is interesting is that both writers envisage similar outcomes, although both of them evaluate them differently. Brzezinski's position is the following:

Of these options, the most likely alternative for the next several years seems to be Option [c], but with a high probability that *perestroika* will gradually lose some of its momentum in the face of internal obstacles. Growing domestic turmoil or eventually renewed stagnation could in turn prompt some renewed efforts on behalf of heightened social and political discipline. The latter could even lead to a military dictatorship, especially if the party proves to be too complacent and incompetent either in promotion of change or in the maintenance of order. Such a turn of events would damage badly Communism's historic prospects. (TGF:100)

Zinoviev's position is that there will be a return to a worse variant of the system that the Gorbachev leadership set out to reform, but that Communism as such still has a future ahead of it and that it is still too soon to speak of a 'post-Communist' era. We shall now review the arguments he marshals in support of that prediction, which applies to the Soviet Union only (IS:188):

(a) The market economy and a parliamentary system of government are attributes of capitalist society, they are a product of that society and they are unworkable in a Communist society. Attempts to introduce these features under Communism will only result in mere imitation, although such imitation could be harmful enough to lead to the collapse of the Communist economy, which in turn would lead to the collapse of the social order (IS:195–6). (Here he seems to contradict what he stated in an earlier section about the subordination of economic relations to social relations.)

(b) *Perestroika* is itself the crisis and can only be overcome by a counter-*perestroika*, which has begun and which is reflected in such phenomena as the prohibition of strikes, the use of the army to restore order in the trans-Caucasus and Central Asia, the arrest and harassment of private entrepreneurs, appeals for the strengthening of public order, etc. It will either be carried out under Gorbachev under the guise of a continuation of *perestroika*, or (by the same people) under Gorbachev's successor as a counter-measure to *perestroika*, which will by then be seen as a mistake, if not a crime (IS:188–90).

(c) Counter-*perestroika* has the support of the overwhelming majority of the population. Very few have gained from *perestroika* and the masses want a return to their normal standard of living. The great wave of anti-Communist propaganda has threatened the real gains of Communism, which people are now beginning to realise they need or want to preserve. That, too, is a form of counter-*perestroika* (IS:190–1).

(d) The reaction of people whose standard of living has deteriorated will increasingly be to regard *perestroika* as counter-revolution, seeking to undo what was achieved by the glorious October Revolution and the whole of Soviet history (IS:192–3). Many people already believe that.

(e) People will become disenchanted with the West. They will discover that it is impossible to transplant desirable Western phenomena onto the basis of the Communist system (IS:193–6). We may comment in passing that this is becoming ever clearer. As Zinoviev notes, there is no 'West Soviet Union' waiting to invest trillions of dollars in its Eastern twin. Germany is finding to its cost that the business of assimilating the former German Democratic Republic is proving much more difficult that the Government of the Federal Republic of Germany appeared (inexplicably) to think it would be.

(f) A major problem for the reformers is the human material at their disposal. All the characteristics of *homo sovieticus* which Zinoviev has tirelessly and mercilessly exposed will guarantee that Soviet people will be incapable of carrying out the reforms to their conclusion (which is to say, to the full destruction of Communism), thereby saving it.[12]

(g) The overwhelming number of people who have to carry out the reforms are 'conservatives', in the sense that they are ordinary Soviet people. Millions appeared to be for *perestroika*, in order to safeguard their positions. As soon as the signal changes, they will be just as eager counter-*perestroikists* (IS:196–9).

(h) There will be a great need to restore the ideological mechanism of Communist society. This will take a long time, and will not be a revision of Marxism-Leninism. Its first task will be to channel and control the dangerous influence of the West (IS:199–200). (Zinoviev invests much hope in the younger generation, which he regards as having been spared the awareness of ideological crisis, and expresses the desire that they will treat their fathers the way their fathers treated their own fathers, who were the builders of Communism. He makes no prediction about the form the new ideology will have. We have noted, however, a swing away from Marxist-Leninist Communism to an all-enveloping 'humanism', subtly weighted against the West.)[13]

(i) Allowing the Baltic republics to secede from the Soviet Union would encourage other republics to do likewise, leading thereby to a grave weakening of the Soviet Union's ability to defend itself. For that reason Gorbachev has to refuse (IS:200).

(j) The removal of Clause 6 of the USSR Constitution which guaranteed the leading role of the CPSU is discounted by Zinoviev. He believes that people voted for its removal in the belief that it would change nothing in practice. Zinoviev also notes with amusement the extent to which the West suddenly takes the Soviet Constitution seriously, having regarded it for decades as not worth the paper it was written on (IS:202–3).

(k) The 'basic link' in the counter-*perestroika* is Gorbachev's construction of a personal dictatorship. He has thereby chosen the Stalinist path. There is no future for a multi-party system, since any such system will merely be a fragmentation of the unified system of power, which will gradually be restored. It is quite possible that the new core of the power system will be an informal combination of elements from the Party apparatus, the KGB, the Soviets, ministries, military establishments, in short, those who wield the real power. This power system will stand above the Party apparatus and will probably be controlled by the President. However, an informal system is unlikely to last beyond a certain period and the Party apparatus is likely to come back into its own (IS:206).

Many of these arguments seem to the present writer to carry conviction. Parliamentary democracy cannot be introduced overnight. The new Soviet Parliament has been an amazing spectacle for the Soviet population and the world at large, but it has quickly revealed itself as a talking-shop more than anything else. The various factions within it do not replicate a multi-party system. The plethora of new laws and decrees have led to the situation best described as the 'war of laws'. Meanwhile, Gorbachev's immense personal power has not yet been put to the ultimate test, yet it is clear that his personal standing is at rock-bottom and that virtually the whole of the Soviet population is heartily sick of him. If he goes, he may be replaced by someone who will relish using that power to initiate a clamp-down.

Arguments (c) to (g), with the exception of (e), seem to this writer to be irrefutable. Disenchantment with the West is very possible. But the prospect of a mass migration westwards is both likely and daunting. The chances of the West offering sufficient material and technical support to the Soviet economy to rescue it are fading. The road to the market economy will prove to be long and hard, and likely to peter out in a Soviet economic bog. Meanwhile, the attractions of the West may prove irresistible to millions of young, disenchanted Soviet citizens and East Europeans, and the countries of Western Europe will have to take counter-measures in the form of highly stringent immigration policy. Argument (i) is sound from a conventional Soviet defence point of view and is one which the Soviet military would probably back up with force, if need be. The argument relating to the abandonment of Clause 6 of the USSR Constitution is likely to turn out to be correct. In the countries of Eastern Europe, the Communist Parties, under a variety of new names, continue to wield a surprising amount of influence, where they do not constitute the major political force. There is every reason to suppose that that situation will be replicated in the Soviet Union. Argument (k) is likewise highly likely to prove to be correct.

How far, then, has Zinoviev 'revised' his model of Communism in *Il superpotere in URSS* ? The 'revisionism' is primarily one of tone rather than of substance. We have given several examples of a pro-conservative sympathy and a vibrant antipathy towards Gorbachev himself, evidence, one might argue, of a growing sense of alarm that the Gorbachev leadership might actually succeed in destroying Communism in the Soviet Union. He has pointed to grave problems which his theory did not predict, including the demise of the official ideology, the fragmentation of the unified system of power, the quite amazing growth of 'informal' organisations and the attempt to take the Soviet Union down the road towards a market economy.

Given his earlier believe in the stability of the system and his continually expressed contempt for Western social science scholarship in the area of Soviet studies, it is something of a come-down for him when he has to account for the origins of the crisis in terms highly reminiscent of precisely these Western social scientists. More than anywhere else in his entire *oeuvre*, Zinoviev acknowledges the 'communalist' effect of pre-Soviet Russian history, which prepared the ground for the successful development of Communism. The origins of the crisis he is now prepared to locate in the Brezhnev years, belatedly, it is true, but again in line with Western opinion.

It is quite clear, or so it seems to the present writer, that Zinoviev has been shocked at the rapidity with which the Communist system in Eastern Europe and the Soviet Union has unravelled. Arguably this sense of shock has affected his sense of judgement. His change of tone, for instance, in relation to Marxism-Leninism is staggering, as is also his blatant regret at the demise of the system as he himself experienced it. His anti-Westernism has also changed in tone. Previously it was one of bewildered despair, tinged with contempt, at the West's apparent inability (a) to comprehend the Soviet Union, (b) to combat its aggression. Currently (at least as reflected in the pages of *Il superpotere in URSS*), it is one almost of hatred. It is as if the West is now not only the aggressor, but a potential conqueror of his native land. Again he seems to be shocked at the totally (for him) unexpected success of the Western 'propaganda-offensive' in the area of human rights, combined with an aggressive economic policy in the area of technology transfer.

However, although on occasions he seems almost too eager to depart from his original model, his thoughts on counter-*perestroika* indicate that his fundamental convictions remain unchanged. *Perestroika* will fail above all because it represents an attempt to solve Communist problems by non-Communist means. The Soviet people, having built Communism (however badly), are now stuck with it. The characteristics fostered by that system over the decades will prevent the Soviet people from destroying it. The collective system will be restored. One way or another, a non-democratic power system with an inner core (*sterzhnevaia chast'*) will be restored, as will a unified ideology, albeit in the longer term.

CONCLUSION

Is Brzezinski's prediction more likely to be correct than Zinoviev's? Will democracy, rather than Communism, dominate the twenty-first century? Brzezinski makes a strong case for his own thesis, but Zinoviev has never paid much attention to *doctrinal* Communism, although he has made a big issue of *participatory* ideology and its consequences for behaviour. He believes that communalist tendencies are universal, so the demise of Communism in the Soviet Union and elsewhere does not necessarily guarantee the future for democracy. Brzezinski's conclusion may well be unwarranted. The doctrine of Marxism-Leninism may well be dead. It is not immediately obvious, however, that the 'classless' egalitarian ideals it allegedly espoused have died with it. There are probably still millions of people who believe in the idea that there should be a more equitable distribution of wealth and resources, that the State should provide a wide range of services free of charge, that wealth-creation and personal endeavour are wholly bad, that the nationalisation of the means of production is wholly good, that egalitarianism is wholly good and that individualism is wholly selfish. Many of these people teach in the educational systems of the Western world.

Capitalism, as Zinoviev used to tell us with approval, was the mainspring of Western civilisation which operated according to the laws of flight. It requires constant effort. Communalism, which is best exemplified by Communism, relies on the principle of least effort, of going with the current, of sinking. The Communist system is in crisis at the moment. But it reflects the aspirations of the majority of the world's population to a greater extent than does capitalism. The East–West conflict is likely to be replaced by a North–South conflict. The prosperous northern hemisphere threatens to be overwhelmed by migration from the southern hemisphere – witness the concern in the USA about illegal immigration from Latin America and similar concerns in Italy and France about illegal immigration from North Africa. Such concern is increasingly accompanied by concern over possible mass immigration from the former Communist empire. Democratic governments are not good at persuading multinational companies to participate in a voluntary distribution of wealth on a world-wide scale. The population explosion is taking place in the southern hemisphere, where need is greatest.

Taking a global perspective, Brzezinsky's prediction may hold for the beginning of the twenty-first century. Present democratic governments, however, almost without exception, are in countries which have a history behind them of exploitation of their own peoples and populations and those of other countries. Wealth creation is not enough. The market requires buyers as well as sellers. The current distribution of wealth on a global scale is so blatantly biased in the direction of a relatively small minority, that the majority of the world's population can never aspire in their lifetime to the standard of living of that minority. Envy and desperation combined with an absence of hope of improvement on the basis of self-help invite communalist-type solutions. To the gross economic imbalance on a global scale which parallels an imbalance between democratic and non-democratic governments we can add an ideological dimension. Apart from world-wide anti-Americanism, there is the growth of fundamentalist Islam, a religion which is by nature anti-Christian, and therefore anti-Western. It is not beyond belief that a major crisis for capitalism could explode even before the twenty-first century has begun.

If, in addition, Zinoviev's prediction turns out to be correct, a revived Soviet Union with an ideology based on 'humanism' and the 'global village' in which the West is the threatening element (with its policy of nuclear deterrence) could act as a focal point of anti-Western resentment and envy, encouraging egalitarian elements *within* Western countries as well as without. Zinoviev points out that it took hundreds of years for capitalism and democracy to develop. Individuals live for less than a hundred years, and they will be much more ready to 'distribute' than to 'create'. Optimists will agree with Brzezinski. Pessimists (of whom the present writer counts himself as one) will reluctantly side with Zinoviev.

Notes

CHAPTER 1: HOMO SOVIETICUS

1. The account of Alexander Zinoviev's life which is offered in this chapter is based on two autobiographies and the volume of memoirs which he has already published (Zinoviev, 1978a:1–11, 1987b:38–43; 1989:323–39; 1990a). Further material has been provided by friends and relatives whom I have been able to interview, and supplemented by observations arising out of my own meetings with the writer. I have also drawn on material in various interviews that Zinoviev has given since his arrival in the West, notably the extended interview which forms the basis of his book *Ich bin für mich selbst ein Staat* (Zinoviev, 1987b), edited by Adalbert and Renée Reif.

2. I. Virabov, 'Syn "antisovetchika" v tylu perestroiki', *Komsomol'skaia pravda* (9 April 1991) 2.

3. Academician Kapitsa was a notable exception. He apparently sent the Zinovievs money quite openly. (See 'An Autobiography', p.20).

4. 'Na anketu IL otvechaiut pisateli russkogo zarubezh'ia', *Inostrannaia literatura*, 2 (1989) 250; A.A. Zinoviev, 'O sebe', ibid., 249.

5. *Moskovskie novosti*, 33 (August 1989) 16; *Gorizont*, 12 (1989) 47–63.

6. France 3, 9 March 1990.

7. *Pravda* (6 June 1990) 8.

8. A.A. Zinoviev, 'Ia ostaius' russkim pisatelem', *Pravda* (9 September 1990).

9. *Moskovskii literator* (15 June 1990) 4–5.

10. *Komsomol'skaia pravda* (8 July 1990) 4.

11. *Izvestiia* (1 July 1990) 4.

12. *Komsomol'skaia pravda* (15 September 1990) 2–3, reprinted (in abridged form) in *Golos rodiny*, 38 (September 1990) 6–7. This article attracted responses, also published in *Komsomol'skaia pravda*, from M.A. Zakharov (20 September 1990), G. Borovik (30 September 1990) and O. Kuchkina (5 March 1991).

13. 'Moi dom – moia chuzhbina', *Sovetskaia literatura*, 11 (1990, pp. 3–34; *Sovetskaia literatura*, 12 (1990) 25–57.

14. 'Idi na Golgofu', *Smena*, (1991) 14–58; *Smena*, 2 (1991) 82–124; *Smena*, 3 (1991) 68–135.

15. *Zhurnalist*, 1 (1991) 32–9.

16. I. Pantin, 'Put' k sebe', *Zhurnalist*, 2 (1991) 32–5.

17. See, for example, the biting article by V. Bushin, 'Esli by ia mog...', *Na boevom postu, Ezhednevnaia gazeta ordena Lenina Zabaikal'skogo voennogo okruga* (8 July 1990), in which the poet Evtushenko and the editor of *Ogonek* Vitalii Korotich are unfavourably compared with

Zinoviev. For an example of a more moderate, 'liberal' interpretation of Zinoviev, see B. Griaznevich, 'Sovetskii soiuz glazami
Aleksandra Zinov'eva', *Literator*, 7 (September 1990) 4–5.

CHAPTER 2: ZINOVIEV'S STYLE AND LANGUAGE

1. See, for example, *V preddverii raia*, p. 246, *Moi dom – moia chuzhbina*, p. 18, *Evangelie dlia Ivana*, p. 98.
2. *Allegra Russia.*
3. Note also Natalia Rubinshteyn's reference to *Ziaiushchie vysoty* as a 'work of art without art' (Rubinshteyn, 1977:147).
4. Quoted in Moskovich (1988:91).
5. Wolf Moskovich's analysis of Zinoviev's language (Moskovich, 1988:89–104) is perhaps the most useful account to date, and the discussion in the main text makes use of some of his data.
6. I am aware, of course, that '*bedro*' and '*rebro*' mean, respectively, 'hip' and 'rib'. I think, however, that the confusion of 'crotch' and 'crux' makes Zinoviev's point more successfully and I used these in my translation of *Zheltyi dom*. See *The Madhouse*, p. 11.
7. There are only eight sentences in the English version, since the English sentence 7 corresponds to the Russian sentences 7 and 8.
8. *Zheltyi dom* I:214–15, 216, 218–19, 222–3, 228–30, 244, 247, 249, 252, 262, 264–5, 269–71, 272, 279–80, 282, 286–7, 289.
9. *Zheltyi dom* I:317–18, 318, 319–20, 321, 323, 325, 325–6, 326, 329, 333–4, 336–7; *Zheltyi dom* II: 207, 213–15, 219–21, 227–8, 231–2, 238–40, 246–7, 256–8, 264–5, 269–70, 292–3, 297–9, 325.

CHAPTER 3: *ZIIAIUSHCHIE VYSOTY*

1. *Kontinent*, 10 (1976) 410.
2. *Ziiaiushchie vysoty* has since appeared in abridged form in the Soviet Union in the first three issues of the journal *Oktiabr'*. See *Oktiabr'*, 1 (1991), 30–97; *Oktiabr'*, 2 (1991) 23–82; *Oktiabr'*, 3 (1991) 59–81.
3. See Kirkwood (1987:104–8).
4. For a philosophical discussion of the 'enterprise' and other aspects of the work in Heidegger terms see J. Rolland, 'Ibansk ou l'époque de la technique', *Exercises de la patience*, No.1/4, Spring 1982, pp. 233–54.
5. The numbers in brackets after the titles in this and subsequent notes refer to the page on which the text in question begins: '*Metodologicheskie printsipy*' (9); '*Shizofrenik*' (13); '*Sotsio-mekhanika*' (14); '*Nauchnye zakony*' (27); '*Boltun*' (30); '*O predvidenii*' (33); '*Sotsial'nye zakony*' (37); '*Sotsial'noe i ofitsial'noe*' (57); '*Sotsial'nyi-individ*' (68); '*O gluposti, podlosti i drugikh priznaniiakh individa*' (70); '*Sotsial'noe deistvie*' (81); '*Sotsial'nye gruppy*' (89); '*Delo gruppy i individ*' (96); '*Sotsial'nye otnosheniia*' (99); '*Rukovoditeli*' (104).

6. '*Zamechenia Sotsiologa*' (15); '*Instruktor*' (15); '*Posviashchenie*' (15);
    '*Somneniia Mazily*' (30); '*Mnenie Sotsiologa*' (40); '*Otklonenie ot
    normy*' (41); '*Evoliutsiia Sotsiologa*' (58); '*Problemy vlasti*' (60); '*Ob
    abstraktsii individa*' (79); '*Koshmary*' (115); '*Itogi*' (118).
7. '*Vremia i mesto*' (10); '*Nachalo*' (11); '*O bespol'ze informatsii* ' (21);
    '*Doklad Sotrudnika*' (33); '*Sotsiolog*' (46); '*Prichina i vina*' (69);
    '*Iuridicheskie pustiaki* ' (76); '*Snimu komnatu*' (83); '*Posledniaia
    vstrecha*' (111); '*Skuka*' (120).
8. '*Instruktor*' (15); '*Traktat o sud'be, svobode, istine, morali, i t.d.*' (17);
    '*O terminologii*' (17); '*Ob odnoi oshibochnoi gipoteze*' (17); '*O khronologii*'
    (18); '*Zdanie shkoly*' (19); '*Sortir*' (20); '*Monument vozhdia*' (22);
    '*Ballada*' (23); '*Uklonist*' (24); '*Ubiitsa*' (25); '*Nachalo*' (44); '*Patriot*'
    (45); '*Paniker*' (46); '*Dostoinstva guby*' (48); '*Nedostatki guby*' (49);
    '*Sosluzhivets i drugie*' (50); '*Literator*' (50); '*Intelligent*' (51); '*Dis-
    kussiia o svobode*' (54); '*Pokhishchenie "Ferdinanda"*' (63); '*Beseda o
    svetlom budushchem*' (63); '*Razgovor ob ume*' (64); '*Diskussiia o
    donosakh*' (73); '*Osnovy sotsial'noi antropologii* ' (94); '*Nemnogo ob
    iskusstve*' (103); '*O sud'be*' (108); '*Konflikt*' (112); '*Besedy o tainakh
    istorii* ' (114); '*Konets*' (119); '*Perspektivy*' (119).
9. '*Epitafiia zhivomu*' (121); '*Iz stat'i Sekretaria*' (122); '*Nekotorye osoben-
    nosti ibanskoi istorii* ' (122); '*Pokhorony Direktora*' (123); '*Perelom*'
    (124); '*Khriak*' (127); '*Prognoz sbivaetsia*' (149); '*Velichie*' (151); '*Dlia
    dela*' (155).
10. '*Pretendent*' (134); '*Neibezhnost' oshibki*' (135); '*Glavnaia oshibka*'
    (138); '*Den' rozhdeniia Pretendenta*' (144); '*Stengazeta*' (153), (159);
    '*Stat'ia Kisa*' (165); '*Vse vzaimopereputano*' (173); '*Reaktsiia sobiraet
    silu*' (175); '*Plagiat*' (189); '*Oshibka naidena*' (199); '*Bol'shomu
    korabliu, bol'shoe plavanie*' (206); '*Neispol'zovannye vozmozhnosti*'
    (218); '*Konets Pretendenta*' (221).
11. '*Krysy*' (133), (136), (140), (142), (144), (145), (149), (153), (155),
    (160), (167), (178); '*Konets krysinogo raia*' (218.
12. '*Nekotorye osobennosti ibanskoi istorii* ' (122); '*Vypiski iz knigi Klevetnika*'
    (143), (147); '*Iz knigi Klevetnika*' (150), (152), (156), (161), (163);
    '*Zametki Klevetnika*' (176), (179), (183), (195); '*Konets zapisok
    Klevetnika*' (196).
13. This question is dealt with at some length in Plaskacz (1982).
14. '*Bezdel'e – nachalo tvorchestva*' (224); '*Psevdonim*' (225); '*Ia**' (225);
    '*Moi khudozhnik**' (227); '*Byt**' (227); '*Byt**' (229); '*Nemnogo istorii**'
    (229); '*Nashi druz'ia**' (231); '*Sotsiologicheskii analiz**' (235); '*My**'
    (236); '*Iazyk**' (240); '*Smyslovaia kompozitsiia**' (248); '*Dvoistven-
    nost'**' (251); '*Potok**' (255); '*Opiat' my i oni**' (273); '*Massovoe ili
    elitarnoe **' (276); '*K probleme vyzhivaniia**' (278). The asterisks
    (present in the original text) denote texts by Chatterer speaking as
    an art critic. Other texts on the subject of art include the following:
    '*Podlinnoe iskusstvo*' (243); '*Tipichnost' iskliucheniia*' (251); '*Podlin-
    nost' iskusstva*' (252); '*Iskusstvo i nauchno-tekhnicheskii progress*' (271);
    '*Trud ne propadaet, no darom*' (279).
15. '*Iunost'*' (230); '*Deti*' (234); '*Zhratva*' (238); '*Iazyk*' (242); '*Baby*'
    (244); '*Pedagogika*' (247); '*Dobavka*' (249); '*Gde spravedlivost'*?'

(252); '*Pravil'noe polozhenie v zhizni*' (254); '*Reshenie*' (258); '*Podkhod k liudiam*' (272); '*Stremitel'naia ataka*' (276); '*Inache nel'zia*' (286).

16. '*Sekrety*' (236); '*Reshenie*' (237); '*Osnovy optimizma*' (242); '*Sotsial'nyi stroi*' (247); '*Podlinnoe iskusstvo*' (252); '*Sotsial'naia orientatsiia*' (256); '*Vlast*'' (258); '*Tip nashikh problem*' (259); '*Kto my*' (269); '*Uchenie o zhizni*' (274); '*Kto my*' (278); '*Personalizm*' (280); '*Kto my*' (282).

17. '*Chas pervyi*' (294); '*Chas vtoroi*' (297); '*Chas tretii*' (301); '*Chas chetvertyi*' (304); '*Chas piatyi*' (311); '*Chas shestoi*' (315); '*Chas sed'moi*' (323); '*Chas vos'moi*' (325); '*Chas deviatyi*' (332); '*Chas desiatyi*' (339), (346); '*Chas odinnadtsatyi*' (365); '*Chas dvenadtsatyi*' (373); '*Chas trinadtsatyi*' (382); '*Chas chetyrnadtsatyi*' (393); '*Chas piatnadtsatyi*' (397); '*Chas vosem'nadtsatyi*' (428); '*Chas deviatnadtsatyi*' (440); '*Chas dvadtsatyi*' (448); '*Chas dvadtsat' pervyi*' (451); '*Chas dvadtsat' vtoroi*' (456); '*Poslednii chas*' (465); '*Konets*' (468).

18. '*Spetskursy*' (321); '*Gosudarstvo*' (329); '*Plata i rasplata*' (332); '*Bratiia*' (346), (356); '*Gosudarstvo*' (360), (389), (399); '*Real'noe i illiuzornoe*' (400); '*Politika*' (406); '*O vlasti*' (410); '*Pravo*' (417); '*Privilegii*' (437).

19. '*Gruppy*' (328); '*O sotsial'nykh sistemakh*' (337), (378), (405), (416).

20. '*Nachalo*' (336); '*Somneniia*' (351); '*Dumy*' (359); '*Dumy*' (367); '*Programma preobrazovanii*' (369).

21. '*Vozvrashchenie*' (469), (472), (473), (476), (479). (482), (487), (488), (493), (498), (503), (505), (510), (513), (526), (535), (536), (540), (544), (547), (549), (551), (556), (558); '*Konets vozvrashcheniia*' (559).

22. '*Pod-Ibansk*' (484), (509); *Vnezemnaia tsivilizatsiia*' (515); '*Vstrecha*' (529); '*Doklad Agenta*' (530); '*Biologicheskie trudnosti*' (533); '*Iazykovye trudnosti*' (537); '*Vzaimoponimanie*' (539); '*Obmen opytom*' (548), (553); '*Vstrechi na vysshem urovne*' (554).

23. '*Potselui ibantsa*' (474); '*Razriadka*' (478); '*Velikaia pobeda*' (480); '*Khmyr*'' (482); '*Pod-Ibansk*' (484); '*Sortir*' (485); '*Psizm*' (486), (490); '*Progress*' (492); '*Zhop*' (497); '*A ty kto takoi*' (501); '*Problema*' (502).

24. '*Prazdnik*' (506); '*Legenda o sebe*' (507); '*Legenda*' (514), (526), (531), (533), (538), (541), (544), (548); '*Konets legendy*' (550).

25. '*Ochered*'' (496), (500), (508); '*Gimn ocheredi*' (511); '*Ochered*'' (528), (532), (537), (544); '*Konets ocheredi*' (558).

26. '*Nuzhna oppozitsiia*' (512); '*Organizatsiia oppozitsii*' (519); '*Proekt programmy oppozitsii*' (529); '*Doklad Agenta*' (530); '*Vozrazhenie Uchitelia*' (536); '*Oppozitsiia za rabotoi*' (545); '*Plan perevorota*' (556); '*Sryv perevorota*' (556); '*Konets oppozitsii*' (557).

CHAPTER 4: *SVETLOE BUDUSHCHEE*

1. See Brown (1978), Lapidus (1977), Breslauer (1976), Cocks (1976).

CHAPTER 5: *ZHELTYI DOM*

1. For a more detailed account than is possible here, see Kirkwood, 1982.
2. See the two examples given at the end of Chapter 2.
3. See '*Toska po drugu*' (ZhD I:200), '*Toska akademika*' (ZhD I:203), '*Toska po Dzhul'ette*' (ZhD I:210), '*Toska prokhvosta*' (ZhD I:219), '*Toska o geroicheskoi zhertve*' (ZhD I:222), '*Toska partiinogo sekretaria*' (ZhD I:227), '*Toska po Rossii*' (ZhD I:235), '*Toska po domu*' (ZhD I:260–1), '*Toska o proshlom*' (ZhD I:274), '*Toska po zhalosti*' (ZhD I:302–3).
4. See, for instance, '*Pritiazhenie goroda*' (ZhD II:197–8) as an example of the former, and '*Gimn kar'ere*' (ZhD II:198–201) as an example of the latter.
5. For details of texts/strands/page references, see Kirkwood, 1982.
6. See Zinoviev, 1986a.
7. '*Nash chelovek*' (ZhD II:260–1, 266–8, 271–2, 284–6).
8. For the texts on 'yearning' see note 3. The following relate to 'loneliness': '*Problema odinochestva*' (ZhD I:203), '*Odinochestvo*' (ZhD I:203, 210, 220–1, 233).
9. The concept of individual sovereignty is central to Zinoviev's philosophy of life. First adumbrated in rules of personal conduct in *Ziiaiushchie vysoty*, it has received ever deeper treatment (Zinoviev, 1985c, 1987, 1990a).
10. '*Problema vykhoda*' (ZhD II:21–2), '*Osnovnoi postulat*' (ZhD II:40–2), '*Postanovka problemy*' (ZhD II:53–4, 62–4), '*Rukovodiashchaia ideia*' (ZhD II:84–5), '*Marksizm-leninizm i sonologiia*' (ZhD II:99–100), '*Estestvennonauchnaia osnova sonologii*' (ZhD II:102–3), '*Moia sotsial'naia kontseptsiia*' (ZhD II:116–17), '*Vvedenie v spunologiiu*' (ZhD II:124–5, 127, 145–6, 154–6, 161–4), '*Moia religiia*' (ZhD II:187–8)
11. This 'epistle' is reproduced in Chapter 2.
12. See the section on town vs. country in this chapter.
13. '*Bitva za urozhai*' (ZhD II:46–8, 73–4).
14. See, for example, '*Nash sarai*' (ZhD II:37), '*I razgovory v sarae*' (ZhD II:39), '*Posle raboty*' (ZhD II:48–9), '*Byt' ili ne byt'*' (ZhD II:49–50), '*Gnev Komissara*' (ZhD II:83–4), '*Razgovory posle raboty*' (ZhD II:87–8), '*Logika Komissara*' (ZhD II:100–1), '*Nedoumenie Dona*' (ZhD II:101–2).
15. '*Matrenadura*' (ZhD II:27–9), '*Iz myslei Matrenadury o Zapade*' (ZhD II:37, 83), '*Matrenadura o Zapade*' (ZhD II:46, 62, 68, 71, 73, 76, 80, 86, 94, 96, 103, 109, 111–12, 116, 119–20, 123–4, 141, 144, 156), '*Matrenadura, my i gomosek*' (ZhD II:67–8), '*Matrenadura o Zapade i o nas*' (ZhD II:106), '*Moskvichi o Matrenadure*' (ZhD II:137–8), '*Filosofiia Matrenadury*' (ZhD II:172–3), '*Obrabotka Matrenadury*' (ZhD II:181–2), '*Nash vklad v "Matrenianu"*' (ZhD II:187), '*Znanie i metod*' (ZhD II:188–9).
16. '*Eshche odna vazhnaia persona*' (ZhD II:86–7), '*Iz rechei Mao Tse-Dun'ki*' (ZhD II:91), '*Iz otkrovenii Mao Tse-Dun'ki*' (ZhD II:92–3), '*Mao Tse-Dun'ka o dissidentakh*' (ZhD II:95–6), '*Mao Tse-Dun'ki ob*

ozhidaemoi smene rukovodstva' (ZhD II:101), '*Iz idei Mao Tse-Dun'ki*' (ZhD II:159).

17. See note 14, plus '*Rasschety Kandidata*' (ZhD II:69–70), '*Zadachka Tokaria*' (ZhD II:76–7), '*Zhaloba Lba*' (ZhD II:76–7), '*Rasskaz Kandidata*' (ZhD II:77–8), '*O zhizni rabochikh*' (ZhD II:78–80), '*Filosofiia Kosti*' (ZhD II:80), '*Problema detei*' (ZhD II:85), '*Ideia Mns*' (ZhD II:89), '*My – mazokhisty*' (ZhD II:91–2), '*Otkrovenie Mns*' (ZhD II:94–5), '*Obychnyi trep na zapadnye temy*' (ZhD II:103–4), '*I opiat' o partii*' (ZhD II:105–7).
18. See note 15.
19. See note 16.
20. See, for instance, Nagirnyi (1985). For an incisive but fair analysis of Zinoviev's views on Stalinism in *Nashei iunosti polet* see Hanson (1988).
21. See ZhD II:353.
22. The relevant texts are the following: '*Bor'ba motivov*' (ZhD II:206–7), '*Stalin*' (ZhD II:207, 213–15, 219–21, 227–8, 231–2, 238–40, 246–7, 256–8, 264–7, 269–70, 292–3, 297–9), '*Konets Stalina*' (ZhD II:325).
23. See the important discussion of this topic in Michael Heller's *Machina i vintiki* (Heller, 1985:36–48).
24. Note especially '*Ob inostrantsakh*' (ZhD II:10–11), '*Vostok i Zapad*' (ZhD I:72–3, 82–3, 90–1, 104), '*Zapad i my*' (ZhD II:59–60, 127–8), '*Obychnyi trep na zapadnye temy*' (ZhD II:103–4), '*My i Zapad*' (ZhD II:131–2), '*Zakon soobshchaiushchikh sistem*' (ZhD II:149), '*Bez illiuzii*' (ZhD II:181), '*Nochnye razgovory*' (ZhD II:316, 345), '*Nakanune ot''ezda*' (ZhD II:350–1).

CHAPTER 6: *KOMMUNIZM KAK REAL'NOST'*

1. Zinoviev's desire to restrain his moralism sometimes lands him in trouble. There is no doubting his contempt for many aspects of Soviet reality, yet he will, almost perversely, refrain from making moral judgements about historically tragic events such as the collectivisation of Soviet agriculture and the behaviour of Joseph Stalin. His book *Nashei iunosti polet* (*Flight of our Youth*) caused great offence to many people, who regarded it as almost a work of Stalinist apologetics. On the other hand, he is by no means the only Soviet citizen to refuse to condemn the actions of people performed over fifty years ago.
2. That means, for Zinoviev, that 'it is unreliable, mendacious, hypocritical, it is boorish from a position of strength, cringes in the face of superior strength, and in addition is absolutely sincere' (KKR:60; TRC:70).
3. The wording of the original and the only available translation in English is as follows: '*maskiruiut fakticheskuiu bespartiinuiu sut' vlasti*' (KKR:132); 'obscure the fact that in reality power is essentially a non-party phenomenon' (TRC:132).

4. See Kirkwood, 1988.
5. This point was strikingly made in Part 1 of the BBC documentary series 'The Hand of Stalin', shown on BBC 2 on 16 October 1990. In Part 2, shown the following evening, a retired KGB Colonel showed the opposite of remorse when speaking about his role in the search for 'enemies of the people' during the 1930s terror.

CHAPTER 7: *GORBACHEVIZM*

1. The individual chapters of *Gorbachevizm* are denoted by the author as 'articles'. See especially 'articles' 18 and 19.
2. *Oktiabr'*, 1 (1991) 36–97; *Oktiabr'*, 2 (1991) 23–82; *Oktiabr'*, 3 (1991) 59–81.
3. The term *samizdat* refers to works produced clandestinely and circulated in secret among friends and acquaintances, copies being produced either by writing or typing. *Tamizdat* denotes works produced in the Soviet Union clandestinely, then smuggled out to the West and published there.
4. For a thorough account see Graffy, 1989.
5. This is not to deny that there exist groups within the Soviet Union who have access to word-processors and have set up distribution systems. They form, however, a vanishingly small proportion of the Soviet press as such.
6. See 'articles' 5, 7, 8, 28, 29, 30.
7. See the relevant chapters in E.W. Lefever and R.D. Vander Lugt (1989.)
8. Substantial corroboration of Zinoviev's prediction is provided in *Perestroika in Crisis?*, Federal Institute for Soviet and International Studies (Longman), 1990.
9. See 'articles' 9, 10, 11, 12, 13, 14, 15, 26, 30.
10. See the account of attempts to implement economic reforms in typical Soviet fashion in G.E. Schroeder (1989:312).
11. There is also the matter of ignorance about how a Western economy works. Gorbachev's reforms have produced precisely the outcomes which Zinoviev predicted. As Schroeder (1989:316) remarks: 'The reforms that are in place now represent a set of inconsistent and contradictory measures that neither dismember the old system of centrally planned socialism, nor create the "socialist regulated market economy" that seems to be Gorbachev's ultimate vision.'
12. See especially 'articles' 2, 6, 9, 14, 21, 24, 25, 32.
13. Since then it has dropped even further. See also Reddaway (1990:131–2).
14. See Almond and Roselle (1989) and Fairbanks (1989).
15. See 'articles' 16 and 17.
16. Zinoviev does not use this word, but I use it to mean the *totality* of the state-owned/regulated economy.

CHAPTER 8: *KATASTROIKA*

1. See texts 1–13.
2. See texts 14–37.
3. This is a reference to the time-worn tradition whereby collectives took on a 'voluntary' commitment to fulfil the five–year plan in four years. As Matrena-Dura observes in *Zheltyi dom*, 'We won't fulfil the plan, that's for sure, but we won't fulfil it ahead of schedule!'
4. See K:59–62.
5. See texts 38–74.
6. See K:99–100, 101–3, 103–5, 109–13, 114–15, 115–16.
7. See for instance K:89–90, 90–1, 91–3, 93, 117, 117–18, 118–20, 121–2, 123.
8. Nina Andreeva is a Leningrad lecturer who became famous overnight as the author of an article-length letter published in the newspaper *Sovetskaia Rossiia* on 13 March 1988 under the heading 'I cannot go against my principles' ('*Ne mogu postupat'sia printsipami*'). It was a conservative counterblast to *perestroika*, full of positive references to Stalin, Marxism–Leninism, the need for vigilance, as well as strong criticism of the 'denigration' of Soviet history and the departure from Leninist principles in the running of the state. The support her letter received from certain members of the top leadership is reflected in the fact that it was not until 5 April that *Pravda* published a rebuttal.
9. See texts 75–101.
10. Potemkin deceived Catherine the Great by constructing village façades on the banks of the Volga in advance of her journey through the Crimea to give the impression of a prosperous, happy peasantry.
11. See Womack, 1991.

CHAPTER 9: *KONETS KOMMUNIZMA?*

1. Although the original Russian version has yet to be published, large parts of it have in fact been incorporated into two articles which Zinoviev has contributed to the Soviet press. See Zinoviev, 1990g and 1991.
2. See TGF: 77–83, 97, 101.
3. See TGF, Chapters 17–20.
4. See IS: 43–8, 147–8.
5. See IS:55–7, 143–7.
6. See IS:52–5, 57–68, 141–3.
7. See IS:68–82, 138–41.
8. See IS:82–89; 149–53.
9. Compare, for instance, IS:149–53 and TGF:77–83.
10. See, for instance, VPR:410–11, 420–1, 430–1, 444–5, 448–9, 455, 539–40, 544, 546.

11. A '*subbotnik*' is a day of unpaid, 'voluntary' labour for the good of society. '*Subbotniki*' performed an important ideological rather than economic function in the pre-Gorbachev era.
12. This point is implicit in Zinoviev's general attitude to *homo sovieticus*, graphically set out in *Katastroika*. The point is not made explicitly in the published version of *Il superpotere in URSS*, although it appears in the original typescript, which has been amended for a forthcoming French translation.
13. See p. 185.

Bibliography

Almond, G.A. and Rosell, L. (1989), 'Model fitting in Communism studies', in Remington, F. (ed.), *Politics and the Soviet System* (London: Macmillan) pp.170–224.

Bar-Sella, Z. (1982) 'Dialektika uroda', *Dvadstat' dva*, 24, 183–93.

Berelowitch, W. (1985), 'Le cauchemar social d'Alexandre Zinoviev: pouvoir et societé soviétiques', *Annales ESC*, juillet-août, 717–36.

Besançon, A. (1982), 'La normalité du communisme selon Zinoviev', *Pouvoirs*, 21, 151–8.

Breslauer, G.W. (1976), 'Krushchev reconsidered', *Problems of Communism*, September–October, Vol. XXV, 18–33.

Brown, A. (1978), 'Political developments: some conclusions and an interpretation', in Brown, A. and Kaiser, M. (eds), *The Soviet Union since the Fall of Khrushchev* (London: Macmillan) pp.218–75.

Brown, A. and Kaiser, M. (eds) (1978), *The Soviet Union since the Fall of Khrushchev* (London: Macmillan).

Brown, A. (ed.) (1989), *Political Leadership in the Soviet Union* (London: Macmillan).

Brown, A. (1990), 'Gorbachev's leadership: another view', *Soviet Economy*, 6, 2 (April–June) 141–54.

Brown, D. (1979), 'Soviet Satyricon', *The Washington Post Book World* (1 July) 1.

Brown, Edward J. (1987), 'Zinoviev, Aleshkovsky, Rabelais, Sorrentino, possibly Pynchon, maybe James Joyce, and certainly *Tristram Shandy*: a comparative study of a satirical mode', in Fleishman, L., Freidin, G., Schupbach, R.D. and Todd, W.M. III (eds), *Stanford Slavic Studies*, Vol. I (Stanford) pp. 307–25.

Brzezinski, Z. (1976), 'Soviet politics: from the future to the past?', in Cocks, P., Daniels, R. and Heer, N. (eds), *The Dynamics of Soviet Politics* (Harvard University Press) pp. 337–51; 414–15.

Brzezinski, Z. (1989), *The Grand Failure* (London: Macdonald).

Carrère-d'Encausse, H. (1978), *L'Empire éclaté*, (Paris: Flammarion).

Cocks, P. (1976), 'The policy process and bureaucratic politics', in Cocks, P., Daniels, R.V. and Heer, N.W. (eds), *The Dynamics of Soviet Politics* (Harvard University Press) pp. 156–78.

Cocks, P. (1977), 'Science policy and Soviet development', in Dallin, A. (ed.), *The Twenty-Fifth Congress of the CPSU* (Hoover Institution Press) pp. 39–52.

Cocks, P., Daniels, R. and Heer, N.W. (eds) (1976), *The Dynamics of Soviet Politics* (Harvard University Press).

Cohen, S.F. (1980), 'The friends and foes of change', in Cohen, S.F., Rabinowitch, A. and Sharlet, R. (eds), *The Soviet Union since Stalin* (Bloomington, Ind.: Indiana University Press) pp. 11–31, reprinted in Hoffmann, E. and Laird, R. (eds), (1984) *The Soviet Polity in the Modern Era*, (New York, Aldine) pp. 85–104.

257

Connor, Walter D. (1975), 'Generations and politics in the USSR' *Problems of Communism*, September–October, Vol. XXIV, 20–31.

Dallin, A. (ed.) (1977), *The Twenty-Fifth Congress of the CPSU: Assessment and Context* (Hoover Institution Press).

Daneil, W. (1988), 'We and Zinoviev: a political view', in Hanson, P. and Kirkwood, M. (eds), *Alexander Zinoviev as Writer and Thinker: An Assessment* (London: Macmillan) pp. 145–53.

Elster, J. (1980) 'Irrational politics', *London Review of Books*, (21 August – 3 September) 11–13.

Elster, J. (1988), 'Active and passive negation', in Hanson, P. and Kirkwood, M. (eds), *Alexander Zinoviev as Writer and Thinker* (London: Macmillan) pp. 118–44.

Fairbanks, C.H. Jr. (1989), 'Soviet bureaucratic politics: the role of leaders and of lower officials', in Remington, T.F. (ed.), *Politics and the Soviet System* ((London: Macmillan) pp. 83–118.

Fassio, F. (1988), *Alexandre Zinoviev, Les fondements scientifiques de la sociologie* (Paris, La Pensée Universelle).

Fassio, F. (1991), *La nature du communisme selon Alexandre Zinoviev* (14780 Lion–sur-mer: Arcane-Beauvieux).

Federal Institute for Soviet and International Studies (1990), *Perestroika in Crisis?* (London: Longman).

Fleischman, L., Freidin, G., Schupbach, R. and Todd, W.M. III (eds) (1987), *Stanford Slavic Studies*, Vol. I (Stanford).

Forrest, L. (1979), 'An indictment of the Soviet system via Rabelaisian satire', *Chicago Tribune Book World* (17 June) 1.

Foucault, M. (1988), 'What is an author?', in Lodge, D. (ed.), *Modern Criticism and Theory* (London: Longman) pp. 197–210.

Franz, N. (1986), 'Komposition und Stil von A. Zinov'evs "Zijajuscie vysoty", in Franz, N. and Meichel, J. (eds), *Russische Literatur der Gegenwart* (Mainz: Liber Verlag) pp. 33–60.

Franz, N. and Meichel, J. (eds) (1986), *Russische Literatur der Gegenwart* (Mainz: Liber Verlag).

Freeborn, R. and Grayson, J. (eds) (1990), *Ideology in Russian Literature* (London: Macmillan).

Graffy, J. (1989), 'The literary press', in Graffy, J. and Hosking, G. (eds), *Culture and the Media in the USSR Today* ((London: Macmillan) pp. 107–57.

Hanson, P. (1982), 'Alexander Zinoviev: totalitarianism from below', *Survey*, Vol. 26, No. 1, 29–48.

Hanson, P. (1988), 'Alexander Zinoviev on Stalinism: some observations on *The Flight of our Youth*', *Soviet Studies*, 1 (January) 125–35.

Hanson, P. (1990), 'Property rights in the new phase of regions', *Soviet Economy*, 6, 2 (April–June) 95–124.

Hanson, P. and Kirkwood, M. (eds) (1988), *Alexander Zinoviev as Writer and Thinker* (London: Macmillan).

Heller, M. (1978), 'The Soviet Swift', *Survey*, Vol. 23, No. 3 (104) (Summer 1977–8) 11–19.

Heller, M. (1985), '*Mashina i vintiki*' (London: Overseas Publications Interchange Ltd).

Hook, S. (1984), 'The myth of necessity', *Times Literary Supplement*, (6 April) 365

Hosking, G. (1980), 'Mediocrity for the millions', *Times Literary Supplement* (23 May) 571–2.

Hosking, G. (1981), *The Times Literary Supplement* (27 March).

Hosking, G. (1988), 'Moralism versus science', in Hanson, P. and Kirkwood, M. (eds), *Alexander Zinoviev as Writer and Thinker* (London: Macmillan) pp. 173–8.

Hosking, G. (1990a), *A History of the Soviet Union* (London: Fontana).

Hosking, G. (1990b), *The Awakening of the Soviet Union* (London: Heinemann).

Hough, J.F. (1976), 'The man and the system', *Problems of Communism* (March–April) Vol.XXV, 1–17.

Hough, J.F. (1989), 'Gorbachev embraces Europe', in Lefever, E.W. and Vander Lugt, R.D. (eds), *Perestroika: How New is Gorbachev's New Thinking?* (Washington DC: Ethics and Public Policy Center) pp. 111–13.

Kennan, G. (1989), 'America's barriers to Gorbachev's success', in Lefever, E.W. and Vander Lugt, R.D. (eds), *Perestroika: How New is Gorbachev's New Thinking?* (Washington DC: Ethics and Public Policy Center) pp. 63–72.

Kirkwood, M. (1982), 'Elements of structure in Zinoviev's *Zheltyi dom*', *Essays in Poetics*, 7, 2, 86–118.

Kirkwood, M. (1983), 'Osnovy zinov'evizma', *Journal of Russian Studies*, 46, 39–48.

Kirkwood, M. (1987), 'Notes on the structure of Alexander Zinoviev's *Ziiaiushchie vysoty*', *Scottish Slavonic Review*, 8, 91–108.

Kirkwood, M. (1988a), 'Ideology in the works of A.A. Zinoviev', in Hanson, P. and Kirkwood, M. (eds), *Alexander Zinoviev as Writer and Thinker* (London: Macmillan) pp. 44–60.

Kirkwood, M. (1988b), 'Stalin and Stalinism in the works of Zinoviev', in Hanson, P. and Kirkwood, M. (eds), *Alexander Zinoviev as Writer and Thinker* (London: Macmillan) pp. 179–99.

Kirkwood, M. (1990a), 'Alexander Zinoviev: seer or scientist?', in Freeborn, R. and Grayson, P.J. (eds), *Ideology in Russian Literature* (London: Macmillan) pp. 174–87.

Kirkwood, M. (1990b), 'The novel approach of A.A. Zinoviev in McMillin, A.B. (ed.), *From Pushkin to Palisandria* (London: Macmillan) pp. 216–28.

Kontinent, 10 (1976) 410.

Koepke, H. (1979), 'Nachrichten aus dem Innern des Kommunismus', *Frankfurter Rundschau Buchmessen-Supplement* (8 October) 8–9.

Krauthammer, C. (1989), 'American Hawks vs. Doves', in Lefever, E. W. and Vander Lugt, R. D. (eds), *Perestroika: How New is Gorbachev's New Thinking?* (Washington DC: Ethics and Public Policy Center) pp. 121–30.

Lapidus, G.W. (1977), 'The Brezhnev regime and directed social change: depoliticisation as political strategy', in Dallin, A. (ed.), *The Twenty-Fifth Congress of the CPSU*, pp. 26–38.

Lefever, E.W. and Vander Lugt, R.D. (eds) (1989), *Perestroika: How New is Gorbachev's New Thinking?* (Washington DC: Ethics and Public Policy Center).

Levin, B. (1981), 'Russia: a society in collapse', *The Sunday Times* (29 March) 43.

Light, M. (1990), 'Foreign policy', in McCauley, M. (ed.), *Gorbachev and Perestroika* (London: Macmillan) pp. 169–88.

Lodge, D. (ed.) (1988), *Modern Criticism and Theory* (London: Longman).

McCauley, M. (1990), *Gorbachev and Perestroika* (London: Macmillan).

McMillin, A.B. (ed.)(1990), *From Pushkin to Palisandria* (London: Macmillan).

Mendras, M (1989), 'Policy outside and politics inside', in Brown, A. (ed.), *Political Leadership in the Soviet Union* (London: Macmillan) pp. 127–62.

Miller, R.F. (1976), 'The scientific-technical revolution and the Soviet administrative debate', in Cocks, P., Daniels, R.V. and Heer, N.W. (eds), *The Dynamics of Soviet Politics* (Harvard University Press) pp. 137–55.

Moskovich, W. (1988), 'Alexander Zinoviev's language', in Hanson, P. and Kirkwood, M. (eds), *Alexander Zinoviev as Writer and Thinker* (London: Macmillan) pp.89–104.

Nagirnyi, V. (1985), 'Aleksandr Zinov'ev kak sovetskii chelovek: kritik Stalina ili apologet stalinizma?', *Forum*, 10, 115–41.

Nivat, G. (1985), 'L'état Zinoviev', *L'Express* (19 April) 44–52.

Panin, D. (1980), 'Zhretsy rezhima', *Sovremennik*, 47–48, 76–89.

Petro, P. (1981), 'A. Zinov'ev's *The Yawning Heights* as an anatomy', *Canadian Slavonic Papers*, Vol. XXIII, No. 1 (March) 70–6.

Plaskacz, B. (1982) 'L'Allégorie du ratorium dans "Les Hauteurs Béantes" de A.A. Zinoviev', *Slavica Candensia*, 9, 83–90.

Reddaway, P. (1978), 'The development of dissent and opposition', in Brown, A. and Kaiser, M. (eds), *The Soviet Union Since the Fall of Khrushchev* (London: Macmillan) pp. 121–55.

Reddaway, P. (1990), 'The quality of Gorbachev's leadership', *Soviet Economy*, 6, 2 (April–June) 125–40.

Remington, T.F. (ed.) (1989), *Politics and the Soviet System* (London: Macmillan).

Remington, T.F. (1989), 'Gorbachev and the strategy of *glasnost"*', in Remington, T.F. (ed.), *Politics and the Soviet System* (London: Macmillan) pp. 56–82.

Remington, T.F. (1990), 'Regime transition in communist systems: the Soviet case', *Soviet Economy*, 6, 2 (April–June) 160–90.

Roche, R. (1982), 'Le travail de la citation chez Alexandre Zinoviev', *Essais sur le discours soviétique*, Vol. III, 136–44.

Rolland, J. (1982), 'Ibansk ou l'époque de la technique', *Exercices de la patience*, 1/4 (Spring) 233–54.

Roviello, A.-M. (1983), 'Zinoviev observateur, théoricien et moraliste', *Esprit* (March) 83–8.

Rubinshteyn, N. (1977), 'Skazanie o zemle ibanskoi', *Vremia i my*, 4, 143–61.

Rubinshteyn, N. (1978), 'Grafomaniia otchaianiia', *Dvadtsat' dva*, 3, 246–9.

Scanlan, J. (1988), 'Reforms and civil society in the USSR', *Problems of Communism* (March–April) 41–6.

Schroeder, G.E. (1989), 'Soviet economic reform: from resurgence to retrenchment?' *The Russian Review*, Vol. 48, 305–19.

Schwab, C. (1984), *Alexandre Zinoviev: Résistance et lucidité* (Lausanne: L'Age d'Homme).

Smith, G. 'The poems in *Yawning Heights*', in Hanson, P. and Kirkwood, M. (eds) (1988), *Alexander Zinoviev as Writer and Thinker* (London: Macmillan) pp. 71–88.

Solzhenitsyn, A. (1981), *The Mortal Danger: How Misperceptions About Russia Imperil America*, 2nd ed. (New York: Harper & Row).

Sorokin, B. (1980) 'Aleksandr Zinov'ev. "Ziiaiuschie vysoty", *Slavonic and East European Journal*, 24, 3 (Fall) 303–6.

Tatu, M. (1987), *Gorbatchev. L'U.R.S.S. va-t-elle changer?* (Paris: Centurion).

Thomson: D. (1981), *England in the Twentieth Century* (London: Penguin).

Urban, G. (1984), 'Portrait of a dissenter as a Soviet man', *Encounter* (April) 8–24.

Vail', P. and Genis, A. (1979), 'Vselennaia bez mozzhechka', *Vremia i my*, 39 (March) 147–58.

Valius, V. (1986), 'Razmyshleniia nad tekstom', *Dvadtsat' dva*, 27, 182–205.

von Ssachno, H. (1977), 'News from nowhere in Ibansk', *Encounter*, Vol. XLVIII, No. 5, 83–85.

Vinokur, T.G. (1965), 'O iazyke i stile povesti A.I. Solzhenitsyna "Odin den' Ivana Denisovicha"', *Voprosy kul'tury rechi*, 6, 16–32.

Warner, G. (1981), 'From affluence to uncertainty', in Thomson, D., *England in the Twentieth Century* (London: Penguin) pp. 291–359.

Wettig, G. (1988), ' "New thinking" on security and East–West relations', *Problems of Communism*, 37 (March–April) 1–14.

Womack, H. (1991), 'Soviet editors fear clampdown', *The Independent* (2 March).

Zheliagin, V. and Popov, N. (1978), 'Svetloe budushchee', *Posev* 8, 33–7.

Zinoviev, A.A. (1976), *Ziiaiushchie vysoty* (Lausanne: L'Age d'Homme).

Zinoviev, A.A. (1978a), 'Autobiography', *Survey*, Vol. 23, No. 3 (104) 1–11.

Zinoviev, A.A. (1978b), 'Avtobiografia', *Posev*, 8, 38–43.

Zinoviev, A.A. (1978c), *Svetloe budushchee* (Lausanne: L'Age d'Homme).

Zinoviev, A.A. (1979a), *Zapiski nochnogo storozha* (Lausanne: L'Age d'Homme).

Zinoviev, A.A. (1979b), *V preddverii raia* (Lausanne: L'Age d'Homme).

Zinoviev, A.A. (1979c), *Bez illiuzii* (Lausanne: L'Age d'Homme).

Zinoviev, A.A. (1980), *Zheltyi dom* (Lausanne: L'Age d'Homme).

Zinoviev, A.A. (1981a), *The Radiant Future* (London: Bodley Head).

Zinoviev, A.A. (1981b), *My i zapad* (Lausanne: L'Age d'Homme).

Zinoviev, A.A. (1981c), *Kommunizm kak real'nost'* (Lausanne: L'Age d'Homme).

Zinoviev, A.A. (1982a), *Gomo sovetikus* (Lausanne: L'Age d'Homme).
Zinoviev, A.A. (1982b) *Moi dom – moia chuzhbina* (Lausanne: L'Age d'Homme).
Zinoviev, A.A. (1983a), *Ni svobody ni ravenstva ni bratstva* (Lausanne: L'Age d'Homme).
Zinoviev, A.A. (1983b) *Nashei iunosti polet* (Lausanne: L'Age d'Homme).
Zinoviev, A.A. (1984a), *Evangelie dlia Ivana* (Lausanne: L'Age d'Homme).
Zinoviev, A.A. (1984b), *The Reality of Communism* (London: Gollancz).
Zinoviev, A.A. (1985a), *Homo Sovieticus* (London: Gollancz).
Zinoviev, A.A. (1985b), *Die Diktatur der Logik* (Munich: Piper).
Zinoviev, A.A. (1985c), *Idi na Golgofu* (Lausanne: L'Age d'Homme).
Zinoviev, A.A. (1986a), *The Madhouse* (London: Gollancz).
Zinoviev, A.A. (1986b), *Die Macht des Unglaubens* (Munich: Piper).
Zinoviev, A.A. (1986c), *Para bellum* (Lausanne: L'Age d'Homme).
Zinoviev, A.A. (1986d), 'Ruka Kremlia', *Kontinent*, 47, 137–84.
Zinoviev, A.A. (1986e), *Der Staatsfreier* (Zürich: Diogenes).
Zinoviev, A.A. (1987a), *Le Gorbatchévisme ou les pouvoirs d'une illusion* (Lausanne: L'Age d'Homme).
Zinoviev, A.A. (1987b), *Ich bin für mich selbst ein Staat* (Zürich: Diogenes).
Zinoviev, A.A. (1987c), 'S chego nachat'?', *Kontinent*, 51, 219–39.
Zinoviev, A.A. (1987d), 'Nauchnaia kritika kommunizma', *Kontinent*, 53, 221–42.
Zinoviev, A.A. (1988a), *Katastroika. Gorbatschows Potemkinsche Dörfer* (Frankfurt/M: Ullstein).
Zinoviev, A.A. (1988b), *Gorbachevizm* (New York: Liberty).
Zinoviev, A.A. (1988c), 'Katastroika. Glavy iz romana.', *Kontinent*, 57, 7–69.
Zinoviev, A.A. (1989a), 'An autobiography', in *Contemporary Authors Autobiography Series*, Vol. 10 (Detroit: Gale Research Inc) pp. 323–39.
Zinoviev, A.A. (1989b), *Zhivi!* (Lausanne: L'Age d'Homme).
Zinoviev, A.A. (1989c), *Allegra Russia* (Milan: Sugarcoedizioni).
Zinoviev, A.A. (1989d), 'Manifest sotsial'noi oppozitsii', *Kontinent*, 60, 207–31.
Zinoviev, A.A. (1990a), *Les confessions d'un homme en trop* (Paris: Olivier Orban).
Zinoviev, A.A. (1990b), *Katasztrojka* (Budapest: Pallas Lap-és Könyvkiadó).
Zinoviev, A.A. (1990c), *Gorbatsovism* (Tallinn: Loomingu Raamatukogu).
Zinoviev, A.A. (1990d), *Katastroika. Povest' o perestroike v Partgrade* (Lausanne: L'Age d'Homme).
Zinoviev, A.A. (1990e), *Gorbachevism*, (London: Claridge Press).
Zinoviev, A.A. (1990f), *Il superpotere in URSS: il communismo è veramente tramontato?* (Milan: Sugarcoedizioni).
Zinoviev, A.A. (1990g), 'Ia khochu rasskazat' vam o Zapade', *Komsomol'skaia Pravda* (15 September) 2–3.
Zinoviev, A.A. (1991), 'Kuda my idem?', *Zhurnalist*, 1, 32–9.

Index

Academy of Sciences, 15, 22, 100,
    108–9, 115–16
Afanas'ev, V.G., 96, 106
agriculture, collectivisation of, 143,
    see also countryside, Soviet
Ambartsumov, E., 26
Andropov, Iu.V., 23, 175–6, 185,
    239

Bar-Sella, Z. (cited), 91, 257
Barthes, R., xi, 31
Berelowich, W. (cited), 84, 257
Besançon, A., (cited), 162, 257
Bez illiuzii, 25, 261
Brezhnev, L.I., 5, 38, 44, 64, 107,
    165, 175, 219
    era, 54, 89, 96–7, 106, 111–12,
        116, 131, 167, 178, 238, 245
    Malaia zemlia (The Little
        Land), 126
Brown, A. (cited), 192, 257
Brown, D. (cited), 63, 257
Brown, E.J. (cited), 63, 257
Brzezinski, Z., 183, 220, 246–7, 257
    see also Grand Failure, The
Bukharin, N.I., 143
bureaucracy, *see under*
    Communism
Burlatsky, F., 108

capitalism, 191, 228, 230–2
    see also economy; propaganda
censorship, 179–80, *see also*
    freedom
clichés, use of, 43–6
Cocks, P. (cited), 107–8, 257

Cohen, S.F. (cited), 109–11, 257
collectivism, *see under* society, Soviet
Communism
    activists, 167, 226
    bureaucracy, 105–6, 189–92, 206,
        208, 210, 227
    crisis of, 81, 194, 205–7, 218–19,
        223, 225, 227–8, 230, 233,
        238–40, 246
    leadership, 182–3, 193, 222–4
    nature of, 67–9, 149–52, 202,
        227–9
    roots of, 225–6
    and stability, 81, 89–90, 112,
        164–70, 228–9
    theory of, xii, 17–18, 74, 120, 148,
        149–70, 222–4, 238, 244–5
    criticisms of, 83–7, 150–4, 219
    see also CPSU; foreign policy;
        ideology; *Kommunizm kak
        real'nost'*; Marxism–Leninism;
        morality; power; propaganda;
        reform; society, Soviet;
        totalitarianism
Communist Party of the Soviet
    Union see CPSU
*Confessions d'un homme en trop,
    Les*, 235–6, 239, 262
Congress of People's Deputies,
    xii–xiii, 243
Connor, W.D. (cited), 111, 112,
    258
conservatism, *see under* society,
    Soviet
counter-*perestroika*, *see under
    perestroika*

Index

analysis of, 37–40, 90–2
Prix Medicis Étranger (1979), 90
publication of, 25, 89
quotations from, 36–7, 97, 99, 100, 106, 114–15
reception of, 90
structure, 32
title, 34–5
see also language; style; texts

tamizdat, 18, 180, 254 n3
Tatu, M. (cited), 173–4, 176–7, 261, 180–1, 261
texts
 analysis of, 31, 37, 54–5, 92–5
 definition, 29–30, 33
 structure of, 66–71, 72, 79–80, 117–26, 149–50, 196
 see also language; style
TGF, *see Grand Failure, The*
Timofeev, L., 177
TM, *(The Madhouse) see Zheltyi dom*
totalitarianism, 152, 169–70, 226
 see also Communism; Stalin, J.V.
translation, difficulty of, 36, 64
TRC, *(The Reality of Communism), see Kommunizm kak real'nost'*
TRF, *(The Radiant Future), see Svetloe budushchee*
Trotsky, L.D., 143

Vail', P. (cited), 62, 63, 65, 261
VAK, 22
Valius, V. (cited), 84–5, 87, 261
Veil, S., 149
verse (in works), 32, 51–4, 55–7, 120–21, 122–3, 135–6
Vinokur, T.G., 34
Visas and Registrations, Department of, 23–4
von Ssachno, H. (cited), 62, 63, 261

Voprosy filosofii, 18, 19, 96
V preddverii raia (VPR), xi, 13, 24, 42–3, 196, 234
 publication of, 25, 47
 structure, 29–33
 see also language; style; texts

war, *see* Second World War
We and the West, see My i zapad
West
 attitudes
  of Soviet Union to, 175–6, 178, 216–18
  to Soviet Union, 26, 75, 144–6, 182–3, 206, 229, 235, 238–9
 its civilisation, 130
 imitation of, 183
 and its scholars, ix, 3, 5, 89, 105–12, 186, 244–5, 246
 see also foreign policy; Gorbachev, M.S.
Wettig, G. (cited), 185, 261
Without Illusions, see Bez illiuzii

Yanaev, G.I., xii
Yeltsin, B.N., xii, 26, 218
YH, *The Yawning Heights, see Ziiaiushchie vysoty*

Zapiski nochnogo storozha, 4, 24, 25, 32, 89, 261
 quotation from, 4
ZhD, *see Zheltyi dom*
Zheliagin, V. (cited), 96, 261
Zheltyi dom, x, xii, 34, 43, 45–6, 114–47, 196, 261
 characters discussed
  Anton Zimin, 115
  Barabanov, 121
  Dobronravov, 120, 138
  Dzerzhinsky (statue), 119
  egos (of JRF), 120, 121, 122,